Dear Reader,

When I first started trying to lose weight, I didn't want to give up my favorite foods. How could I say no to chocolate, nachos, and wine? I knew there **had to be a way** to incorporate them into my diet while also working toward my goals.

I firmly believe if there's a will, there's a way, and I'm so thankful I discovered macros when I did. I was able to lose 25 pounds without restricting myself or "dieting," and I discovered a whole new way of living. That was nearly two decades ago, and I've maintained my weight loss ever since.

Over the years, I've had the pleasure of sharing this macro lifestyle and recipes with my nutrition clients and social media followers. Eating well within your macros doesn't need to be difficult if you **have the right resources**. The recipes in this cookbook are intended to help you reach your goals and discover total food freedom without spending hours in the kitchen.

I hope this book and its recipes help you find a truly livable (and delicious) way of eating. And, if done correctly and confidently, know that macro counting **sets you up for success**, not just as a "diet," but for the rest of your life.

Tina Haupert

Welcome to the Everything® Series!

These handy, accessible books give you all you need to tackle a difficult project, gain a new hobby, comprehend a fascinating topic, prepare for an exam, or even brush up on something you learned back in school but have since forgotten.

You can choose to read an Everything® book from cover to cover or just pick out the information you want from our four useful boxes: Questions, Facts, Alerts, and Essentials. We give you everything you need to know on the subject, but throw in a lot of fun stuff along the way too.

question	fact
Answers to common questions.	Important snippets of information.

alert	essential
Urgent warnings.	Quick handy tips.

We now have more than 600 Everything® books in print, spanning such wide-ranging categories as cooking, health, parenting, personal finance, wedding planning, word puzzles, and so much more. When you're done reading them all, you can finally say you know Everything®!

PUBLISHER Karen Cooper

MANAGING EDITOR Lisa Laing

COPY CHIEF Casey Ebert

PRODUCTION EDITOR Jo-Anne Duhamel

ACQUISITIONS EDITOR Lisa Laing

DEVELOPMENT EDITOR Lisa Laing

EVERYTHING® SERIES COVER DESIGNER Erin Alexander

THE
EVERYTHING®
MACRO
DIET
COOKBOOK

TINA HAUPERT
of *Carrots 'N' Cake*

300 SATISFYING RECIPES FOR SHEDDING POUNDS AND GAINING LEAN MUSCLE

ADAMS MEDIA

NEW YORK   LONDON   TORONTO   SYDNEY   NEW DELHI

Dedication

To my boys: I love you to the moon and back.

Acknowledgments

Thank you to each and every *Carrots 'N' Cake* follower and nutrition client. This book was inspired by more than a decade of your support and interactions online and in person. Without you, it wouldn't be possible.

Adams Media
An Imprint of Simon & Schuster, Inc.
100 Technology Center Drive
Stoughton, MA 02072

An Everything® Series Book.
Everything® and everything.com® are registered trademarks of Simon & Schuster, Inc.

First Adams Media trade paperback edition August 2020

ADAMS MEDIA and colophon are trademarks of Simon & Schuster.

For information about special discounts for bulk purchases, please contact Simon & Schuster Special Sales at 1-866-506-1949 or business@simonandschuster.com.

The Simon & Schuster Speakers Bureau can bring authors to your live event. For more information or to book an event contact the Simon & Schuster Speakers Bureau at 1-866-248-3049 or visit our website at www.simonspeakers.com.

Interior design by Colleen Cunningham
Photographs by Kelly Jaggers

Manufactured in the United States of America

11 10 9 8 7

Library of Congress Cataloging-in-Publication Data
Names: Haupert, Tina, author.
Title: The everything® macro diet cookbook / Tina Haupert of Carrots 'N' Cake.
Description: First Adams Media trade paperback edition. | Avon, Massachusetts: Adams Media, 2020.

Series: Everything® series. | Includes index.
Identifiers: LCCN 2020013333 | ISBN 9781507213957 (pb) | ISBN 9781507213964 (ebook)
Subjects: LCSH: Macrobiotic diet--Recipes. | Reducing diet--Recipes. | LCGFT: Cookbooks
Classification: LCC RM235 .H38 2020 | DDC 641.5/63--dc23
LC record available at https://lccn.loc.gov/2020013333

ISBN 978-1-5072-1395-7
ISBN 978-1-5072-1396-4 (ebook)

Contains material adapted from the following title published by Adams Media, an Imprint of Simon & Schuster, Inc.: *The Everything® Guide to Macronutrients* by Matt Dustin, CSCS, Pn1, copyright © 2017, ISBN 978-1-5072-0416-0.

Contents

4: SALADS 77

5: CHICKEN AND TURKEY 101

9: PASTA AND PIZZA 203

10: SIDES AND SAUCES 221

11: APPETIZERS AND SNACKS 241

Introduction

You've fallen off the wagon and vowed to get back on track a million times in the past, only to end up right back where you started: frustrated and overwhelmed with all of the conflicting diet and nutrition out there.

Should you try intermittent fasting or carb cycling? Drink protein shakes? Cut out gluten and dairy? What about the keto diet or Whole30? Maybe you've tried them all, but nothing has stuck for more than a few weeks because you feel restricted and lose motivation.

Many of these diets rely on you eliminating all of your favorite foods, and suddenly all you can think about is what you can't eat. Donuts, pizza, and beer are not allowed; it's all about eating "clean." No fun allowed! But how many sad salads with dressing on the side can you eat before you dive headfirst into a plate of gooey brownies?

Diets also force us to miss out on the best parts of life—brunch with friends, happy hour with coworkers, and ice cream dates with our kids. Obviously, this (antisocial) way of living is not enjoyable or sustainable. But what if there's a way to have your carrots and eat cake too?

When you focus on macronutrients, there are no restrictive rules or limitations. Instead, you use macros as a tool to help you find real balance within your diet by making you more aware of your food choices and eating habits. Not only will you know how much you consume each day, but you'll also keep track of the macronutrient breakdown of everything you eat and drink. You'll also begin to be aware of any habits that might trip you up and get in the way of weight loss. This awareness makes working toward your goals that much easier because you have data to back up your choices.

Instead of changing your lifestyle to match a specific diet, when you count macros, you create a personalized plan for yourself. First you'll figure out your individual daily macro goals (see Appendix A for a simple calculation) and then plan the foods you want to eat each day. What you come up with is completely tailored to your taste preferences and lifestyle. What's more, macro diets can fit into any way of eating. On Paleo? Get your protein from meat and fish. Going vegan? Substitute that protein with tofu, tempeh, and seitan instead.

It might seem like this diet requires a lot of calculation and work up front and you're right, it does. But like anything else worthwhile, the more you practice, the easier it becomes. With practice and patience, you'll learn how to track your food and eat for your needs. Even after just a few weeks, you'll find that tracking your macros becomes second nature.

When you're following a diet built around foods you love, it's much easier and more realistic to implement. You won't need to second-guess your "good" and "bad" choices. Nothing is off-limits. You can enjoy all of your favorite foods on a weekly basis. You just need to plan ahead and enjoy them in moderation. And when you satisfy your cravings on a regular basis, you're less likely to binge, which means you can find consistency in your diet. Consistency wins over perfection every time.

This book includes a wide variety of recipes—everything from Overnight Peanut Butter Protein Oats (Chapter 2) and Lentil Taco Lettuce Wraps (Chapter 8) to Pizza Cottage Pie (Chapter 6) and Lemon Coconut Protein Balls (Chapter 11). There's a great mix of "healthy" and "fun" recipes, so you always have a dish to pique your interest and keep you excited about what you're cooking up next in the kitchen. You'll no longer need to scour the Internet for recipes that "fit your macros" because there are 300 here to keep you motivated and on track with your choices.

In Appendix B, you'll find sample meal plans that demonstrate how you can use the recipes to create a weekly macro-balanced menu. Each day includes a different macro ratio and calorie count, so you'll likely need to make some tweaks to fit your personal goals, but they are still a good framework for demonstrating what balanced eating looks like. They'll get you started with creating the perfect plan for you.

There are no hidden secrets or fancy biohacks to magically losing weight and getting healthy. It takes a basic understanding of nutrition and calorie deficit, a solid plan, motivation, and consistency. This can happen one of two ways: giving up all of your favorite foods or consuming them regularly in moderation. It's up to you, but the latter is a lot more enjoyable. The macro diet is powerful, and now it's time for you to experience it for yourself. Cheers to the last "diet" you'll ever try!

CHAPTER 1

What Are Macronutrients?

Macronutrients are the building blocks of any diet—proteins, carbohydrates, and fats—and where your calories come from. Macronutrients supply the energy, fuel, and nutrients you need to live. Each macronutrient serves a specific purpose and should be consumed In the proper amount for optimal health. Quite a few variables come into play when setting up macronutrient ratios, but first, you must understand what they are, what they do, and what foods they come from.

The Building Blocks of Nutrition

Macronutrients form the basis of any nutrition plan. Regardless of whether you follow a strict diet plan or just eat whatever you feel like, you take in macronutrients every single day. Without an adequate macronutrient intake, your body would stop working. The number of macronutrients in a given food determines how many calories are in that food. By figuring out exactly how many macronutrients your body needs each day and then eating just that balanced amount, you can achieve your health and weight loss goals.

> **essential**
>
> Macronutrients are proteins, carbs, and fat. An easy trick to remember this is remembering that macro means large. Micronutrients on the other hand, while essential, don't have any calories. Micronutrients would include vitamins, minerals, antioxidants, and other things found in food that don't have any calories.

To understand macronutrients, you need a very basic understanding of how your body operates. Every single process your body goes through every day, from brushing your teeth to digesting food and even breathing, requires energy. You may not feel physically tired from sitting on the couch watching television, but even the simple act of staying alive requires a little bit of energy. Your body gets the energy it needs from calories. Some foods have quite a few calories while some have very little, but all foods contain calories, even if they are found in very small amounts.

> **fact**
>
> A calorie is a measure of energy. In scientific terms, a calorie is the amount of energy needed to increase the temperature of 1 kilogram of water by 1°C. Thus, the more calories a food contains, the more energy it supplies to your body. A calorie isn't "good" or "bad"—it just is. Different foods will offer more nutritional benefits than others, but ultimately a calorie is still a calorie and nothing more than a measure of energy.

If you have a very active lifestyle, your body will use, or "burn," a greater number of calories to function every day. Activities that make you feel physically tired, like running, playing sports, yard work, or significant walking, will burn more calories than sitting around doing nothing.

Do You Need All Three?

Calories come from macronutrients, and there are three different macronutrients, or macros for short. They are protein, carbohydrates, and fats. Each of these macros plays a unique role in how your body functions. If fat loss and body composition were a pyramid, total calories would form the base of that pyramid, as that is the most important factor. However, the next level would be the actual quantities of macronutrients you consume each day.

You must have a proper balance of the three macros. Having too much or too little of any of the three will lead to less than optimal health and body functioning, as all three play important roles, and none of them are bad or evil. Having a better understanding of each macronutrient will allow you to make the best choices for your health and diet goals.

Carbohydrates: Fuel for Life

Carbohydrates, or carbs for short, come from starchy foods like potatoes, rice, beans, oatmeal, vegetables, and fruit. They are the body's preferred source of energy as they provide a quick form of energy. Where protein and fats are slow to digest, and not used as easily for energy, stored carbohydrates are very easy for your body to digest and use for energy. When you need a fast energy supply, you don't want to mess around with proteins and fats, which digest slowly. Every gram of carbohydrate contains four calories.

It's worth mentioning that carbohydrates are the only nonessential macronutrient. You may feel miserable if you remove them completely from your diet, but assuming your protein and fat intake is correct, you won't suffer any dangerous side effects. If your protein or fat levels drop too low, you'll be looking at some real health problems, but you can live without carbohydrates. Removing them completely is an extreme form of dieting and not sustainable for most people, but it's a viable option if you really want to try it.

question

Is alcohol a carbohydrate?

A gram of alcohol has seven calories, but as it doesn't provide any nutrition or any significant protein, carbohydrates, or fat, it's considered an "empty calorie." It gets you closer to your daily calorie goal without providing any value. If you consume alcohol and want to still hit your calorie goal for the day, you'll have to take away some calories from your daily food intake, and you'll lose that nutritional value.

Simple versus Complex Carbs

Typically, when someone talks about "bad carbs," they are referring to sugary, processed carb sources. These are things like candy, soda, fruit juice, or just about anything else that's sweet, delicious, and comes from a box. These are typically referred to as simple carbs, and they are fast-digesting with regard to the speed at which they are broken down, digested, and absorbed into your bloodstream.

On the other hand, complex carbs, often known as "good carbs," are slow-digesting. They're higher in fiber, which makes them more filling and a good option for weight control. Complex carbs also pack in more nutrients than simple carbs.

There are two kinds of fiber: soluble fiber and insoluble fiber. Insoluble fiber is a tough, dense fiber that can't be broken down by the gut. It moves through the digestive system, adding bulk to your waste, which promotes regular bowel movements. This fiber is commonly found in dense leafy greens, the skin of fruits and vegetables, and certain whole grains.

Soluble fiber absorbs water and liquid and has many benefits when consumed in the proper quantity. As it absorbs water, it forms a thick, gel-like substance. In addition to this gel helping keep you regular and feeling full, soluble fiber can bind to sugar and cholesterol, slowing or completely preventing their absorption into the bloodstream. This is why high-fiber diets can lower blood sugar and cholesterol levels, which in turn reduces the risk of heart disease later in life.

All carbohydrates are made up of simple sugar molecules. When fully broken down by your body's digestive system, carbohydrates are made up of either glucose or fructose, two simple sugar molecules. It doesn't matter if you get 40 grams of carbs from cake or from brown rice; your body reacts to the 40 grams of carbs. But here's the big difference: Whole foods will be significantly higher in fiber and micronutrients, which are the vitamins and minerals you need to stay healthy. You'll get those in high quantities from fresh fruit and vegetables, and you'll get virtually none from processed sweets like donuts and candy.

For optimal health, you should be getting your carbs from whole foods. However, the occasional treat, assuming it fits into your daily calorie allotment, isn't going to derail your progress. It's much better to allow yourself to enjoy these treats in moderation if it helps you stay on track, rather than attempt to eliminate them completely and end up binge eating a whole cake on the weekend. Don't make a habit of getting all of your carbs from cookies, but understand that those cookies are not bad in and of themselves.

alert

Fiber absorbs water, which you've probably noticed if you've ever made oatmeal. When you consume high-fiber foods, they will tend to absorb the water in your body and can cause cramping or an upset stomach. Be sure to drink plenty of water to avoid any stomach discomfort from your fiber intake.

To help you plan your diet, here is a list of whole foods that contain primarily carbohydrates. Some foods will contain high amounts of multiple macronutrients, but these foods are mostly carbs. There will be similar lists for proteins and fats as well. The best way to learn what macros are in what foods is to start checking the nutritional information labels of the foods you buy, but the following lists will give you a quick reference guide to look at.

Carbohydrate Sources
- Rice
- Oatmeal
- Beans
- Fruit
- Whole-grain bread
- Potatoes
- Squash

Why Protein Is So Important

Of all the nutrients, protein may be the most misunderstood. People are quick to vilify carbohydrates and fats, claiming they are all sorts of evil, but no one seems to know what to think about protein. Some say it damages your liver; others say you need incredibly high amounts of protein in your diet.

The answer is somewhere in the middle. Protein in proper quantities won't have any negative effects, but you probably don't need as much as most people claim. For optimal recovery from training, satiety, and a healthy body, 0.6 gram–1.0 gram of protein per pound of lean body weight is a pretty good guideline. Not getting enough protein can cause you to lose muscle, as your body will break down your muscle tissue for the amino acids it contains.

Proteins are made up of amino acids, which are the building blocks of most of the cells in the human body. Without amino acids, you'd be unable to replace the skin cells you lose every day, grow hair and fingernails, or rebuild and repair damaged muscle tissue. Proteins are essential for optimal health and body functioning. Every gram of protein has four calories.

Not All Proteins Are Created Equal

Just like carbohydrates are classified as simple or complex, proteins also come in two varieties: complete and incomplete. Remember how proteins are made up of amino acids? Well, of those amino acids, nine are referred to as essential amino acids. Essential amino acids cannot be produced by the human body and must be obtained through food or supplements.

Protein is what allows you to rebuild your body and recover from the daily wear and tear you place on it. Often people associate high protein intake with gaining muscle, but that's just one role protein plays in the body. Every day, your body is regenerating hair, skin, fingernails, and, yes, muscle tissue. It uses amino acids to do this, so if you aren't consuming enough from your diet, your body will start to rip apart and break down your muscle tissue to get those amino acids.

> **fact**
>
> In terms of digestion, there is something called the *thermic effect of food*. Remember how every process in your body requires energy? Digestion is no different. Every food you eat requires some energy to break it down, absorb it, and put it to use or store for later. Protein has a high thermic effect, which means your body burns quite a few calories simply from digesting it. You shouldn't try to adjust the total calorie content based on this, but it's good to know.

The other main benefit of protein is its ability to keep you feeling full. Whole-food protein sources are tough for your body to digest. This means that when you consume protein sources like meat, fish, or eggs, it's going to take your body longer to break them down compared to foods that consist of simple carbohydrates. If fat loss is your goal, increasing your protein intake is a fantastic way to keep yourself feeling full throughout the day, making your diet easier and preventing muscle breakdown as your food intake gets lower and lower.

If a protein source contains all nine essential amino acids, it's considered a complete protein. If it's lacking any of the essential amino acids, it's considered an incomplete protein. It's important that you get plenty of complete proteins throughout the day, whatever your diet of choice may be.

If you're a vegan or vegetarian, you still need complete proteins if you want to live a healthy life. Unfortunately, most plant-based proteins just aren't complete. Soy protein is one of the few complete plant proteins available, but excess soy consumption can have negative side effects, so try not to go overboard with the soy protein. If you follow a vegan diet, especially if you are active, you should strongly consider investing in a plant-based protein supplement to ensure you are reaching your daily goals.

Protein Sources
- Chicken
- Turkey
- Beef
- Fish
- Soy
- Dairy products
- Eggs
- Protein powder

Repeat after Me: "Fat Is Not Bad"

Fat rounds out the trio of key macronutrients and, like protein, it is essential to live. The right kinds of fat support healthy joints, cellular health, heart health, brain functioning, mood, and a whole host of other functions in the body. Unlike carbohydrates and proteins, however, certain fats are less than stellar and should be avoided for the most part. Whereas carbs and proteins each have four calories per gram, fat has nine calories per gram.

question

Doesn't fat make me fat?

No. This is a very common belief because they share the same name, but this is not true. Dietary fat that you eat in your food is essential for your body in certain amounts. Adipose tissue, or body fat, is simply stored calories. While eating foods high in fat *can* result in excess adipose tissue, consuming dietary fat in the correct amounts will not make you fat.

Dietary fat is simply another form of energy and nutrition; it does not directly correlate at all to actual body fat. The right fats supply the body with energy, help it retain crucial vitamins that require fat for absorption, protect the organs, and encourage healthy skin and hair.

Why You Need Fat to Live

Contrary to common belief, fat is not evil. The word itself sounds bad because it's often associated with body fat, which many people want to lose. The truth is you *need* dietary fat for your body to function. There are good fats and bad fats, and some are better than others, but without adequate fat intake, you'll run into all sorts of health problems.

First, let's define body fat and dietary fat. When you talk about body fat, the stuff you probably want to lose, you're actually referring to what's known as *adipose tissue*. Adipose tissue contains adipose cells, which are storage units for energy.

If your diet provides more calories than you are able to burn, you'll store those calories in fat cells, causing you to store more body fat. Keep in mind that dietary fat intake does not cause body fat gain; excess calories from any macronutrient causes body fat gain. Dietary fat is simply another source of energy, just like proteins and carbs. Body fat is extra energy stored for later, but it can come from *any* food. Eating fat does not automatically make you fat.

There are several very important functions of dietary fats. In addition to being a good source of sustained, slow-releasing energy, they help support your cellular health and functioning. Without proper fat intake, many of the cells in your body wouldn't be able to operate at 100 percent efficiency. Certain essential nutrients, like vitamins A, D, E, and K, are fat-soluble, which means they can't be absorbed by your body without enough fat intake. If you take these vitamins or find them in foods that don't include some fat, your body won't be able to absorb and use them properly, and you may run into deficiencies.

> **fact**
>
> Saturated fats are not bad fats, at least not in the proper amounts, but they aren't exactly good, either. Saturated fats are typically found in red meat, as well as in certain dairy products. You do need some saturated fats, and it would be pretty hard to avoid them completely, but try to limit them. They won't kill you, like some claim, but they aren't as good as the unsaturated fats.

The last important function of dietary fat is hormonal support. Fat supplies cholesterol, which is generally classified as HDL or LDL cholesterol. Too much cholesterol, particularly too much LDL cholesterol, can cause plaque formation and buildup in your heart. However, not getting enough cholesterol is also bad. Cholesterol is important for producing many hormones in the body, including important reproductive hormones, which is why those who follow very low-fat diets often report negative hormonal changes after a while. There's no need to go overboard with fat, but don't be afraid of including the right fats in your diet.

Good Fats and Bad Fats

Fat gets confusing, and for good reason—there are quite a few types. You don't really need to understand how exactly these are classified; you just need to understand the difference between good and bad fats. Let's skip the science lesson; just know that unsaturated fats are the best, saturated fats are decent, and trans fats should be avoided whenever possible. You also have monounsaturated fats and polyunsaturated fats, but the easiest thing is just to remember which foods provide the "good" fats—there will be a list later on in this section for you to reference.

To start, trans fat is the only truly bad fat. Trans fats are often found in fried and heavily processed foods and usually have negative effects on your cholesterol and heart health. Whenever possible, avoid any food containing trans fats. Most trans fats are artificially created, so if you see that a food contains trans fats, put it down and walk away.

When it comes to good fats, unsaturated fats are the ones you want. You'll see monounsaturated and polyunsaturated fats, and these are both good types of fat. These are very anti-inflammatory; good for your heart, skin, and brain; and will help you achieve a better quality of life. Unsaturated fats have also been shown to lower levels of bad cholesterol while promoting levels of good cholesterol. You can get these healthy fats from whole eggs, nuts, and avocados.

Foods that are high in omega-3s are considered to be good fats. There are two common omegas: omega-3 fatty acids and omega-6 fatty acids. Omega-3s are found in fatty cuts of fish, egg yolks, avocados, and nuts, as well as other foods. Getting enough in your diet can be done by supplementing with a high-quality fish oil or just by making an effort to eat wild-caught fish two to three times per week.

fact

Omega-3 fatty acids have been associated with a very long list of health benefits, beyond simply providing a balance with omega-6s. They have been associated with increased mental function and focus, improved mood, decreased inflammation and joint pain, decreased risk of cardiovascular disease, improved insulin sensitivity for easier fat loss, and many more benefits. If you don't eat fatty cuts of wild-caught fish on a regular basis, you may want to consider using a daily fish oil supplement.

Omega-6 fatty acids are very common in processed and fried foods like salad dressings, pizza, French fries, and sausages, in addition to certain cooking oils, such as vegetable oil. Omega-6 fatty acids are a tricky subject. They are essential, in that your body needs them and cannot produce them, but it's important to have the right balance between omega-6 and omega-3 fatty acids. If your omega-6 fatty acid intake outweighs your omega-3 intake, you may run into health problems, like increased inflammation and increased risk of cardiovascular disease. To get as close to a one-to-one ratio of omega-6 and omega-3 fatty acids as possible, be sure to eat plenty of good fats on a regular basis.

Fat Sources
- Egg yolks
- Avocados
- Nuts
- Coconut oil
- Red meat
- Fatty cuts of fish
- Cooking oils such as olive oil and macadamia nut oil

Balancing Macronutrients for Optimal Health

A healthy diet will consist of a balance of all three macronutrients. The total number of calories in your diet is determined by your macronutrient intake. If you decrease your total calorie intake, all of your macronutrient numbers will decrease as well. For a healthy, safe approach to weight loss, you should keep a balance of all three nutrients in your diet, rather than eliminating one altogether.

If your goal is to lose body fat, you need to maintain a caloric deficit. You can do this by reducing your food intake or burning more calories through exercise, but without this deficit, fat loss will not happen. There is no magic pill or one evil food you can eliminate to instantly lose fat, no matter what magazine covers may claim. If you are trying to gain weight, you simply need to eat more calories than your body needs.

Some of the more common diet strategies can have negative side effects and aren't optimal for a healthy, sustainable body change. Always remember that any changes you make to your diet should be sustainable, lasting, and healthy, not short-term fixes that set you up to gain all of your weight back as soon as you stop the diet.

The Science Behind the Diet

The macronutrient diet doesn't always make sense. After all, you've probably been told your entire life that you can lose weight only by eating "clean" foods. Candy bars and pizza? Those foods make you fat. If you want to lose weight, you can eat only grilled chicken, sweet potatoes, egg whites, spinach, and asparagus.

This information is well-meaning—most of the time. A lot of so-called experts truly believe that you must eat these clean food sources if you want to lose weight and get healthy. Eating indulgent foods is not bad, not by any means. But a diet full of whole foods is going to have significantly more nutritional benefit than a diet full of processed and packaged foods.

You must understand that the "clean eating" diet isn't the *only* way. It's very possible, and in fact more sustainable in the long term, to eat the foods you enjoy in moderation on a regular basis. The idea of giving up any one food forever is a scary idea, but if you know you can enjoy your favorite foods whenever you want, guilt-free, so long as you account for them, it makes the prospect of long-term dieting much easier. You can have it all, just not all at once.

Macronutrients versus Micronutrients

You may be wondering, if macros are proteins, carbohydrates, and fats, where do all of those vitamins and minerals come from? Surely those are important.

The important nutritional value your food provides comes from micronutrients. These are the vitamins and minerals that allow your body to function at an optimal level. They are required only in small amounts, which is why they are called micronutrients, but they are very important. These micronutrients come from nutrient-dense foods, such as fruits, vegetables, lean meats, and healthy fats, and these should be main staples in your diet.

It's important to care about your internal health and how you feel, not just how you look. You can dramatically change your body composition and reduce fat by cutting your caloric intake, but this doesn't mean you're healthy on the inside. Vitamins and minerals are essential to your immune system, hormones, hair and skin health, brain functioning, heart health, energy levels, and so many other important things.

The issue with eating processed foods is that they are generally lacking in these micronutrients. Spending your macros on processed foods means you'll have fewer available for whole foods that provide those good nutrients. Many people try to use a multivitamin or greens supplement as nutritional insurance, which isn't a bad idea, but nothing will be as good as eating whole foods every day.

While it's possible to change your body composition with just about any sort of food you'd like, assuming the calories add up, your overall health is far more important than the number on the scale. You may think you're cheating the system if you try to get all of your daily calories from foods that are lacking in micronutrients, but this isn't ideal if you care about your long-term health.

How to Build Your Perfect Diet

In order to build your perfect diet plan, you must first decide what your goals are. Are you looking to just lose weight? Are you looking to gain more muscle? Your final goal will influence your eating plan and how many macros you will require each day. Once you have your goals in mind, you can calculate the proper number of calories and macronutrients that you should be eating each day. To find your actual numbers, follow the steps in Appendix A to figure out your total calorie goal and calculate your macros.

Use these calculations to figure out your individual daily needs for total calories and total macros and use those numbers to plan your days and meal plans. Remember, these numbers are just a best guess and will have to be adjusted as you go. Once you get in the habit of accurately consuming these numbers, which takes practice, it's very easy to adjust your diet when progress stalls.

Build Your Perfect Meal Plan

There's a famous quote about planning that states:

Failing to plan is planning to fail.

When it comes to dietary adherence, this is 100 percent true. If you aren't planning your nutrition ahead of time, there's no way you can have any shot at consistently hitting your macros. Rather than take a reactive approach to your diet and adjust as you go, be proactive and plan your days ahead of time. This way, before the day even starts, you'll see exactly what your macro intake will look like, and you can plan ahead to fill any gaps, or adjust as needed.

If you prefer a more rigid schedule, try planning out two or three perfect days that hit your macros dead-on, and then just follow those meal plans. When coming up with your plans, make sure at least 80 percent of your food is unprocessed, whole foods and make sure they're realistic.

> **essential**
>
> Remember that it's okay to enjoy life, and you shouldn't feel guilty, especially if you plan ahead. If you start to feel guilty, it's easy to bring yourself down, and the temptation to just give up entirely is much stronger. Plan ahead, do your best, and if you slip up, just get back on track as soon as you can.

If you work the night shift at a hospital, your food choices and meal frequency will be different than someone who works from home and has access to a kitchen; there really is no one-size-fits-all approach. Plan ahead, make this process as painless and thought-free as possible, and you'll be good to go.

There are sample meal plans at the end of this book, but if you want to start from scratch, here are the basic steps.

STEP ONE: FIGURE OUT YOUR SCHEDULE

Start by looking at an average day in your life. How many meals can you eat? When are you the busiest? When do you have the most time to cook?

If you work from home, chances are you'll have an easier time preparing three to four meals per day. If you're a busy executive who's constantly working long days and rushing in and out of meetings, you may find that you need a quick and easy breakfast, a few snacks, and a big dinner.

Regardless of your schedule, figure out what sort of meal plan would be easy for you to follow in terms of timing and write those meals down, times and all.

STEP TWO: DIVIDE YOUR MACROS

Now that you have your meal times, and total number of meals, attempt to evenly split your macros across each meal. If your goal is 140 grams of protein per day, and you eat four meals, you'd want to aim for around 35 grams with each meal. This makes hitting your macros much more manageable, rather than trying to get all of your protein at once.

If you're working out that day, put most of your carbs before and after your workout; otherwise you can spread them around however you'd like. For each meal, write down the total number of macronutrients and calories you'll need for that meal.

STEP THREE: CHOOSE YOUR FOODS

Finally, you have the framework. Time to fill it in. Look at each meal and figure out what foods will give you that meal's required calories and macros. This is where you can have fun and get really creative.

The recipes in this book include nutrition calculations that will tell you exactly how many macros are in each serving. This makes planning easy, though of course you can use any food you like.

essential
When choosing food sources, keep in mind that foods high in fiber will keep you full the longest, making it easier to diet. Choose leafy greens, whole grains, and assorted fruits and vegetables to fight off hunger during the day. With a little planning, you should have a sample meal plan that fits your schedule, allows you to hit your macros, and uses foods of your choosing. You can write out the foods you want by hand, or use an app for a food log, like MyFitnessPal or Cronometer. This way you can plan the next day ahead of time and see where any gaps may be that you need to fill. Planning, and sticking to the plan, sets you up for the best possible chance at success as it's a plan perfectly engineered for your needs, schedule, and preferences.

How to Indulge and Still See Results

On to the most fun part of the book: How to eat all the foods you love without sabotaging your progress. The beauty of the macronutrient diet lies in the freedom to choose what you enjoy. This may be the only diet in existence that not only allows you to eat your favorite foods but encourages it. Forget referring to your favorite indulgences as "cheat meals." There's such a negative connotation, and the name couldn't be further from the truth. These meals and snacks should fit into your diet without causing guilt or stress about your choices.

The most effective diet is the one you can stick to for a long time. Making a lasting change takes time, and bouncing from diet to diet, losing and gaining the same five pounds over and over, isn't going to get you anywhere. If having a cookie every night after dinner helps you finally reach your goal weight, that's significantly better than trying to cut out all sweets and resorting to binge eating every weekend, making no long-term progress.

The biggest mistake you can make is seeing a food you love, eating as much of it as you want, and then planning the rest of the day around your indulgence. Not only can an unplanned indulgence send you way over your daily or even weekly calories, but this is the most common cause of dietary guilt. If you've been tracking your macros consistently and suddenly you get thrown way off track by a cheat meal, it can make you feel like a failure,

and it'll be hard to get back on track. This is dangerous for long-term success.

The trick to eating foods you enjoy is planning ahead. If you know that tomorrow night is pizza night, open up tomorrow's food log, plug in however much pizza you want to eat, and adjust the rest of your day accordingly. Being proactive about this will allow you to go through your day stress-free, knowing you'll hit your targets even with that added pizza, and you can enjoy your treat without feeling bad.

essential

If a lot of your macros come from foods that are particularly high in carbs and sodium, you may notice the scale jump up seemingly overnight. These foods can cause extra water retention because the high carb and sodium content pulls water into the cells of your body. If you wake up the next day feeling bloated, there's no need to panic. Just drink plenty of water, and your body will balance itself out after a day or two.

This works for anything, not just pizza. Plan it ahead of time and adjust your day to fit that treat in. It takes moderation, but it can be done. Once you get comfortable with planning small treats and indulgences into your diet, you'll soon realize that the macronutrient diet doesn't require you to give up any of your favorite foods or drinks; you just have to make room for them.

Real-Life Macros in Practice

In a perfect world, all of your food would come from fresh, whole-food sources and supply perfectly balanced nutrition. In the real world, this simply isn't realistic for most people. Life is meant to be enjoyed, and you shouldn't have to make yourself miserable or become obsessed with your food choices to be healthy and maintain the body you want.

Most people find they are able to manage their nutrition while still enjoying themselves by following the 80/20 rule of nutrition. Eighty percent of the time try to eat whole, unprocessed foods. These are the foods that supply the nutrition you need to feel your best. The other 20 percent of the time, have some fun with your choices. Think of a few treats you love and figure out how to work them into your meal plan. You can do a small treat every day, or eat whole foods most of the week and have one or two fun meals. The choice is yours. Just keep in mind that the more processed foods you eat, the greater risk you have of feeling less than optimal, as you're lowering your nutrient intake.

If you can learn to fit those indulgences into your daily macronutrients without losing control and binge eating an entire pizza in one sitting, you'll find you can enjoy the foods you love on a regular basis and still see great results. It's possible for anyone to enjoy the foods they love guilt-free and still work toward the healthy body they want to have.

CHAPTER 2

Breakfast

Mediterranean Scrambled Eggs

SERVES 1	
Per Serving:	
Calories	328
Fat	26g
Sodium	349mg
Carbohydrates	6g
Fiber	1g
Sugar	1g
Protein	17g

Amp up the flavor profile of your traditional morning eggs with flavors of the Mediterranean. Spinach, sun-dried tomatoes, and crumbled feta combine with creamy eggs to satisfy both your taste buds and appetite with a variety of bold flavors and healthy fats.

1 tablespoon olive oil

1 cup baby spinach

2 large eggs, beaten

1 tablespoon jarred sun-dried tomatoes, drained, rinsed, and chopped

2 tablespoons crumbled feta cheese

1 Heat oil in a medium skillet over medium heat.
2 Add spinach and sauté for 1 minute until wilted.
3 Add eggs and sun-dried tomatoes to the skillet. Continue to sauté for another 1–2 minutes until eggs are fully cooked. Stir in feta cheese.
4 Transfer to a plate and serve.

Egg White and Roasted Red Pepper Pitas

SERVES 2	
Per Serving:	
Calories	251
Fat	8g
Sodium	534mg
Carbohydrates	26g
Fiber	4g
Sugar	3g
Protein	19g

There's no excuse to skip breakfast when it's this nutritious, delicious, and fast. Keep just four main ingredients on hand, and you'll always have a healthy and satisfying breakfast ready in just minutes.

½ tablespoon olive oil

½ cup jarred roasted red pepper slices, drained

¼ teaspoon salt

1 cup liquid egg whites

1 (8") whole-wheat pita bread, halved

¼ cup crumbled feta cheese

1 Heat oil in a large skillet over medium heat. Add pepper slices and salt and sauté for 1 minute.
2 Add egg whites and sauté until cooked, about 2–3 minutes.
3 Spoon half of the egg white mixture into each pita half and top the sandwiches with feta cheese. Serve immediately.

Tortilla Breakfast Quiche

This quiche is high in protein, packed with flavor, and almost too pretty to eat. You need only a few ingredients, many of which you likely already have in your kitchen.

8 ounces ground Italian sausage

1½ cups frozen pepper and onion strips

3 large eggs

½ cup nonfat plain Greek yogurt

1 teaspoon Italian seasoning

⅛ teaspoon salt

⅛ teaspoon ground black pepper

1 (10") flour tortilla

1 Preheat oven to 350°F.

2 Heat a large skillet over medium heat. Add sausage and sauté 8–10 minutes until fully browned. Using a slotted spoon, transfer sausage to a large mixing bowl.

3 In the same skillet, sauté pepper and onion strips until softened, about 5–7 minutes. Transfer vegetables to the mixing bowl.

4 In a small bowl, whisk together eggs, yogurt, Italian seasoning, salt, and black pepper. Add egg mixture to sausage mixture and stir.

5 Line a 9" round baking dish with tortilla and press to cover the bottom and partway up the sides.

6 Pour sausage and egg mixture over tortilla and bake 55 minutes or until the center is firm and top is lightly browned.

7 Cool 5 minutes before cutting into six pieces and serving.

The Easiest Frittata You'll Ever Make

SERVES 4	
Per Serving:	
Calories	37
Fat	0g
Sodium	256mg
Carbohydrates	1g
Fiber	0g
Sugar	0g
Protein	8g

This egg white frittata is high in protein and low in carbs and fat. A slice on a toasted English muffin makes a quick breakfast sandwich. If you don't have fresh basil on hand, substitute a teaspoon of dried basil.

8 large egg whites

¼ cup unsweetened almond milk

¼ teaspoon salt

¼ teaspoon ground black pepper

1 medium tomato, sliced

4 basil leaves, cut into thin strips

1 Preheat oven to 375°F.

2 In a large bowl, whisk together egg whites, almond milk, salt, and pepper.

3 Spray a medium oven-safe skillet with nonstick cooking spray and heat over medium heat. Pour the egg white mixture into the skillet and top with tomato and basil. Cook for 2 minutes, occasionally lifting the edges and tilting the pan to allow the uncooked egg to reach the bottom of the pan.

4 Place the skillet in the oven and bake for 10–12 minutes until egg whites are firm and cooked all the way through. Remove frittata from the oven, cut into quarters, and serve immediately.

Egg and Cheese Muffins

These portable muffins are easy to eat hot or cold and can be made in large batches and frozen until ready to serve. A healthy amount of protein and fiber will keep you feeling full all day. If you want to lower the fat, replace the whole eggs with egg whites. Customize the muffins with your favorite vegetables or cheese.

1 teaspoon olive oil

4 cups chopped cooked broccoli

4 large eggs

1 cup liquid egg whites

¼ teaspoon salt

¼ teaspoon ground black pepper

¼ cup shredded Cheddar cheese

1 Preheat oven to 350°F. Brush eight cups of a muffin tin with oil.
2 Divide broccoli among the eight muffin cups.
3 In a medium bowl, beat eggs, egg whites, salt, and pepper.
4 Pour egg mixture into muffin cups over broccoli, filling cups no more than three-quarters full. Top with cheese.
5 Bake 15–20 minutes or until puffed and golden. Cool in pan 1 minute, then remove muffins from the pan. Serve warm or cold.

SERVES 8	
Per Serving:	
Calories	104
Fat	4g
Sodium	174mg
Carbohydrates	8g
Fiber	3g
Sugar	2g
Protein	10g

Strawberry and Walnut Yogurt Bowl

A nutritious and macro-balanced breakfast doesn't get easier than this. Prepare the ingredients ahead of time and store them in the refrigerator for a delicious grab-and-go breakfast.

1 cup full-fat vanilla Greek yogurt

2 tablespoons finely chopped walnuts

½ cup chopped strawberries

¼ teaspoon ground cinnamon

1 Place ½ cup yogurt in a small bowl or Mason jar.

2 Top with 1 tablespoon walnuts, ¼ cup strawberries, and ⅛ teaspoon cinnamon. Layer remaining yogurt, walnuts, strawberries, and cinnamon on top.

3 Serve immediately or refrigerate, covered, overnight.

SERVES 1	
Per Serving:	
Calories	292
Fat	17g
Sodium	81mg
Carbohydrates	13g
Fiber	1g
Sugar	13g
Protein	22g

STREAMLINE YOUR TRACKING

At the beginning of the week, create two or three complete, macro-balanced days in your tracking app and then repeat them throughout the week. Of course, you can make small tweaks here and there, but the majority of the planning is done for you. No need to reinvent the wheel each day!

"Cheesy" Tofu Scramble

SERVES 4	
Per Serving:	
Calories	134
Fat	7g
Sodium	190mg
Carbohydrates	6g
Fiber	3g
Sugar	2g
Protein	12g

Turmeric and nutritional yeast give this scramble the look and taste of cheesy scrambled eggs. Even traditional egg lovers will enjoy it!

2 teaspoons olive oil

½ medium red bell pepper, seeded and chopped

½ medium yellow onion, peeled and chopped

14 ounces extra-firm tofu, drained and pressed to remove water

2 tablespoons nutritional yeast

¼ teaspoon ground turmeric

¼ teaspoon salt

3 cups baby spinach

1 Heat oil in a medium skillet over medium heat. Add pepper and onion and sauté for 8–10 minutes.

2 Add tofu to skillet. Use the back of a wooden spoon to break it apart into smaller pieces.

3 Stir in nutritional yeast, turmeric, and salt.

4 Add baby spinach to the pan and stir until wilted, about 1 minute.

5 Remove from heat and serve.

French Toast Scramble

If you're watching your carbs, a plate of French toast can easily push you over your daily goal. Try this high-protein, low-carb alternative instead. It's made with just a handful of ingredients and comes together in a matter of minutes. Add a spoonful of your favorite nut butter for more protein.

1 medium banana, peeled and mashed

1 large egg

3 large egg whites

1 teaspoon ground cinnamon

½ teaspoon honey

1 teaspoon vanilla extract

½ teaspoon coconut oil

SERVES 1	
Per Serving:	
Calories	279
Fat	8g
Sodium	231mg
Carbohydrates	36g
Fiber	3g
Sugar	17g
Protein	16g

1 In a medium mixing bowl, combine banana, egg, egg whites, cinnamon, honey, and vanilla. Mix well.

2 Melt coconut oil in a small skillet over medium heat. Pour in batter.

3 Cook, stirring, until eggs are no longer runny, about 3–4 minutes.

4 Remove from pan and serve.

Sautéed Sausage and Plantain

Just grab a pan and two main ingredients, and a hearty breakfast is ready in just 10 minutes. Protein-packed sausage and satisfying plantains will fill you up and give you energy all morning long.

¼ teaspoon ground cinnamon

2 large ripe plantains, peeled and sliced

1 tablespoon olive oil

1 (11-ounce) package precooked sweet Italian-style chicken sausage, sliced

SERVES 4	
Per Serving:	
Calories	316
Fat	9g
Sodium	401mg
Carbohydrates	47g
Fiber	4g
Sugar	1g
Protein	12g

1 Sprinkle cinnamon over plantain slices.

2 Heat oil in a large skillet over medium-high heat.

3 Add plantain and sausage slices and sauté for about 10 minutes or until golden brown and cooked through.

4 Transfer to plates and serve immediately.

Low-Carb Protein Waffle

SERVES 1	
Per Serving:	
Calories	190
Fat	6g
Sodium	115mg
Carbohydrates	5g
Fiber	0g
Sugar	1g
Protein	29g

This low-carb breakfast will leave you feeling worlds better than the traditional high-sugar frozen waffle. Swap out the vanilla protein powder with your favorite flavor—try chocolate or peanut butter for a fun variation.

¼ cup vanilla protein powder

1 teaspoon baking powder

1 teaspoon ground cinnamon

1 large egg

½ cup water

1 Preheat a waffle maker for 5 minutes.

2 Add protein powder, baking powder, and cinnamon to a medium bowl and mix well. Stir in egg and water.

3 Pour the batter into the waffle maker and close the top.

4 Cook waffle 1–2 minutes and serve immediately.

Overnight Peanut Butter Protein Oats

SERVES 2	
Per Serving:	
Calories	354
Fat	8g
Sodium	260mg
Carbohydrates	41g
Fiber	8g
Sugar	4g
Protein	28g

Overnight oats are perfect for busy mornings. Whip up a batch (or enough for the whole week) the night before. In the morning, all you need to do is grab a spoon and dig in. These oats also make a great well-balanced snack. Just divide the recipe in half for fewer calories per serving.

1 cup rolled oats

¼ cup vanilla protein powder

½ cup nonfat plain Greek yogurt

¼ cup powdered peanut butter

1½ cups unsweetened almond milk

1 Combine all ingredients in a medium bowl. Divide mixture between two Mason jars or containers with lids.

2 Cover and refrigerate overnight.

3 Serve cold.

Four-Ingredient Pancake

Even during the busiest work week, you can make this hot and healthy breakfast. And the ingredients are much more nutritious than traditional pancake batter.

1 small banana, peeled and mashed

1 large egg

1 large egg white

⅛ teaspoon ground cinnamon

1 teaspoon coconut oil

1 In a small mixing bowl, combine banana, egg, egg white, and cinnamon and mix well.
2 Melt coconut oil in a small skillet over medium-low heat.
3 Pour banana mixture into skillet and flatten slightly with the back of a spatula.
4 Cook the pancake for about 5–6 minutes until the middle starts to bubble and the edges easily pull away from the pan with a spatula. Flip the pancake and cook the other side for 2 minutes.
5 Remove from pan and serve.

SERVES 1	
Per Serving:	
Calories	218
Fat	10g
Sodium	121mg
Carbohydrates	22g
Fiber	3g
Sugar	12g
Protein	11g

Rice Cakes with Avocado and Egg

This quickie breakfast, loaded with protein and healthy fats, comes together in no time. It's also extremely satisfying and will keep you full and happy for hours.

½ **medium avocado, peeled, pitted, and mashed**

2 **lightly salted rice cakes**

2 **large hard-cooked eggs, peeled and sliced**

⅛ **teaspoon salt**

⅛ **teaspoon ground black pepper**

1 Spread avocado onto rice cakes. Top each with a sliced egg.
2 Sprinkle with salt and pepper and serve immediately.

Strawberry Cheesecake Overnight Oats

Fresh strawberries and crushed graham crackers will make you feel like you're having (cheese) cake for breakfast.

1 **graham cracker**

½ **cup rolled oats**

½ **cup low-fat cottage cheese**

2 **tablespoons strawberry preserves**

½ **cup vanilla almond milk**

½ **teaspoon vanilla extract**

1 **cup chopped strawberries**

1 Break graham cracker into pieces and place them inside a zip-top plastic bag. Use a rolling pin to crush cracker into crumbs.
2 In a medium bowl, combine oats, cottage cheese, preserves, almond milk, vanilla, and strawberries. Stir to mix well.
3 Divide the mixture between two Mason jars or containers with lids. Sprinkle with graham cracker crumbs.
4 Cover and refrigerate overnight. Serve cold.

Coconut Almond Overnight Oats

Here's an easy and satisfying breakfast for a busy morning. Made with chocolate, coconut, and almond just like the classic candy bar, it's sweet and decadent, but it won't blow up your macros for the day.

⅓ cup rolled oats

¼ cup chocolate protein powder

½ teaspoon cocoa powder

1 teaspoon maple syrup

⅓ cup unsweetened vanilla almond milk

1 tablespoon almond butter

1 tablespoon shredded coconut

SERVES 1	
Per Serving:	
Calories	447
Fat	17g
Sodium	532mg
Carbohydrates	46g
Fiber	8g
Sugar	15g
Protein	27g

1 Combine all ingredients in a container with a lid or a Mason jar and mix well.

2 Cover and refrigerate overnight. Serve cold.

Overnight Protein Oats

Top these oats with your favorite ingredients—berries, sliced bananas, chopped nuts, shredded coconut, or dried fruit. Anything goes! Triple the recipe for nearly a full week's worth of make-ahead breakfasts.

1 cup rolled oats

1 tablespoon chia seeds

¼ cup vanilla protein powder

1¼ cups unsweetened almond milk

SERVES 2	
Per Serving:	
Calories	269
Fat	7g
Sodium	138mg
Carbohydrates	33g
Fiber	8g
Sugar	2g
Protein	19g

1 In a large bowl, combine oats, chia seeds, protein powder, and almond milk. Stir to combine.

2 Divide between two Mason jars or containers with lids.

3 Cover and refrigerate overnight.

4 Serve cold or heat for 2–3 minutes on high in the microwave.

Overnight Carrot Cake Oats

SERVES 1

Per Serving:

Calories	405
Fat	14g
Sodium	177mg
Carbohydrates	37g
Fiber	11g
Sugar	5g
Protein	31g

This super satisfying breakfast tastes like a decadent dessert, while providing a healthy (and balanced) dose of protein, carbs, and fat.

⅓ cup rolled oats

¼ cup vanilla protein powder

½ cup unsweetened almond milk

2 tablespoons grated carrot

½ tablespoon chopped walnuts

½ tablespoon unsweetened flaked coconut

1 teaspoon maple syrup

1 teaspoon chia seeds

½ teaspoon ground cinnamon

⅛ teaspoon ground ginger

1 Combine all ingredients in a Mason jar or a container with a lid.
2 Serve cold or heat for 2–3 minutes on high in the microwave.

Mocha Overnight Oats

SERVES 4

Per Serving:

Calories	443
Fat	15g
Sodium	624mg
Carbohydrates	47g
Fiber	14g
Sugar	2g
Protein	24g

Start your day with a coffee and chocolate buzz. This easy breakfast might sound decadent, but it's actually nutritious and macro-friendly.

2 cups rolled oats

¼ cup cocoa powder

½ cup chocolate protein powder

¼ cup chia seeds

1 cup freshly brewed coffee

2 cups unsweetened almond milk

¼ cup cacao nibs

1 teaspoon salt

1 Combine all ingredients in a large mixing bowl and stir thoroughly.
2 Divide oat mixture between four Mason jars or containers with lids.
3 Cover and refrigerate overnight.
4 Serve cold or heat for 2–3 minutes on high in the microwave.

Pumpkin Pie Overnight Oats

Thick and creamy overnight oats with real pumpkin, warm spices, and chia seeds make a nutritious breakfast, snack, or dessert.

⅓ cup rolled oats

⅓ cup canned pumpkin purée

⅓ cup unsweetened almond milk

1 teaspoon chia seeds

1 teaspoon pumpkin pie spice

1 teaspoon maple syrup

1 teaspoon chopped pecans

SERVES 1	
Per Serving:	
Calories	264
Fat	8g
Sodium	76mg
Carbohydrates	39g
Fiber	12g
Sugar	6g
Protein	8g

1 In a medium jar or container with a lid, combine oats, pumpkin, almond milk, chia seeds, pumpkin pie spice, and maple syrup. Mix well.

2 Cover and refrigerate overnight.

3 In the morning, top with pecans and serve cold or heat for 2–3 minutes on high in the microwave.

Peachy Cottage Cheese Toast

This cottage cheese toast is one of the simplest breakfasts you can make in the morning. Just top your favorite whole-grain toast with cottage cheese and a few nutritional powerhouse ingredients. This toast works with just about any fresh fruit, so feel free to try your favorites.

¼ cup low-fat cottage cheese

¼ teaspoon maple syrup

⅛ teaspoon ground cinnamon

1 tablespoon almond butter

1 (1-ounce) slice whole-grain bread, toasted

½ small peach, pitted and thinly sliced

1 teaspoon hemp hearts

SERVES 1	
Per Serving:	
Calories	243
Fat	11g
Sodium	293mg
Carbohydrates	22g
Fiber	3g
Sugar	8g
Protein	14g

1 In a small bowl, combine cottage cheese, maple syrup, and cinnamon.

2 Spread almond butter on toasted bread and top with cottage cheese mixture, peach slices, and hemp hearts. Serve immediately.

Smoked Salmon Avocado Toast

SMOKED SALMON IS NOT LIKE OTHER FISH

Smoked salmon can be purchased in regular grocery stores as well as specialty food shops. It's a quick source of protein, rich in omega-3 fatty acids. Its sodium content is higher than other fish, so it's something to consider if you're watching your intake.

Smoked salmon is loaded with protein, healthy omega-3 fats, and flavor. When paired with avocado and whole-grain toast, it makes a well-balanced and macro-friendly breakfast you'll want to eat every morning of the week.

½ medium avocado, peeled, pitted, and mashed

2 (1-ounce) slices whole-grain bread, toasted

2 ounces smoked salmon

¼ small red onion, peeled and thinly sliced

1 Spread avocado on toasted bread. Top with salmon and onion.

2 Serve immediately.

"Oatmeal" Minus the Oats

Per Serving:

Calories	320
Fat	11g
Sodium	426mg
Carbohydrates	31g
Fiber	6g
Sugar	14g
Protein	25g

This low-carb porridge is a warm and hearty breakfast that can be made on the stovetop or in the microwave for a quick, protein-packed breakfast. Add your favorite toppings—berries, raisins, or nut butter—just as you would for a traditional bowl of oatmeal.

¾ cup liquid egg whites or 6 large egg whites

½ cup unsweetened almond milk

2 tablespoons chopped walnuts

1 tablespoon ground flaxseed

1 teaspoon ground cinnamon

1 medium banana, peeled and mashed

½ teaspoon vanilla extract

1 In a medium saucepan, whisk together egg whites and almond milk. Stir in walnuts, flaxseed, cinnamon, banana, and vanilla; blend well.

2 Place the saucepan over medium heat and cook, stirring frequently, until the "oatmeal" reaches the desired consistency; this should take 2–3 minutes. Serve immediately.

Loaded Banana Toast

Per Serving:

Calories	303
Fat	7g
Sodium	221mg
Carbohydrates	53g
Fiber	5g
Sugar	22g
Protein	11g

If you have only a few minutes to make breakfast, here's an easy and nutritious on-the-go recipe for you. All you need are a few minutes and a handful of common kitchen ingredients. There's no excuse to skip breakfast with this recipe in your repertoire.

1 medium banana, peeled and mashed

1 tablespoon hemp hearts

1 teaspoon honey

½ teaspoon ground cinnamon

2 (1-ounce) slices whole-grain bread, toasted

1 In a small bowl, mix together mashed banana, hemp hearts, honey, and cinnamon.

2 Spread mixture on toasted bread and serve immediately.

Bacon Roasted Potatoes

These potatoes are a versatile breakfast side dish. But they're just as good at dinnertime too.

6 slices thick-cut bacon

4 medium russet potatoes, peeled and cut into 1" pieces

2 medium sweet potatoes, peeled and cut into 1" pieces

1 medium red bell pepper, seeded and chopped

1 medium yellow onion, peeled and chopped

1 tablespoon Montreal Steak Seasoning

SERVES 8	
Per Serving:	
Calories	183
Fat	5g
Sodium	220mg
Carbohydrates	29g
Fiber	4g
Sugar	4g
Protein	6g

1 Preheat oven to 400°F. Spray a large baking sheet with nonstick cooking spray.

2 Place bacon in a large skillet. Place over medium heat and cook 8–10 minutes until crisp, turning often. Remove bacon from pan and drain on paper towels. Cool 5 minutes, then chop into small pieces. Set aside. Reserve ¼ cup bacon drippings from the pan and set aside.

3 Place potatoes, sweet potatoes, pepper, and onion in a large mixing bowl. Drizzle reserved bacon drippings over vegetables and mix well. Sprinkle seasoning over the mixture.

4 Transfer potato mixture to prepared baking sheet.

5 Bake 10 minutes. Remove from oven and toss. Return to oven and bake 10 minutes more.

6 Adjust oven setting to broil and cook for another 5–7 minutes or until potatoes are crispy around the edges.

7 Transfer potatoes to a serving bowl. Add bacon and toss.

8 Serve immediately or refrigerate in an airtight container for up to 5 days.

Hash Brown Breakfast Casserole

SERVES 6	
Per Serving:	
Calories	270
Fat	19g
Sodium	417mg
Carbohydrates	11g
Fiber	1g
Sugar	4g
Protein	15g

POWER YOUR BRAIN WITH FAT

Fat is a slow-digesting source of energy—it makes you feel full and helps you avoid energy crashes. Many people report improved mental functioning when they consume high-fat breakfasts in the morning, so try this kind of meal when working on big projects. Depending on your goals, you can adjust egg recipes to have more or less fat. Use whole eggs and full-fat cheese if you want more fat or all egg whites and low-fat cheese if you want a meal with less fat.

Whip up this hearty breakfast at the beginning of the week and just reheat in the morning. Enjoy it alone or tuck a slice into a toasted English muffin for a quick, travel-friendly breakfast sandwich.

1½ cups shredded Cheddar cheese, divided

5 large eggs

1½ cups whole milk

¾ cup frozen pepper and onion strips

1 teaspoon onion powder

¼ teaspoon ground black pepper

¼ teaspoon salt

6 (1-ounce) frozen hash brown patties

1 Preheat oven to 350°F.

2 Coat a 9" × 13" baking pan with nonstick cooking spray.

3 Spread 1 cup cheese on the bottom of the prepared baking pan in a thin layer.

4 In a large bowl, whisk together eggs, milk, pepper and onion strips, onion powder, black pepper, and salt.

5 Pour egg mixture over cheese in the pan and layer hash brown patties on top.

6 Bake for 35 minutes. Remove from oven and top with remaining ½ cup cheese.

7 Bake for another 20–25 minutes until top is golden brown.

8 Remove from the oven and cool 5 minutes before serving.

Salsa Breakfast Bake

Made with only four ingredients, this nutritious vegetarian breakfast is delicious and super satisfying. A spicy salsa gives it quite a kick to start your morning! Bake the squash the night before to save time in the morning.

1 (2-pound) spaghetti squash, halved and seeded

2 teaspoons olive oil

¾ cup mild or medium salsa

5 large eggs

1 cup shredded Cheddar cheese

SERVES 4	
Per Serving:	
Calories	301
Fat	19g
Sodium	219mg
Carbohydrates	17g
Fiber	3g
Sugar	6g
Protein	16g

1 Preheat oven to 400°F. Line a baking sheet with parchment paper.

2 Place spaghetti squash halves, cut side up, on the prepared baking sheet. Drizzle with oil, then turn the halves cut side down.

3 Roast until fork-tender, about 35–40 minutes. Remove from oven, then adjust oven temperature to 350°F.

4 Spray a 9" square baking dish with nonstick cooking spray. Set aside.

5 Cool squash slightly, then use a fork to separate the flesh into strands. Transfer strands to a large bowl. Add salsa and eggs and mix well. Pour mixture into prepared baking dish and smooth the top with a spatula.

6 Top with cheese.

7 Bake for 30–35 minutes until cooked through and cheese is lightly browned. Remove from oven and cool 5 minutes. Cut into four pieces and serve.

Overnight Honey Bread Pudding

SUGAR IS SUGAR IS SUGAR?

Typically, yes, but high-quality, raw, unfiltered honey contains bee pollen, which is associated with reducing inflammation, boosting liver health, and strengthening the entire immune system.

Made with both nutritious and decadent ingredients, this twist on traditional bread pudding is just as satisfying as it is delicious. Mix up a few batches on Sunday for a quick and easy dessert-like breakfast all week.

1 (1-ounce) slice whole-grain bread

¼ cup nonfat vanilla Greek yogurt

¼ cup unsweetened almond milk

2 teaspoons honey, divided

2 tablespoons vanilla protein powder

¼ teaspoon ground cinnamon

1 Cut bread into 16 small squares and place in a Mason jar or container with a lid.

2 In a small bowl, combine yogurt, almond milk, 1 teaspoon honey, protein powder, and cinnamon.

3 Pour yogurt mixture over bread, allowing it to fully soak in. Cover and refrigerate overnight.

4 In the morning, drizzle remaining 1 teaspoon honey on top and serve.

Peanut Butter and Jelly Chia Pudding

Your childhood favorite gets a nutritional upgrade in this sweet and comforting breakfast pudding. Chia seeds are packed with protein, fiber, and omega-3 fatty acids that have important benefits for your body and brain. Chia seeds are high in protein and fiber, both of which have been shown to aid weight loss. The fatty acids can increase memory, concentration, and learning in those who suffer from ADHD.

¼ cup chia seeds

1 cup unsweetened almond milk

1 cup raspberries

2 tablespoons creamy natural peanut butter

SERVES 2	
Per Serving:	
Calories	205
Fat	14g
Sodium	165mg
Carbohydrates	15g
Fiber	13g
Sugar	3g
Protein	7g

1 In a medium bowl, stir together chia seeds and almond milk. Mix well.
2 In a small bowl, mash raspberries using the back of a spoon.
3 Divide half of the chia seed mixture between two small Mason jars or containers with lids and top with raspberries. Add the remaining chia mixture to each container.
4 Cover and refrigerate overnight.
5 In the morning, top each with 1 tablespoon peanut butter and serve.

Morning Glory Muffins

What a glorious and delicious way to start the day! Moist, nutritious, and slightly sweet, these muffins are a healthy treat.

1 cup mashed sweet potato

1 cup shredded coconut

1 cup raisins

1 cup chopped walnuts

½ cup honey

¼ cup shredded carrot

4 large eggs

1½ cups almond flour

1 teaspoon ground cinnamon

1 teaspoon vanilla extract

2 teaspoons baking powder

1 Preheat oven to 350°F. Spray a twelve-cup muffin tin with non-stick cooking spray or line with paper liners.

2 Combine all ingredients in a large mixing bowl. Stir to mix.

3 Pour batter into muffin tin.

4 Bake 28–30 minutes or until a toothpick inserted into the center of a muffin comes out clean.

5 Cool 2 minutes in muffin tin, then remove from tin and cool on a wire rack.

MAKES 12 MUFFINS

Per Serving (1 muffin):

Calories	328
Fat	14g
Sodium	34mg
Carbohydrates	46g
Fiber	4g
Sugar	33g
Protein	7g

TO WEIGH OR NOT TO WEIGH (YOUR FOOD)

Owning a food scale is important for figuring out what a proper portion size looks like, especially in the beginning of your macro journey. Look for a scale that measures food in ounces, grams, or milliliters.

Meal Prep Ninja Breakfast Cookies

MAKES 18 COOKIES

Per Serving (2 cookies):

Calories	167
Fat	8g
Sodium	40mg
Carbohydrates	16g
Fiber	2g
Sugar	5g
Protein	8g

BREAKFAST PREP MAKES YOUR WEEK EASIER

Breakfast is one of the easiest meals to prepare in advance. Find two breakfasts that you love and alternate them Monday through Friday. Make and pack them up once, and you're ready for the week. Switch up the recipes the following week to prevent boredom.

These delicious morsels are packed with wholesome ingredients containing fiber and protein to keep you satisfied for hours. And they're sneaky, like ninjas—they taste so good, you probably won't even notice that they're healthy for you!

2 medium bananas, peeled and mashed

2 large eggs

1 medium carrot, peeled and grated

½ cup creamy almond butter

2 tablespoons coconut oil, melted

2 tablespoons maple syrup

1½ cups rolled oats

½ cup almond flour

½ cup vanilla protein powder

¼ cup pumpkin seeds

½ cup raisins

1 teaspoon ground cinnamon

1 Preheat oven to 350°F. Line a large baking sheet with parchment paper.

2 In a large mixing bowl, combine all ingredients and mix well.

3 Roll dough into eighteen large balls and place on prepared baking sheet. Flatten each ball slightly with your hands.

4 Bake for 25–30 minutes until cookies are golden brown.

5 Remove and cool slightly on the baking sheet. Transfer cookies to a wire rack and cool completely. Serve immediately or store in an airtight container.

Pumpkin Spice Protein Bars

One of these Pumpkin Spice Protein Bars is the perfect make-ahead breakfast for hectic mornings (or low-key weekends). The best part about this recipe is just how delicious and satisfying it can be to start your day off on the right foot with oats, pumpkin, eggs, cottage cheese, and walnuts.

1½ cups quick oats

⅔ cup low-fat cottage cheese

1 cup canned pumpkin purée

⅓ cup maple syrup

2 large eggs

½ cup liquid egg whites or 3 large egg whites

2 teaspoons pumpkin pie spice

1 teaspoon ground cinnamon

1 teaspoon vanilla extract

2 tablespoons finely chopped walnuts

1 Preheat oven to 350°F. Spray a 9" square baking pan with non-stick cooking spray.

2 Combine oats, cottage cheese, pumpkin, maple syrup, eggs, egg whites, pumpkin pie spice, cinnamon, and vanilla in a food processor and pulse for about 1 minute. Batter should be a little chunky.

3 Pour batter into the prepared pan. Smooth the top of the batter with a spatula and top with walnuts.

4 Bake for 32–34 minutes until a toothpick inserted into the center comes out clean.

5 Remove from oven and cool in the pan for 5 minutes before slicing and serving.

SERVES 9	
Per Serving:	
Calories	133
Fat	3g
Sodium	78mg
Carbohydrates	20g
Fiber	2g
Sugar	9g
Protein	7g

PUMPKIN MIGHT SURPRISE YOU

Pumpkin is low in calories because it consists of 90 percent water. One cup of canned pumpkin has less than 100 calories. The same-sized serving of sweet potato has three times as many calories. Pumpkin also has more fiber than kale and more potassium than bananas, and it's full of heart-healthy magnesium and iron.

Sweet Potato and Parsnip Breakfast Hash

SERVES 2	
Per Serving:	
Calories	339
Fat	10g
Sodium	450mg
Carbohydrates	52g
Fiber	9g
Sugar	14g
Protein	12g

This hash is protein-packed, fiber-rich, and nutrient-dense. Prep it ahead of time and reheat it in the morning. Or cook it for dinner and save the leftovers for breakfast the next day.

6 ounces ground pork sausage

1 medium sweet potato, peeled and diced

2 medium parsnips, peeled and diced

1 small yellow onion, peeled and chopped

1 small apple, peeled, cored, and diced

¼ teaspoon ground cinnamon

⅛ teaspoon salt

3 cups chopped kale

1 Sauté sausage in a medium skillet over medium heat until browned, about 8 minutes. Using a slotted spoon, transfer sausage to a plate and set aside.

2 In the same skillet, sauté sweet potato and parsnips for 6–8 minutes until tender.

3 Add onion, apple, cinnamon, and salt and cover skillet with a lid. Cook for another 2–3 minutes until apple is softened.

4 Uncover skillet and add kale. Cook, stirring, until wilted, about 2 minutes.

5 Return sausage to the skillet and stir until warmed through, about 2 minutes more.

6 Divide mixture into two bowls and serve.

CHAPTER 3

Soups, Sandwiches, and Wraps

Creamy Potato Soup

SERVES 5	
Per Serving:	
Calories	186
Fat	9g
Sodium	609mg
Carbohydrates	19g
Fiber	3g
Sugar	3g
Protein	7g

This hearty meal combines all the flavors of a traditional baked potato in a creamy and comforting soup. It's perfect as a warm and filling lunch, especially on a cold or rainy day.

2 medium russet potatoes

1 small head cauliflower, cored, outer leaves removed, and chopped

1½ cups low-sodium chicken broth

1½ cups whole milk

½ cup sour cream

½ cup shredded Cheddar cheese

6 tablespoons chopped chives

1 teaspoon salt

1 teaspoon ground black pepper

3 slices bacon, cooked and crumbled

1 Preheat oven to 400°F.

2 Place potatoes on a baking sheet and bake 1 hour. Cool 10 minutes, then cut potatoes in half. Scoop the flesh from each half and roughly dice. Set aside.

3 Place cauliflower in a steamer basket. In a medium saucepan, bring 1" of water to a boil. Place steamer basket in saucepan, cover, and reduce heat to medium-low. Steam cauliflower for 5 minutes.

4 Combine potatoes, broth, and milk in a large saucepan and bring to a boil over medium-high heat. Stir in cauliflower.

5 Remove from heat, then transfer soup to a blender and process until smooth (or use a handheld blender).

6 Return soup to pot and place over low heat and stir in sour cream, cheese, chives, salt, and pepper. Simmer 10 minutes, stirring frequently.

7 Top with bacon before serving.

Sweet Potato Soup

This savory and colorful soup is just what you need on a chilly day. Serve it alongside a few whole-grain crackers or a mixed green salad for a nutritious meal. Sweet potatoes are packed with essential nutrients and fiber, making them one of the healthiest starchy carb sources you can eat.

6 large sweet potatoes, peeled and chopped

1 large onion, peeled and chopped

3 stalks celery, chopped

2 teaspoons poultry seasoning

4 cups low-sodium chicken broth

2 cups milk

SERVES 4	
Per Serving:	
Calories	178
Fat	3g
Sodium	121mg
Carbohydrates	29g
Fiber	4g
Sugar	12g
Protein	8g

1 Add sweet potatoes, onion, celery, and poultry seasoning to a large pot. Add broth and top off with water until vegetables are just covered.

2 Bring to a boil over high heat. Reduce heat to medium-low and simmer 10–15 minutes until vegetables are tender.

3 Remove from heat, then transfer soup to a blender and process until smooth (or use a handheld blender). Return soup to pot and stir in milk. Heat over medium-low heat for 5 minutes. Serve hot.

Garlic Cheddar Cauliflower Soup

SERVES 2

Per Serving:

Calories	351
Fat	23g
Sodium	485mg
Carbohydrates	18g
Fiber	7g
Sugar	8g
Protein	18g

If you've ever been intimidated by making your own soup, this cauliflower soup is a great one to start with. The ingredient list is small, and the simple instructions make it foolproof. The soup is nutritious, delicious, and cheesy, and it's sure to please everyone, even those who don't like cauliflower.

2 tablespoons olive oil

1 small yellow onion, peeled and chopped

2 cloves garlic, peeled and minced

1 medium head cauliflower, cored, outer leaves removed, and chopped

4 cups low-sodium chicken broth

½ cup shredded sharp Cheddar cheese

¼ cup grated Parmesan cheese

1 Heat oil in a large saucepan over medium heat. Sauté onion and garlic 5 minutes.
2 Add cauliflower and broth. Increase heat to high and bring to a boil.
3 Reduce heat to medium-low and simmer 20 minutes until cauliflower is soft.
4 Remove from heat, then transfer soup to a blender and process until smooth (or use a handheld blender).
5 Return soup to pot, stir in Cheddar and Parmesan, and heat, stirring constantly, over medium heat 5 minutes until cheeses melt. Serve hot.

Broccoli and "Cheese" Soup

You'd never guess that there's no dairy in this rich, creamy broccoli "cheese" soup. It's made from a savory and nutritious blend of broccoli, coconut milk, and nutritional yeast. It's so delicious, you won't even miss the cheese.

1 teaspoon olive oil

1 medium yellow onion, peeled and chopped

2 teaspoons minced garlic

3 cups low-sodium chicken broth

1 cup full-fat coconut milk

5 cups roughly chopped broccoli florets

⅓ cup nutritional yeast

¼ teaspoon salt

SERVES 4	
Per Serving:	
Calories	208
Fat	17g
Sodium	178mg
Carbohydrates	11g
Fiber	1g
Sugar	6g
Protein	3g

1 Heat oil in a large pot over medium heat. Add onion and garlic and sauté for 3–4 minutes until softened.

2 Add chicken broth, coconut milk, broccoli, nutritional yeast, and salt. Stir to combine.

3 Reduce heat to medium-low and simmer for 12–15 minutes until broccoli is tender.

4 Remove from heat, then transfer soup to a blender and process until smooth or until desired consistency is reached (or use a handheld blender). Serve immediately.

Instant Pot® Chicken and White Bean Soup

SERVES 6	
Per Serving:	
Calories	270
Fat	5g
Sodium	820mg
Carbohydrates	25g
Fiber	5g
Sugar	1g
Protein	32g

THE BEST WAY TO COOK CHICKEN?

Pressure cooking might just be the best way to cook chicken. Baking and grilling are fine, but you could easily end up with dry chicken. Pressure-cooked chicken will fall apart and shred very easily and retain a lot of its moisture.

With an Instant Pot®, you can make a super flavorful meal within minutes. You probably already have most of the ingredients on hand for this hearty protein-packed soup. Keep the ingredients in your pantry so you can make this last-minute on a weeknight anytime.

1½ pounds boneless, skinless chicken breasts

3 cups low-sodium chicken broth, divided

2 tablespoons salted butter

¾ cup diced onion

1 tablespoon minced garlic

1 (4.5-ounce) can chopped green chilies, drained

1 tablespoon ground cumin

1 teaspoon dried oregano

1 teaspoon salt

½ teaspoon ground black pepper

2 (15-ounce) cans white beans, drained and rinsed

¼ cup chopped fresh cilantro

1 Place chicken, 2 cups broth, butter, onion, garlic, chilies, cumin, oregano, salt, and pepper in an Instant Pot®.

2 Close lid, set steam release to Sealing, press the Manual button, and set time to 19 minutes. When the timer beeps, quick-release the pressure until the float valve drops and open the lid.

3 Transfer chicken to a plate and cool 5 minutes. Shred chicken with two forks and return it to the Instant Pot®. Stir in beans and the remaining 1 cup broth. Let soup stand on the Keep Warm setting for 5 minutes.

4 Garnish soup with fresh cilantro before serving.

Taco Corn Chowder

Per Serving:

Calories	412
Fat	12g
Sodium	857mg
Carbohydrates	67g
Fiber	4g
Sugar	12g
Protein	13g

BE CONSCIOUS, NOT OBSESSIVE

Tracking macros is an effective way to lose weight because it focuses your attention on the amount and types of food you are eating. While mindfulness of your consumption is important, it's okay to loosen the reins occasionally on how strict you are about meeting the exact percentages and grams in your diet every day. When you find a balance within your diet, there's a higher likelihood you'll stick with tracking.

Traditional corn chowder gets a zesty upgrade with a kick of taco seasoning for a simple and delicious one-pot weeknight dinner. It's perfect for dinner on a cool fall night or packed in a thermos for a portable and fuss-free lunch.

2 tablespoons olive oil

8 cups frozen corn kernels, thawed

1 medium yellow onion, peeled and diced

1 tablespoon taco seasoning

1 teaspoon salt

6 cups low-sodium chicken broth

½ cup shredded pepper jack cheese

1 In a large pot over medium-high heat, heat oil. Add corn, onion, taco seasoning, and salt.

2 Sauté for 7–8 minutes until onion is soft.

3 Remove one-third of the mixture and set aside.

4 Add broth to the pot and bring to a boil. Reduce heat to medium-low and simmer for 15 minutes.

5 Remove from heat, then transfer soup to a blender and process until smooth (or use a handheld blender).

6 Return soup to pot and stir in the reserved corn mixture. Simmer over medium-low heat for 3 minutes.

7 Ladle soup into four bowls and top with cheese. Serve immediately.

Slow Cooker Black Bean Soup

Made with fresh carrots, celery, and onion, this lightly creamy black bean soup is packed with nutrients and flavor. Leftovers can be stored in the refrigerator and reheated whenever you need an easy, protein-packed lunch.

2 tablespoons olive oil

2 medium carrots, peeled and chopped

2 stalks celery, chopped

1 medium onion, peeled and chopped

¼ cup tomato paste

3 cloves garlic, peeled and minced

1½ teaspoons ground cumin

3 (15-ounce) cans black beans, drained and rinsed

1 cup frozen or canned corn

3 cups vegetable broth

1 Heat oil in a medium skillet over medium-high heat.

2 Add carrots, celery, and onion to the pan and sauté 5 minutes until slightly softened.

3 Stir in tomato paste, garlic, and cumin and continue to cook 2 minutes, stirring frequently.

4 Transfer mixture to a 4- to 6-quart slow cooker. Stir in beans, corn, and broth. Cook on high for 4 hours.

5 Serve warm or allow to cool and refrigerate for up to 5 days.

SERVES 6	
Per Serving:	
Calories	392
Fat	6g
Sodium	102mg
Carbohydrates	66g
Fiber	2g
Sugar	6g
Protein	18g

CANNED VERSUS DRIED BEANS

Nutrition-wise, cooked and canned beans are about the same. Dried beans are much more cost-effective, and some say they taste better than canned, but they take a fair amount of time to cook because they require soaking, often overnight. Canned beans don't require advance planning, and they're relatively inexpensive, but they're higher in sodium than cooked beans. If you have the time, it might be worth it to make your own beans at home, but for convenience, having a few cans in the pantry is certainly handy in a mealtime time-crunch.

Turkey Pumpkin Chili

SERVES 4

Per Serving:

Calories	253
Fat	12g
Sodium	785mg
Carbohydrates	14g
Fiber	4g
Sugar	7g
Protein	24g

Turkey, pumpkin, and traditional chili ingredients combine to make a flavorful dish that's loaded with protein and fiber. This cold-weather recipe utilizes the best flavors of the season and will warm you right up.

1 tablespoon olive oil

1 pound ground turkey

1 medium yellow onion, peeled and diced

1 tablespoon minced garlic

2 tablespoons chili powder

1 tablespoon ground cumin

1 teaspoon paprika

½ teaspoon pumpkin pie spice

1 cup canned crushed tomatoes

1 cup canned pumpkin purée

1½ cups water

1 teaspoon salt

1 Heat oil in a large skillet over medium-high heat. Add ground turkey, onion, and garlic and sauté for about 7–8 minutes, or until turkey is no longer pink.

2 Add chili powder, cumin, paprika, pumpkin pie spice, tomatoes, pumpkin, water, and salt. Bring to a boil.

3 Reduce heat to low and simmer 20 minutes.

4 Ladle into four bowls and serve.

Spicy Ranch Chili

This easy vegetarian chili is full of flavor—a comforting bowl with a spicy kick of hot sauce. Feel free to add as little or as much as you wish. No matter what you decide, this chili might just become your very favorite.

2 (15-ounce) cans chili beans

2 tablespoons olive oil

1 small yellow onion, peeled and diced

2 medium red bell peppers, seeded and diced

2 tablespoons ranch seasoning mix

2 teaspoons chili powder

1 (28-ounce) can diced tomatoes with juice

2 tablespoons sriracha sauce

SERVES 6	
Per Serving:	
Calories	154
Fat	4g
Sodium	391mg
Carbohydrates	20g
Fiber	6g
Sugar	6g
Protein	7g

1 Drain and rinse 1 can of chili beans. Set aside.
2 In a large saucepan, heat oil over medium-high heat. Add onion and peppers and sauté until softened, about 6–8 minutes.
3 Stir in ranch seasoning and chili powder. Add drained and undrained beans, tomatoes, and sriracha and bring to a boil.
4 Reduce heat to medium-low. Simmer for 15–20 minutes until thickened. Serve immediately.

Creamy Pumpkin Soup

SERVES 4	
Per Serving:	
Calories	363
Fat	30g
Sodium	340mg
Carbohydrates	21g
Fiber	2g
Sugar	9g
Protein	1g

You don't need to wait until fall—this light yet comforting soup can be enjoyed year-round. Packed with sweet and savory flavors, it'll fill you up without weighing you down. Make a double batch and freeze some in individual containers for later.

4 cups low-sodium chicken broth

1 (15-ounce) can pumpkin purée

2 cups full-fat coconut milk

½ teaspoon salt

½ teaspoon ground cinnamon

¼ teaspoon ground ginger

¼ teaspoon ground nutmeg

1 Place all ingredients in a large saucepan and stir to combine.
2 Bring to a boil over high heat. Reduce heat to low, cover, and simmer for 12–15 minutes until fully warmed.
3 Serve hot.

Turkey Reuben Sandwiches

SERVES 2	
Per Serving:	
Calories	577
Fat	28g
Sodium	954mg
Carbohydrates	59g
Fiber	2g
Sugar	8g
Protein	22g

A Reuben is traditionally a high-calorie meal, but this version drastically lowers the high fat content typically found in Reubens. Despite the lower fat profile, the flavor is anything but lacking.

1 tablespoon olive oil

4 slices rye bread

4 ounces sliced turkey breast

2 slices Swiss cheese

½ cup sauerkraut, drained

¼ cup Thousand Island dressing

1 Heat oil in a medium skillet over medium heat.
2 Place 2 slices of bread on a flat surface. Top each with turkey, cheese, sauerkraut, and dressing. Top with the remaining slices of bread.
3 Cook sandwiches in the skillet 3–4 minutes per side until bread is toasted. Serve warm.

Turkey and Spinach Focaccia Sandwiches

These sandwiches are not your run-of-the-mill turkey sandwiches. They provide lean protein from the turkey, as well as micronutrients from spinach and sun-dried tomatoes, and a ton of flavor from basil, the tomatoes, and red pepper.

2 tablespoons mayonnaise

2 tablespoons chopped fresh basil

2 tablespoons diced sun-dried tomatoes

¼ teaspoon crushed red pepper

4 (1-ounce) slices focaccia bread

8 ounces sliced turkey breast

1 cup baby spinach

SERVES 2	
Per Serving:	
Calories	539
Fat	25g
Sodium	1,042mg
Carbohydrates	58g
Fiber	3g
Sugar	4g
Protein	20g

1 In a small bowl, mix mayonnaise, basil, tomatoes, and crushed red pepper.

2 Place 2 slices bread on a flat surface. Spread each with mayonnaise mixture, then top with turkey and spinach. Cover with the remaining 2 slices bread. Cut in half and serve.

Apple and Cheddar Waffle Sandwich

If you're in a comfort food mood, here's just the sandwich to satisfy your craving. Cheddar cheese and sliced apple are a winning flavor combo, and convenient frozen waffles take the place of sliced bread.

2 frozen whole-grain waffles

2 teaspoons honey mustard

1 (1-ounce) slice Cheddar cheese

½ small apple, cored and thinly sliced

SERVES 1	
Per Serving:	
Calories	278
Fat	10g
Sodium	691mg
Carbohydrates	37g
Fiber	4g
Sugar	9g
Protein	11g

1 Toast waffles in a toaster oven for 2 minutes.

2 Spread 1 teaspoon honey mustard on each waffle.

3 Top 1 waffle with Cheddar cheese and the other with apple slices.

4 Return waffles to the toaster oven and toast for another 2 minutes or until cheese is melted and bubbly.

5 Carefully remove waffles from toaster oven. Press waffles together with Cheddar and apples on the inside. Serve immediately.

Turkey and Cheese Pressed Sandwiches with Raspberry Jam

SERVES 2	
Per Serving:	
Calories	347
Fat	9g
Sodium	987mg
Carbohydrates	44g
Fiber	9g
Sugar	10g
Protein	20g

This hearty recipe includes the opposing yet complementary flavors of sweet raspberry jam and creamy spreadable Swiss cheese. It's filled with flavor and nutrients, and it's delicious!

2 teaspoons raspberry jam

2 (.75-ounce) wedges creamy Swiss spreadable cheese

4 (1-ounce) slices multigrain bread, toasted

6 ounces sliced turkey breast

1 cup coarsely chopped baby spinach

1 In a small bowl, combine jam and cheese.
2 Spread half of the cheese mixture on 2 slices of toast. Top each with half of turkey and spinach. Cover each sandwich with the remaining slices of toast. Cut sandwiches in half and serve immediately.

Smashed Chickpea and Avocado Sandwiches

SERVES 2	
Per Serving:	
Calories	442
Fat	14g
Sodium	829mg
Carbohydrates	64g
Fiber	22g
Sugar	2g
Protein	19g

These sandwiches are a perfect macro-friendly lunch, with a well-balanced ratio of protein, carbs, and fat. The salad can also be served on mixed greens or eaten as a dip with crackers or vegetables.

1 (15-ounce) can chickpeas, drained, rinsed, and dried

1 large ripe avocado, peeled and pitted

¼ cup chopped fresh cilantro

2 tablespoons lime juice

⅛ teaspoon salt

⅛ teaspoon ground black pepper

4 (1-ounce) slices multigrain bread

1 Using a fork or potato masher, mash chickpeas and avocado together in a medium bowl.
2 Stir in cilantro, lime juice, salt, and pepper.
3 Spread the chickpea mixture on 2 slices of bread. Top with the remaining slices of bread. Cut each sandwich in half and serve immediately.

Fig and Bacon Grilled Cheese Panini

All you need are four ingredients and 10 minutes for an indulgent treat that is great for not only lunch or an easy dinner, but breakfast too!

4 (1-ounce) slices whole-wheat bread

4 tablespoons fig spread

2 (1-ounce) slices Cheddar cheese

4 slices bacon, cooked

SERVES 2	
Per Serving:	
Calories	422
Fat	21g
Sodium	920mg
Carbohydrates	39g
Fiber	4g
Sugar	21g
Protein	20g

1 Preheat a panini press or grill pan.
2 Spread each slice of bread with 1 tablespoon fig spread.
3 Place 1 cheese slice and 2 bacon slices on each of 2 slices of bread. Top with remaining bread slices.
4 Grill sandwiches in the panini press or on the grill pan until cheese has melted and bread is toasted and golden, about 8 minutes.
5 Slice each sandwich in half and serve immediately.

Cilantro Chicken and Avocado Burritos

If you have leftover chicken, this recipe can be assembled in minutes. Use grilled or roasted chicken strips from the store or make your own using your favorite chicken recipe. Instant Pot® Shredded Chicken (see recipe in Chapter 5) works particularly well for these burritos.

4 (8") flour tortillas

1 pound boneless, skinless chicken breasts, cooked and shredded

1 medium avocado, peeled, pitted, and diced

1 cup shredded Mexican-blend cheese

1 cup salsa verde

½ cup sour cream

4 tablespoons chopped fresh cilantro

SERVES 4	
Per Serving:	
Calories	425
Fat	22g
Sodium	499mg
Carbohydrates	20g
Fiber	2g
Sugar	0g
Protein	32g

1 Place tortillas on a work surface.
2 Equally distribute chicken, avocado, cheese, salsa, sour cream, and cilantro among tortillas.
3 Roll up tortillas and serve.

Open-Faced BLATs

They're not just BLTs—they're better than that. They're crispy, creamy, salty, and juicy—all in one sandwich. BLAT stands for Bacon, Lettuce, Avocado, and Tomato, and these sandwiches truly taste like a bite of heaven. This is a great lunch if you're watching your carbs, since each sandwich contains only one slice of bread.

12 slices center-cut bacon

1 medium avocado, pitted and peeled

¼ teaspoon salt

¼ teaspoon ground black pepper

4 (1-ounce) slices whole-grain bread, toasted

4 leaves romaine lettuce

1 medium tomato, cut into 8 slices

1 Cook bacon in a large skillet over medium heat until crisp, 8–10 minutes. Transfer to a paper towel–lined plate and set aside.

2 Mash avocado in a medium bowl with salt and pepper.

3 Spread avocado mixture on each slice of toast.

4 Top each with 3 pieces of bacon, 1 lettuce leaf, and 2 tomato slices. Serve immediately.

SERVES 4	
Per Serving:	
Calories	205
Fat	13g
Sodium	592mg
Carbohydrates	14g
Fiber	4g
Sugar	6g
Protein	8g

AVOCADO AS A GOOD SOURCE OF…FIBER?

You might know that beans are a good source of fiber, but did you know that avocados are too? That's right! The creamy flesh of an avocado is a great fiber source. A medium avocado contains around 10 grams.

The Red Onion Sandwich

WHAT'S THE BEST BREAD?

In terms of pure calories, there isn't a huge variety among bread manufacturers. You'll likely find most slices range from 80–140 calories. For maximum health, however, a sprouted whole-grain bread will be full of fiber and beneficial nutrients.

Inspired by the Red Onion Cafe in Burlington, Vermont, this sandwich is legendary, and you'll see why with your very first bite. The combination of flavors and textures might sound a little unusual, but the ingredients work their magic when together on a sandwich. Turkey breast, sharp Cheddar, bacon, green apple, red onion, and sun-dried tomato mayonnaise...your taste buds won't know what hit them—in the best way possible, of course!

1½ tablespoons mayonnaise

1 tablespoon finely chopped sun-dried tomatoes, drained

2 (1-ounce) slices whole-grain bread

3 ounces sliced turkey breast

1 (1-ounce) slice sharp Cheddar cheese

2 slices thick-cut bacon, cooked

⅓ medium Granny Smith apple, cored and thinly sliced

2 thin slices red onion

1 In a small bowl, combine mayonnaise and sun-dried tomatoes. Use the back of a spoon to muddle and break up sun-dried tomatoes as much as possible.

2 Spread mayonnaise mixture on 1 bread slice. Top with turkey, cheese, bacon, apple, and onion.

3 Place the other bread slice on top and toast for 1–2 minutes in a toaster oven until bread is lightly browned and cheese is fully melted.

4 Slice in half and serve immediately.

Buffalo Chicken Mini Wraps

These bite-sized wraps are the perfect grab-and-go lunch or snack. Once prepared, they're ready to go when you are. Wrap the chicken mixture in lettuce leaves instead of tortillas if you don't want the extra carbs.

3 (6-ounce) boneless, skinless chicken breasts, cut into ½" cubes

¾ cup Frank's RedHot Original Cayenne Pepper Sauce, divided

15 (4") corn tortillas

1 medium avocado, peeled, pitted, and diced

½ cup ranch dressing

SERVES 15	
Per Serving:	
Calories	142
Fat	7g
Sodium	543mg
Carbohydrates	11g
Fiber	2g
Sugar	1g
Protein	9g

1 Place chicken in a large bowl or zip-top plastic bag. Pour ½ cup hot sauce over chicken, toss to coat, and refrigerate 2 hours.

2 Spray a large skillet with nonstick cooking spray and heat over medium heat. Add marinated chicken to pan and sauté 10–12 minutes until fully cooked.

3 Remove from heat and add remaining ¼ cup hot sauce to chicken. Toss to coat, then set aside to cool for 5 minutes.

4 Place tortillas on a flat surface. Divide chicken mixture among tortillas and top with avocado. Drizzle with dressing.

5 Roll each filled tortilla into a cylinder. Serve warm or refrigerate for up to 3 days.

Turkey Kale Wraps

SERVES 4

Per Serving:

Calories	137
Fat	5g
Sodium	690mg
Carbohydrates	11g
Fiber	2g
Sugar	2g
Protein	12g

These light wraps check all the boxes when it comes to quick, easy, and healthy. Buy the four ingredients at the beginning of the week to ensure that you have a tasty and macro-friendly meal ready to go whenever hunger strikes.

4 large leaves lacinato kale

⅔ cup garlic hummus

8 ounces sliced turkey breast

½ small cucumber, thinly sliced

1 Place kale leaves on a flat surface.

2 Spread hummus on kale and top with turkey and cucumber.

3 Roll leaves into cylinders and serve immediately.

Pesto Chicken Collard Wraps

SERVES 4

Per Serving:

Calories	297
Fat	16g
Sodium	590mg
Carbohydrates	24g
Fiber	7g
Sugar	2g
Protein	16g

Of course you can make your pesto from scratch, but you can save yourself a bunch of time purchasing the pre-made kind. Stir in some chopped walnuts for some extra crunch and you've got yourself a tasty low-carb meal.

2 cups Instant Pot® Shredded Chicken (see recipe in Chapter 5)

1 tablespoon chopped walnuts

½ cup pesto

4 large leaves collard greens, stems removed

1 Place chicken, walnuts, and pesto in a large bowl and toss to combine.

2 Lay collard leaves on a flat surface. Fill each leaf with about ½ cup of the chicken mixture and roll into cylinders. Serve immediately.

Barbecue Chicken Lettuce Wraps

Here's a delicious weeknight meal that requires very minimal effort on your part. The chicken is sweet and fall-apart tender, and ranch dressing adds a tangy complementary flavor.

2 cups Instant Pot® Shredded Chicken (see recipe in Chapter 5)

½ cup barbecue sauce

8 large soft leaves Boston lettuce

2 tablespoons ranch dressing

1 In a medium bowl, stir together chicken and barbecue sauce.
2 Lay lettuce leaves on a flat surface. Spoon ¼ cup chicken mixture onto the center of each leaf. Drizzle with ranch dressing.
3 Roll up each leaf to contain filling and serve immediately.

SERVES 4	
Per Serving:	
Calories	207
Fat	4g
Sodium	762mg
Carbohydrates	33g
Fiber	5g
Sugar	13g
Protein	10g

Greek Spinach Wrap

A wrap sandwich makes a perfect breakfast, lunch, or snack when you're short on time. This vegetarian version is loaded with lean protein, fiber, and powerful antioxidants.

3 large egg whites

1 cup chopped baby spinach

¼ cup crumbled feta cheese

1 (8") whole-wheat tortilla

2 tablespoons diced sun-dried tomatoes

1 In a small bowl, beat egg whites. Stir in spinach.
2 Spray a small skillet with nonstick cooking spray and heat over medium heat.
3 Pour egg mixture into the pan and cook, stirring, for 1–2 minutes until eggs are almost set.
4 Remove from heat, add feta cheese, and mix well.
5 Place tortilla on a flat surface and top with egg mixture and tomatoes. Roll tortilla into a cylinder and serve immediately.

SERVES 1	
Per Serving:	
Calories	318
Fat	10g
Sodium	664mg
Carbohydrates	33g
Fiber	5g
Sugar	8g
Protein	23g

Buffalo Chicken Lettuce Wraps

No breading is needed on the chicken when you have so many flavors in one meal. These wraps are a healthy and filling lunch or dinner your whole family will love. If you don't have blue cheese crumbles on hand, a drizzle of blue cheese dressing works just as well.

2 cups Instant Pot® Shredded Chicken (see recipe in Chapter 5)

½ cup diced tomato

½ cup diced cucumber

½ cup Buffalo-style hot sauce

8 large soft leaves Boston lettuce

½ cup crumbled blue cheese

1 Place chicken, tomato, and cucumber in a large mixing bowl. Add Buffalo sauce and toss to combine.

2 Lay lettuce leaves on a flat surface. Fill each leaf with about ¼ cup chicken mixture and top with cheese. Roll filled lettuce into cylinders and serve immediately.

Southwest Chicken Lettuce Wraps

Simple, nutritious, and delicious, these wraps require only three main ingredients, so they're perfect for busy weeknights.

1 pound ground chicken

1 cup Cowboy Caviar (see recipe in Chapter 8) or salsa with black beans and corn

8 large soft leaves Boston lettuce

3 tablespoons guacamole

1 Spray a medium skillet with nonstick cooking spray and heat over medium-high heat. Add ground chicken to the skillet. Sauté, using a wooden spoon to break up meat, until no pink remains, about 5 minutes.

2 Stir in Cowboy Caviar or salsa, reduce heat to medium-low, and cook for another 2 minutes.

3 Lay lettuce leaves on a flat surface. Fill each leaf with about ¼ cup chicken mixture and top with guacamole. Roll filled lettuce into cylinders and serve immediately.

CHAPTER 4
Salads

Spinach, Bacon, and Sweet Potato Salad

SERVES 4	
Per Serving:	
Calories	279
Fat	17g
Sodium	412mg
Carbohydrates	24g
Fiber	5g
Sugar	6g
Protein	8g

This sweet potato salad might just become one of your favorites. Make it the day before and allow the flavors to combine overnight in the refrigerator.

2 large sweet potatoes, peeled and cut into chunks

4 tablespoons olive oil, divided

¼ teaspoon salt

¼ teaspoon ground black pepper

2 slices thick-cut bacon

1 small red onion, peeled, halved, and thinly sliced

1 pound baby spinach

¼ cup Honey Dressing (see recipe in Chapter 10)

1 Preheat oven to 400°F.

2 Place sweet potatoes on a large baking sheet, drizzle with 2 tablespoons oil, and sprinkle with salt and pepper. Toss to coat.

3 Roast potatoes for 30 minutes, tossing occasionally, until crisp and brown outside and tender inside.

4 While potatoes cook, place bacon in a small skillet over medium heat. Cook until crisp, about 8 minutes. Drain bacon on paper towels and pour off fat from skillet. Roughly chop bacon and set aside.

5 Return skillet back to medium heat and add remaining 2 tablespoons oil. Add onion and sauté until just softened, about 5 minutes. Stir in bacon.

6 Place spinach in a large bowl. Add potatoes, onion mixture, and dressing. Toss to combine. Serve immediately.

Chicken and Kale Caesar Salad

If you're not careful, a seemingly "healthy" salad can turn into a calorie bomb. This version of the popular chicken Caesar salad is macro-friendly and a whole lot more nutritious than the original. Kale leaves hold up much better than romaine lettuce, so the salad will last all week in the refrigerator—it's a great option for meal prep.

¼ cup grated Parmesan cheese

¼ cup nonfat plain Greek yogurt

¼ cup lemon juice

½ teaspoon Worcestershire sauce

3 tablespoons olive oil, divided

1 teaspoon minced garlic

1 pound boneless, skinless chicken breasts

½ teaspoon salt

½ teaspoon ground black pepper

4 cups trimmed and chopped kale

SERVES 4	
Per Serving:	
Calories	280
Fat	13g
Sodium	789mg
Carbohydrates	9g
Fiber	1g
Sugar	2g
Protein	33g

1 Combine cheese, yogurt, lemon juice, Worcestershire sauce, 2 tablespoons oil, and garlic in a food processor and pulse until combined. Set aside.

2 Season chicken with salt and pepper.

3 Heat remaining 1 tablespoon oil in a large skillet over medium heat.

4 Place chicken in skillet and cook 6–8 minutes per side until no longer pink. Remove from skillet and set aside to cool for 5 minutes.

5 Place chicken in a large bowl and shred, using two forks. Add kale and dressing. Toss to coat.

6 Divide mixture among four bowls and serve.

Loaded Baked Potato Chicken Salad

SERVES 6

Per Serving:

Calories	387
Fat	18g
Sodium	895mg
Carbohydrates	28g
Fiber	4g
Sugar	2g
Protein	30g

MACRO TRACKING ISN'T RESTRICTIVE

Counting macros doesn't mean denying yourself—it's a way of making sure you get to enjoy your favorite foods. When you keep yourself in balance, you are living a healthy life to feel good about. You don't have to avoid foods because they don't fit your macros or because you think they're too caloric or "bad." Plan them in and enjoy!

This main-dish salad takes a little time to prep with all the various ingredients, but once they're cooked and ready to go, it comes together in no time. It also makes great leftovers, so schedule it into your weekly food prep day.

5 medium red potatoes, peeled and cut into 1" chunks

2 tablespoons olive oil, divided

¼ teaspoon salt, divided

¼ teaspoon ground black pepper, divided

12 ounces Brussels sprouts, cut in half

½ medium red onion, peeled and chopped

6 slices bacon

2 (9-ounce) packages grilled chicken strips

3 tablespoons mayonnaise

3 tablespoons Dijon mustard

1 tablespoon minced garlic

2 teaspoons garlic powder

1 Preheat oven to 375°F. Line two baking sheets with parchment paper.

2 In a large mixing bowl, toss potatoes with 1 tablespoon oil, ⅛ teaspoon salt, and ⅛ teaspoon pepper. Pour mixture onto a baking sheet.

3 In another large bowl, toss Brussels sprouts and red onion with remaining oil, salt, and pepper. Transfer mixture to the remaining baking sheet.

4 Place potatoes in the oven and bake for 20 minutes. Remove from oven and toss gently. Return baking sheet to oven along with the Brussels sprouts. Bake 20 minutes until tender and lightly browned.

5 While vegetables are roasting, cook bacon in a large skillet over medium heat until crisp, about 10 minutes, turning often. Drain on paper towels, then chop roughly.

6 In a large bowl, add roasted vegetables, chicken, bacon, mayonnaise, mustard, garlic, and garlic powder. Mix well and serve warm.

Buffalo Blue Chicken Salad

If you don't have crumbled blue cheese on hand, blue cheese salad dressing works just as well. But this salad is so flavorful, you can skip the cheese, which of course saves you calories (and macros) in the long run.

3 cups mixed salad greens

½ small cucumber, chopped

1 cup Buffalo-Style Shredded Chicken (see recipe in Chapter 5)

2 tablespoons crumbled blue cheese

1 In a large bowl, combine greens, cucumber, and shredded chicken.
2 Top with cheese and serve immediately.

SERVES 1	
Per Serving:	
Calories	378
Fat	12g
Sodium	1,306mg
Carbohydrates	25g
Fiber	6g
Sugar	11g
Protein	43g

Avocado Chicken Salad

Take chicken salad to a whole new level by adding creamy avocado. Serve it on bread, inside a tortilla or lettuce wrap, with crackers, or on top of mixed greens.

1 large avocado, peeled and pitted

¼ cup diced red onion

2 teaspoons lime juice

¾ teaspoon garlic powder

½ teaspoon salt

2 cups Instant Pot® Shredded Chicken (see recipe in Chapter 5)

1 Place avocado in a large bowl and mash until almost smooth. Stir in onion, lime juice, garlic powder, and salt.
2 Add shredded chicken and stir to combine.
3 Serve immediately or refrigerate for 1–2 days.

SERVES 2	
Per Serving:	
Calories	383
Fat	13g
Sodium	1,218mg
Carbohydrates	48g
Fiber	15g
Sugar	6g
Protein	20g

Hummus Chicken Salad

SERVES 2	
Per Serving:	
Calories	389
Fat	12g
Sodium	811mg
Carbohydrates	48g
Fiber	14g
Sugar	7g
Protein	22g

This salad is super versatile—try different flavors of hummus and switch up the type of chopped vegetables. Make a big batch at the start of the week for a delicious and versatile protein lunch option.

2 cups Instant Pot® Shredded Chicken (see recipe in Chapter 5)
½ cup hummus
½ cup chopped red bell pepper
½ cup chopped celery

Combine all ingredients in a large bowl and mix well. Serve immediately.

Veggie Burger and Hummus Chopped Salad

SERVES 1	
Per Serving:	
Calories	397
Fat	20g
Sodium	817mg
Carbohydrates	32g
Fiber	12g
Sugar	12g
Protein	23g

Super quick and easy, this vegetable- and protein-packed bowl is ready in 10 minutes or less. Choose your favorite brand of veggie burger and flavor of hummus, and you're more than halfway to a delicious, nutritious, and seriously satisfying meal.

1 frozen veggie burger patty
3 cups chopped romaine lettuce
¼ cup hummus
⅓ cup halved grape tomatoes
¼ cup chopped cucumber
¼ cup crumbled feta

1 Cook veggie burger patty according to package instructions. Crumble or chop patty and set aside.
2 In a salad bowl, combine lettuce with hummus and mix well. Add tomatoes, cucumber, and cheese. Stir to combine.
3 Top with crumbled veggie burger and serve immediately.

Caprese Salad Quinoa Bowls

A traditional caprese salad—nothing more than fresh mozzarella, juicy tomatoes, and fragrant basil—is the inspiration for this satisfying and fresh-tasting recipe. Make it in the late summer when local tomatoes are at their best.

⅔ cup quinoa, rinsed

1⅓ cups water

½ teaspoon salt

2 tablespoons balsamic vinegar, divided

6 slices thick-cut bacon

2 cups halved grape tomatoes

2 cups baby arugula

4 ounces Ciliegine ("cherry-sized") fresh mozzarella balls

1 In a medium saucepan, add quinoa and water. Cook on high heat and bring to a boil. Once boiling, reduce to a simmer and cover. Allow to simmer for 12–15 minutes, or until water is fully absorbed.

2 Remove lid and then stir in salt and half the balsamic vinegar. Set aside.

3 Meanwhile, cook the bacon in a large skillet over medium-low heat until crisp, about 10 minutes. Transfer to a paper towel–lined plate. Once cooled, chop into pieces.

4 Divide the quinoa, bacon, tomatoes, arugula, and mozzarella balls between two bowls.

5 Drizzle with the remaining balsamic vinegar. Serve immediately.

SERVES 2	
Per Serving:	
Calories	607
Fat	31g
Sodium	1,283mg
Carbohydrates	49g
Fiber	7g
Sugar	5g
Protein	33g

QUINOA, THE COMPLETE PROTEIN

On a vegetarian diet, it's very important to ensure you are getting complete protein sources that have all the amino acids you need. Quinoa is one of the most complete protein sources in the plant world and should be a staple in your diet if you're avoiding meat.

Avocado Southwestern Salad

SERVES 4

Per Serving:

Calories	141
Fat	8g
Sodium	354mg
Carbohydrates	14g
Fiber	5g
Sugar	1g
Protein	3g

AVOCADO IS A POWER FAT

Avocados are a very good source of potassium and monounsaturated fat (the good kind of fat). They can be used for much more than guacamole—add slices to a sandwich, salad, or grain bowl.

This super satisfying southwestern-style salad is packed with fiber-rich beans and healthy fats from the avocado. Serve it as a side dish at dinner or on its own for lunch.

¼ **cup olive oil**

¼ **cup lime juice**

½ **teaspoon ground cumin**

1 **teaspoon salt**

1 **teaspoon ground black pepper**

12 **cups torn romaine lettuce**

2 **medium avocados, peeled, pitted, and cubed**

1 **(15-ounce) can black beans, drained and rinsed**

1 **cup frozen corn kernels, thawed**

½ **medium red onion, peeled and diced**

½ **cup chopped fresh cilantro**

1 Whisk together oil, lime juice, cumin, salt, and pepper in a small bowl until emulsified. Set aside.

2 Toss lettuce, avocados, beans, corn, onion, and cilantro in a large bowl.

3 Drizzle with dressing, toss to coat, and serve.

Spicy Burrito Rice Bowls

Meal prep can make your weeknight dinners stress-free. Make a big batch of this healthy, Mexican-inspired meal, portion it into individual containers, and reheat it throughout the week. It's great for lunch too.

1 cup white rice

1½ cups water

1½ teaspoons salt, divided

1 pound ground turkey

1 tablespoon taco seasoning

2 tablespoons hot sauce

¼ cup low-fat plain Greek yogurt

1 (15-ounce) can black beans, drained and rinsed

1 In a medium saucepan, combine rice, water, and ½ teaspoon salt. Bring to a boil. Stir once, cover, and reduce heat to low. Simmer 18–20 minutes. Remove from heat and fluff with fork. Set aside.

2 Brown ground turkey in a medium skillet over medium heat until no longer pink, about 8 minutes. Strain excess fat and season turkey with taco seasoning and remaining salt.

3 In a small bowl, combine hot sauce and yogurt, mixing well.

4 Scoop rice into four serving bowls, and top with turkey and beans. Drizzle with spicy yogurt sauce and serve.

Warm Farro Salad with Asparagus, Peas, and Feta

Farro is an excellent source of protein, fiber, and nutrients, including magnesium, zinc, and some B vitamins. Its sweet and nutty flavor complements asparagus, peas, and feta to create a nutritious warm salad.

1 cup farro, rinsed

3 cups water

1¾ teaspoons salt, divided

1 cup frozen green peas, thawed

1 bunch asparagus, trimmed

4 tablespoons olive oil, divided

2 tablespoons lemon juice

1 tablespoon Dijon mustard

½ cup crumbled feta cheese

¼ cup slivered almonds

SERVES 4	
Per Serving:	
Calories	433
Fat	22g
Sodium	511mg
Carbohydrates	45g
Fiber	9g
Sugar	7g
Protein	17g

1 Preheat oven to 400°F. Line a large baking sheet with parchment paper.

2 Place farro, water, and 1 teaspoon salt in a medium saucepan. Bring to a boil over high heat. Reduce heat to low and simmer for 30 minutes. Stir in peas and cover saucepan with a lid.

3 While farro cooks, place asparagus on the prepared baking sheet. Drizzle with 1 tablespoon oil and sprinkle with ½ teaspoon salt. Roast asparagus for 10–15 minutes until softened and tips are lightly browned. Remove from oven and allow to cool slightly. Cut spears into 2" pieces. Set aside.

4 In a small bowl, whisk together the remaining 3 tablespoons oil, lemon juice, mustard, and the remaining ¼ teaspoon salt.

5 Divide farro mixture among four plates. Top with asparagus, feta, and almonds.

6 Drizzle dressing on top and serve immediately.

Taco Salad

This family-favorite salad is topped with zesty ground beef and traditional taco toppings.

1 pound 90% ground beef

2 tablespoons taco seasoning

1 cup salsa with black beans and corn

2 heads romaine hearts, chopped

1 cup chopped cherry tomatoes

½ cup guacamole

1 cup shredded sharp Cheddar cheese

1 Place beef in a medium skillet over medium-high heat. Using a wooden spoon, break meat into very small pieces and cook until no longer pink, about 8 minutes. Drain any excess fat from beef.

2 Add taco seasoning and salsa to beef and stir to combine. Stir and heat over medium heat for 3 minutes.

3 Place lettuce on four plates and top evenly with beef mixture, tomatoes, guacamole, and cheese. Serve immediately.

Summer Fruit Salad

Fresh, light, and sweet, this is the perfect fruit salad for a backyard barbecue or other summer occasion. It's loaded with antioxidants, nutrients, and fibers, so you'll feel good about eating it. Pair it with a main dish or serve it for a healthy dessert.

1 medium cantaloupe, seeded and chopped

½ small seedless watermelon, chopped

2 cups blueberries

1 medium kiwi, peeled and sliced

1 tablespoon lime juice

1½ teaspoons honey

1 In a large bowl, combine all ingredients together and toss to combine.

2 Cover and refrigerate 1 hour before serving.

Chickpea Waldorf Salad

A typical Waldorf salad is made with healthy ingredients like apples, celery, and walnuts, but often dressed in copious amounts of mayonnaise, which adds a ton of extra fat to your meal. This version swaps Greek yogurt for the mayonnaise and adds chickpeas for a tasty source of plant-based protein. Vegetarians and meat eaters alike will enjoy this wonderfully sweet and savory salad.

½ cup low-fat plain Greek yogurt

2 tablespoons apple cider vinegar

1 teaspoon Dijon mustard

½ teaspoon honey

½ teaspoon salt

¼ teaspoon ground black pepper

1 (15-ounce) can chickpeas, drained and rinsed

2 stalks celery, finely chopped

1 medium apple, cored and chopped

1 cup halved red grapes

½ cup diced red onion

⅓ cup chopped walnuts

4 cups baby spinach

1 In a small bowl, combine yogurt, vinegar, mustard, honey, salt, and pepper. Whisk until smooth.
2 In a large bowl, combine chickpeas, celery, apple, grapes, onion, and walnuts.
3 Stir in the dressing and toss until evenly coated.
4 Serve over baby spinach.

SERVES 4

Per Serving:	
Calories	243
Fat	6g
Sodium	546mg
Carbohydrates	39g
Fiber	9g
Sugar	17g
Protein	11g

BEAN COMBINING FOR PROPER PROTEIN

One of the biggest challenges with following a vegan or vegetarian diet can be getting adequate protein. Even if your goal isn't to build muscle, you need protein to live and function. While beans contain some protein, they don't necessarily have all the essential amino acids you need to get in your diet. Combining bean sources is a good way to make sure you're getting a variety of amino acids.

Strawberry and Feta Summer Salad

This light and simple Mediterranean salad is a lively mixture of baby spinach, strawberries, almonds, and feta tossed in a sweet and tangy homemade dressing. Add grilled chicken, shrimp, or salmon for an extra boost of protein.

1 teaspoon minced garlic

2 teaspoons honey mustard

1 tablespoon strawberry jam

2 tablespoons balsamic vinegar

2 teaspoons maple syrup

2 tablespoons olive oil

6 cups baby spinach

2 cups sliced strawberries

2 tablespoons sliced almonds

1 cup crumbled feta cheese

1 In a small bowl, whisk together garlic, mustard, jam, vinegar, maple syrup, and oil until well blended. Set aside.

2 Toss spinach, strawberries, almonds, and cheese in a large bowl. Drizzle with dressing and toss to coat.

3 Divide salad between two bowls and serve immediately.

SERVES 2	
Per Serving:	
Calories	508
Fat	32g
Sodium	841mg
Carbohydrates	35g
Fiber	7g
Sugar	20g
Protein	21g

WATER, WATER, EVERYWHERE

Drink half of your body weight in ounces of water. For instance, if you weigh 140 pounds, aim to drink 70 ounces of water. Set a reminder on your phone or computer or, better yet, plan "checkpoints" into your day. For instance, drink 40 ounces of water by noon, 20 ounces by dinner, and 10 ounces by the end of the day.

White Bean, Cranberry, and Pecan Salad on Toast

WHY CLEAN EATING DOESN'T WORK

Eating clean does *not* mean you'll automatically lose weight. The quality of food is important, but so is the quantity of food you consume. Plus, clean eating prevents you from enjoying your favorite foods, and if you're missing out on brunch with friends, happy hour with coworkers, or cake at a birthday party, you're likely feeling deprived. And that's not enjoyable or sustainable. By counting macros, you can satisfy your cravings on a regular basis, which means you're less likely to binge.

This flavorful and hearty salad will fill you up and leave you feeling completely satisfied. If you're watching your carbs, skip the bread and serve it on a bed of lettuce.

3 tablespoons tahini

2 tablespoons apple cider vinegar

1 teaspoon maple syrup

1 tablespoon water

⅛ teaspoon ground cinnamon

1 (15-ounce) can cannellini beans, drained and rinsed

½ cup diced celery

¼ cup dried cranberries

¼ cup chopped pecans

¼ cup thinly sliced scallions

¼ teaspoon salt

¼ teaspoon ground black pepper

4 (1-ounce) slices whole-wheat bread, toasted

1 In a small bowl, combine tahini, vinegar, maple syrup, water, and cinnamon. Set aside.
2 Place beans in a medium bowl and roughly mash with potato masher or fork. Stir in celery, cranberries, pecans, scallions, salt, and pepper.
3 Drizzle with dressing and toss to coat.
4 Spread mixture on toast and serve immediately.

Salmon Salad Toast

This salmon salad is easy to make, high in protein and omega-3 fats, and wonderful to keep on hand in the refrigerator.

1 (5-ounce) can boneless, skinless salmon

1½ teaspoons mayonnaise

1 teaspoon Dijon mustard

1½ tablespoons sweet relish

⅛ teaspoon salt

⅛ teaspoon ground black pepper

2 (1-ounce) slices whole-grain bread, toasted

SERVES 2	
Per Serving:	
Calories	210
Fat	10g
Sodium	464mg
Carbohydrates	11g
Fiber	1g
Sugar	1g
Protein	19g

1 In a small bowl, combine salmon, mayonnaise, mustard, relish, salt, and pepper. Stir together until well combined.

2 Spread salmon mixture on toasted bread. Serve immediately.

Avocado, Chickpea, and Quinoa Salad

Avocado and chickpeas are excellent sources of healthy fats and fiber, and quinoa is packed with vitamins and minerals as well as protein and carbs, making it one of the healthiest grains available. Make a big batch of this salad and store in the refrigerator for a quick cold meal or side dish.

1 cup cooked quinoa

1 (15-ounce) can chickpeas, drained and rinsed

2 tablespoons minced red onion

2 tablespoons minced fresh cilantro

4 tablespoons lime juice

¼ teaspoon salt

¼ teaspoon ground black pepper

1 cup diced cucumber

1 medium avocado, peeled, pitted, and diced

SERVES 4	
Per Serving:	
Calories	249
Fat	8g
Sodium	448mg
Carbohydrates	35g
Fiber	9g
Sugar	6g
Protein	9g

1 Combine quinoa, chickpeas, onion, cilantro, lime juice, salt, and pepper in a large bowl.

2 Stir in cucumber and avocado and serve immediately.

Curried Chickpea Salad

SERVES 4

Per Serving:

Calories	219
Fat	8g
Sodium	239mg
Carbohydrates	31g
Fiber	4g
Sugar	15g
Protein	5g

The perfect blend of flavors and textures, this flavorful salad is packed with fresh vegetables, dried cranberries, and a subtly sweet dressing for the perfect healthy meal or side dish. Make it ahead of time and store in the refrigerator for up to a week for easy to-go lunches.

2 tablespoons extra-virgin olive oil

1½ tablespoons lime juice

1½ tablespoons maple syrup

1 tablespoon curry powder

1 (15-ounce) can chickpeas, drained and rinsed

1 small apple, peeled, cored, and finely chopped

1 stalk celery, finely chopped

¼ cup chopped red onion

¼ cup dried cranberries

¼ cup chopped fresh cilantro

⅛ teaspoon salt

⅛ teaspoon ground black pepper

1 In a small bowl, whisk together oil, lime juice, maple syrup, and curry powder.

2 In a large bowl, combine chickpeas, apple, celery, onion, cranberries, and cilantro. Pour dressing on top and toss to coat.

3 Season with salt and pepper and serve immediately.

Lentil and Feta Tabbouleh

This naturally gluten-free and vegetarian salad can be made ahead of time and kept for several days in the refrigerator. It will fill you up with healthy plant-based protein and gut-friendly fiber.

1 (6.9-ounce) package ready-to-eat lentils

2 medium tomatoes, diced

⅔ cup crumbled feta cheese

4 cups chopped fresh parsley

½ cup minced red onion

¼ cup extra-virgin olive oil

1½ tablespoons lemon juice

1 tablespoon ground cinnamon

½ teaspoon salt

SERVES 4	
Per Serving:	
Calories	275
Fat	21g
Sodium	579mg
Carbohydrates	12g
Fiber	4g
Sugar	2g
Protein	10g

1 In a large bowl, toss together all ingredients until evenly combined.

2 Serve immediately or refrigerate for up to 5 days.

Salmon Chickpea Salad

This sophisticated salad, made with tender salmon, filling chickpeas, and a hint of lemon, is a slam dunk when you're hungry and short on time.

2 tablespoons extra-virgin olive oil

3 tablespoons lemon juice

¼ teaspoon salt

1 (15-ounce) can chickpeas, drained and rinsed

1 (5-ounce) can salmon, drained

4 scallions, chopped

½ cup chopped fresh parsley

SERVES 4	
Per Serving:	
Calories	189
Fat	10g
Sodium	437mg
Carbohydrates	14g
Fiber	3g
Sugar	0g
Protein	12g

In a large bowl, whisk oil, lemon juice, and salt. Stir in chickpeas, salmon, scallions, and parsley. Serve immediately.

Chili Lime Shrimp Taco Salad

SERVES 4

Per Serving:

Calories	298
Fat	15g
Sodium	1,015mg
Carbohydrates	12g
Fiber	5g
Sugar	4g
Protein	28g

MAKE YOUR OWN SALSA

Salsa is an incredibly versatile and low-calorie snack that goes well with anything. Store-bought salsas are great, but it's very easy to make at home, and there are countless recipes. Use this base recipe: Mix together 2 chopped tomatoes, ¼ cup chopped onion, 2 tablespoons chopped cilantro, and 1 tablespoon minced garlic. From there, add any flavor enhancers or extra ingredients that you enjoy.

Shrimp is a versatile and quick-cooking protein source, so it's an easy way to increase your intake without adding a lot of fat to your daily macro goals. Marinate the shrimp the night before for a stronger flavor.

1 pound large shrimp, peeled and deveined

2 tablespoons lime juice, divided

2 tablespoons extra-virgin olive oil

2 teaspoons garlic powder

2 teaspoons chili powder

½ teaspoon salt, divided

4 cups shredded purple cabbage

8 cups mixed greens

1 medium ripe avocado, peeled, pitted, and mashed

1 In a large bowl, combine shrimp, 1 tablespoon lime juice, oil, garlic powder, chili powder, and ¼ teaspoon salt. Set aside to marinate for 15 minutes.

2 Meanwhile, combine cabbage with the remaining 1 tablespoon lime juice and remaining ¼ teaspoon salt in a large bowl. Toss to coat and set aside.

3 Heat a large nonstick skillet over medium-high heat. Add shrimp and cook just until they turn pink, 2–3 minutes, flipping once.

4 Divide greens among four plates and top with avocado, cabbage mixture, and shrimp. Serve immediately.

Italian Pasta Salad

SERVES 4

Per Serving:

Calories	386
Fat	18g
Sodium	811mg
Carbohydrates	49g
Fiber	2g
Sugar	5g
Protein	7g

WHICH SALAD DRESSING IS BEST?

The best salad dressings are typically very simple with few ingredients. While bottled dressings are convenient, making your own allows you to control what goes into it. But if store-bought dressings make sense for your lifestyle, look for a variety made with olive or avocado oil, a short list of ingredients, and no added sugars.

This fuss-free pasta salad is perfect for a satisfying lunch, a quick weeknight dinner, or a dish for a summer potluck party. It's loaded with flavor from a variety of fresh vegetables and Italian dressing, and it's incredibly easy to prepare. If you have time, make it the day before and let the flavors come together in the refrigerator overnight. Top the salad with feta or fresh mozzarella cheese if you like.

8 ounces rotini

1 tablespoon salt

⅓ cup chopped green bell pepper

½ cup sliced cherry tomatoes

⅓ cup sliced black olives

⅓ cup diced red onion

¾ cup Italian salad dressing

1 Bring a large pot of water to a boil. Add rotini and salt and boil for 9 minutes. Drain pasta and rinse with cold water.
2 In a large bowl, combine pasta, bell pepper, tomatoes, olives, onion, and Italian dressing. Toss to combine.
3 Refrigerate for at least 30 minutes before serving.

Italian Tuna Salad

If the thought of traditional tuna salad bores you, one simple ingredient (one you probably already have in your refrigerator) might just change your tune. You'll love the zesty flavor that classic Italian salad dressing adds in place of mayonnaise.

1 (5-ounce) can tuna, drained

2 tablespoons Italian salad dressing

2 scallions, sliced

2 romaine hearts, chopped

1 In a small bowl, combine tuna, salad dressing, and scallions.

2 Divide romaine between two plates and top with tuna mixture. Serve immediately.

SERVES 2	
Per Serving:	
Calories	143
Fat	9g
Sodium	567mg
Carbohydrates	3g
Fiber	1g
Sugar	2g
Protein	13g

Avocado and Tuna Salad

If you have guacamole in your refrigerator, you can whip up this simple salad in a matter of minutes. Serve it on whole-grain bread, over mixed greens, or on crackers for a healthy snack.

1 (5-ounce) can solid white albacore tuna, drained

½ cup chopped cucumber

¼ cup chopped celery

¼ cup chopped red bell pepper

2 tablespoons guacamole

¼ cup sweet pickle relish

⅛ teaspoon salt

⅛ teaspoon ground black pepper

Combine all ingredients in a medium bowl. Mix well. Serve immediately.

SERVES 2	
Per Serving:	
Calories	121
Fat	3g
Sodium	598mg
Carbohydrates	8g
Fiber	1g
Sugar	3g
Protein	15g

Avocado Egg Salad

SERVES 2	
Per Serving:	
Calories	273
Fat	22g
Sodium	435mg
Carbohydrates	3g
Fiber	2g
Sugar	1g
Protein	16g

There's no mayonnaise here! Cook eggs ahead of time and store them in the refrigerator so all you need to do is assemble the ingredients when mealtime rolls around. This salad is best eaten right after it's made.

5 large eggs

½ medium avocado, peeled, pitted, and mashed

1 teaspoon Dijon mustard

⅛ teaspoon salt

⅛ teaspoon ground black pepper

1 Place eggs in a medium saucepan and add water to cover. Bring to a boil over high heat. Remove from heat, cover pan, and set aside for 10 minutes.

2 Remove eggs with a slotted spoon and place in a medium bowl. Fill bowl with cold water and let cool for 5 minutes.

3 Peel and dice eggs.

4 In a medium bowl, gently stir eggs and avocado together. Stir in mustard, salt, and pepper.

5 Serve immediately at room temperature or refrigerate at least 2 hours and serve cold.

CHAPTER 5

Chicken and Turkey

Instant Pot® Shredded Chicken

SERVES 8

Per Serving:

Calories	188
Fat	5g
Sodium	410mg
Carbohydrates	0g
Fiber	0g
Sugar	0g
Protein	36g

SLOW COOKER SHREDDED CHICKEN

If you don't own an Instant Pot®, you can use a slow cooker to make shredded chicken. Place 2 pounds boneless, skinless chicken breasts in a slow cooker along with enough low-sodium chicken broth or water to cover. Add ½ teaspoon each salt and ground black pepper. Cover and cook on low for 6 hours or until the chicken is tender. Remove the chicken from the slow cooker and shred it with two forks or a hand mixer.

Make a large batch of this chicken on Sunday, and you'll have the basis for a whole week's worth of meals. Low in fat and high in protein, shredded chicken can be added to soups, salads, sandwiches, pasta dishes—the possibilities are endless!

3 pounds boneless, skinless chicken breasts

1 cup low-sodium chicken broth

¾ teaspoon salt

¼ teaspoon ground black pepper

1 Place chicken, broth, salt, and pepper in an Instant Pot®.
2 Close lid, set steam release to Sealing, press the Manual button, and set time to 14 minutes.
3 When the timer beeps, let pressure release naturally for 5 minutes, then quick-release any remaining pressure until the float valve drops.
4 Open lid and remove chicken from liquid. Set aside to cool for 5–10 minutes.
5 Place chicken in a large bowl and shred using two forks or a hand mixer.
6 Use immediately or cool to room temperature and refrigerate in an airtight container for up to 5 days. Chicken can also be frozen for up to 3 months.

Buffalo-Style Shredded Chicken

Use this flavorful chicken to fill lettuce or tortilla wraps, top salads, or mix with rice and beans. Make a double batch for a convenient source of protein that's ready when you are.

2 cups Instant Pot® Shredded Chicken (see recipe in this chapter)
½ cup Frank's RedHot Original Cayenne Pepper Sauce

In a medium bowl, combine chicken and hot sauce. Stir to combine.

SERVES 2	
Per Serving:	
Calories	254
Fat	2g
Sodium	650mg
Carbohydrates	41g
Fiber	10g
Sugar	4g
Protein	18g

Barbecue-Style Shredded Chicken

Sweet, salty, savory, and satisfying, Barbecue-Style Shredded Chicken is a flexible source of protein for everything from sliders to a chopped salad.

2 cups Instant Pot® Shredded Chicken (see recipe in this chapter)
½ cup barbecue sauce

In a medium bowl, combine chicken and barbecue sauce. Stir to combine.

SERVES 2	
Per Serving:	
Calories	342
Fat	7g
Sodium	710mg
Carbohydrates	24g
Fiber	0g
Sugar	20g
Protein	48g

Baked Buffalo Chicken Nuggets

SERVES 4

Per Serving:

Calories	135
Fat	3g
Sodium	680mg
Carbohydrates	3g
Fiber	0g
Sugar	0g
Protein	24g

Healthier than traditional fried Buffalo wings, these nuggets are still spicy and delicious. Serve with ranch or blue cheese dressing or try using them to top off a salad.

½ teaspoon garlic powder

½ teaspoon paprika

½ teaspoon chili powder

⅛ teaspoon ground black pepper

¼ cup panko bread crumbs

2 tablespoons Frank's RedHot Original Cayenne Pepper Sauce

2 teaspoons olive oil

1 pound boneless, skinless chicken breasts, cut into 40 bite-sized pieces

1 Preheat oven to 425°F. Spray a large baking sheet with nonstick cooking spray.
2 Combine garlic powder, paprika, chili powder, pepper, and bread crumbs in a shallow bowl and mix well.
3 In another shallow bowl, mix hot sauce and oil until well blended.
4 Dip chicken pieces in hot sauce mixture, roll in bread crumb mixture, and place on the prepared baking sheet.
5 Bake 12–15 minutes or until golden brown, removing halfway through to turn over.
6 Serve hot.

Pesto Chicken Quesadilla

Quesadillas are so quick to throw together, especially if you use pre-made ingredients. Cook and eat these fresh or make ahead on your food prep day so all you need to do is reheat them later. Quesadillas work well as a packed lunch for work or school and quick dinner after a long day.

1 (8") whole-grain tortilla

2 tablespoons pesto

4 ounces Instant Pot® Shredded Chicken (see recipe in this chapter)

½ cup baby spinach

¼ cup crumbled feta cheese

1 Place tortilla on a flat surface and spread with pesto.

2 Top one-half of tortilla with chicken, spinach, and cheese. Fold tortilla in half.

3 Heat a small nonstick skillet over medium heat. Place quesadilla in pan. Cook until the bottom is golden brown, about 3 minutes. Flip tortilla and brown the other side for 2–3 minutes.

4 Remove from pan, cut into wedges, and serve.

SERVES 1	
Per Serving:	
Calories	485
Fat	29g
Sodium	798mg
Carbohydrates	15g
Fiber	6g
Sugar	2g
Protein	40g

EASY HOMEMADE PESTO

Store-bought pesto is convenient, but if you have the time and some fresh basil, make your own. All you need is 2 cups basil, 2 cloves of garlic, 2 tablespoons pine nuts, ½ cup extra-virgin olive oil, and ½ cup grated Parmesan cheese. Pulse in a blender or food processor.

One Pan Chicken Fajitas

SERVES 4

Per Serving:

Calories	649
Fat	42g
Sodium	744mg
Carbohydrates	36g
Fiber	2g
Sugar	5g
Protein	24g

These fajitas are versatile and easy to make. Once cooked and pre-pared, the chicken and vegetables can be reheated and eaten alone or served with tortillas and rice for extra carbs. Top with shredded Mexican-style cheese and sour cream for a truly complete meal.

1½ pounds chicken breast tenders

½ teaspoon salt

½ teaspoon ground black pepper

1 medium red bell pepper, seeded and sliced

1 medium green bell pepper, seeded and sliced

1 large yellow onion, peeled and sliced

4 tablespoons salted butter or ghee, melted

2 tablespoons fajita seasoning

1. Preheat oven to 400°F.
2. Place chicken in a 9" × 13" baking dish and sprinkle with salt and black pepper. Top with bell peppers and onion.
3. In a small bowl, stir together butter and fajita seasoning.
4. Pour butter mixture over chicken and vegetables.
5. Bake for 38–40 minutes until chicken reaches an internal temperature of 165°F. Serve immediately.

Lemon and Herb Grilled Chicken Salad

This low-carb, high-protein dish is light, refreshing, and perfect for the summer. Prep the chicken and dressing ahead of time, so all you need to do is assemble the salad when you're ready to eat.

4 ounces grilled chicken breast, sliced

1 cup mixed greens

1 tablespoon olive oil

1 tablespoon lemon juice

½ teaspoon garlic salt

¼ teaspoon dried rosemary

½ tablespoon sunflower seeds

Toss all ingredients together in a medium bowl. Serve immediately.

SERVES 1	
Per Serving:	
Calories	290
Fat	16g
Sodium	1,261mg
Carbohydrates	3g
Fiber	1g
Sugar	1g
Protein	34g

Pulled-Chicken BBQ Sandwich

You don't need to wait for a summer barbecue to enjoy barbecue chicken. Prepare the pulled chicken ahead of time, so all you need to do is grab a bun for a delicious meal.

4 ounces Instant Pot® Shredded Chicken (see recipe in this chapter)

2 tablespoons barbecue sauce

1 whole-grain hamburger bun

¼ cup Cabbage Slaw (see recipe in Chapter 10)

4 bread and butter pickle slices

1 Place chicken in a small microwave-safe bowl. Microwave on high for 90 seconds.

2 Add barbecue sauce and toss until chicken is coated completely.

3 Spoon chicken mixture onto hamburger bun. Top with Cabbage Slaw and pickles and serve.

SERVES 1	
Per Serving:	
Calories	437
Fat	16g
Sodium	933mg
Carbohydrates	39g
Fiber	9g
Sugar	18g
Protein	38g

Greek-Style Stuffed Chicken

This dish is bursting with Mediterranean flavors, and you'll want to make it again and again.

1 pound boneless, skinless chicken breasts

2 tablespoons pesto

½ cup crumbled feta cheese

1 (8-ounce) package sun-dried tomatoes

¼ teaspoon salt

½ teaspoon ground black pepper

1 Preheat oven to 350°F.

2 Lay chicken breasts on a flat surface. With a sharp knife, butterfly each chicken breast, stopping about ½" from the edge.

3 Open each breast like a book and spread with pesto. Top with cheese and sun-dried tomatoes. Fold the breasts closed over the filling. Use toothpicks to hold stuffed breasts shut, if necessary.

4 Place stuffed breasts in a 9" × 13" baking dish and sprinkle with salt and pepper.

5 Bake for 35–40 minutes or until the internal temperature reaches 165°F. Serve hot.

SERVES 4	
Per Serving:	
Calories	376
Fat	13g
Sodium	582mg
Carbohydrates	33g
Fiber	7g
Sugar	22g
Protein	35g

LOG IT BEFORE YOU EAT IT

If you can't plan a whole day in advance, keep this rule in mind: Log it before you eat it. Most of the time, if you log it before you eat it, you will be successful in hitting your macros.

Microwave Chicken and Bean Burrito

SERVES 1	
Per Serving:	
Calories	561
Fat	8g
Sodium	367mg
Carbohydrates	75g
Fiber	8g
Sugar	3g
Protein	50g

Make this easy burrito for a quick lunch or make a half dozen or so, wrap and freeze them, and just grab and reheat when you're ready. Top with low-fat sour cream or fat-free Greek yogurt for some extra protein and creaminess.

½ cup cooked pinto beans

2 teaspoons taco seasoning

2 tablespoons medium salsa

1 (8") whole-wheat tortilla

½ cup cooked rice

3 ounces Instant Pot® Shredded Chicken (see recipe in this chapter)

2 tablespoons low-fat Mexican-blend shredded cheese

1 Place beans, taco seasoning, and salsa in a food processor and pulse until smooth.
2 Place tortilla on a large plate and top with rice, bean mixture, and chicken. Sprinkle cheese on top. Roll tortilla into a cylinder.
3 Microwave 15–25 seconds until cheese is melted. Serve immediately.

Southwestern Chicken

SERVES 4	
Per Serving:	
Calories	247
Fat	18g
Sodium	42mg
Carbohydrates	4g
Fiber	0g
Sugar	4g
Protein	17g

This recipe is perfect for when you need dinner on the table fast. Serve it hot over white rice and fajita vegetables or enjoy it cold, sliced, and served with a salad and avocado.

5 tablespoons olive oil, divided

¼ cup lime juice

¼ teaspoon crushed red pepper flakes

1 tablespoon honey

½ teaspoon ground cumin

2 (6-ounce) boneless, skinless chicken breasts

1 In a small bowl, combine 4 tablespoons oil, lime juice, red pepper flakes, honey, and cumin and mix well.
2 Place chicken in a medium bowl or dish and pour marinade on top. Cover and marinate at least 1 hour in the refrigerator.
3 Heat a grill pan or large skillet over medium-high heat and brush with remaining 1 tablespoon oil. Cook chicken 6–8 minutes per side until the internal temperature reaches 165°F. Serve hot.

Salsa Verde Chicken

This southwestern-style chicken is low in fat and high in flavor. The salsa verde can easily be swapped for different types of salsa, so feel free to experiment with your favorites.

1 pound boneless, skinless chicken breasts

1 tablespoon olive oil

1 teaspoon garlic salt

1 (16-ounce) jar salsa verde

1½ cups shredded Monterey jack cheese

¼ cup chopped fresh cilantro

1 medium lime, cut into wedges

1 Preheat oven to 400°F.

2 Arrange chicken breasts in a 9" × 13" baking dish. Brush with oil and sprinkle with garlic salt. Pour salsa over chicken, spreading it evenly all over.

3 Bake 30–35 minutes until chicken reaches an internal temperature of 165°F. Remove baking dish from the oven. Turn on broiler.

4 Top chicken with cheese and broil 1–2 minutes until cheese is melted.

5 Garnish with cilantro and lime wedges and serve.

SERVES 4	
Per Serving:	
Calories	320
Fat	17g
Sodium	1,450mg
Carbohydrates	5g
Fiber	0g
Sugar	4g
Protein	33g

Chicken Taco Skillet

SERVES 4

Per Serving:

Calories	244
Fat	12g
Sodium	641mg
Carbohydrates	13g
Fiber	5g
Sugar	8g
Protein	21g

HOME COOKING IS GOOD FOR YOUR HEALTH

Homemade meals are almost always more nutrient-dense and filled with fewer calories than takeout or ready-made options at your grocery store. Preparing your own recipes and ingredients for the week allows you to make better food choices.

This one pan meal comes together in no time, thanks to quick-cooking ground chicken (turkey or lean ground beef would also work) and frozen vegetables. Salsa and taco seasoning add a ton of flavor without using one of everything from your spice rack. Serve this chicken with guacamole, over rice or cauliflower rice, inside a wrap, or with tortilla chips.

1 pound ground chicken

1 (16-ounce) bag frozen pepper and onion strips

½ cup frozen corn

2 tablespoons taco seasoning

12 ounces mild or medium salsa

1 Place ground chicken in a large skillet over medium heat. Cook chicken, breaking it up with a wooden spoon or spatula, for 4–5 minutes, until no longer pink.

2 Stir in pepper and onion strips, corn, and taco seasoning. Cook, stirring occasionally, for 5 minutes.

3 Add salsa, stir, and cook 2 more minutes until warm. Serve immediately.

Baked Parmesan Caesar Chicken

Here's your new favorite meal—it's packed with flavor and couldn't be easier to make. Once you try it, it'll likely become part of your regular dinner rotation. For a lower fat option, swap the sour cream for nonfat plain Greek yogurt.

4 (6-ounce) boneless, skinless chicken breasts

1 cup creamy Caesar salad dressing

½ cup sour cream

2 cups frozen broccoli florets

½ cup grated Parmesan cheese

1 Preheat oven to 375°F.

2 Spray an 8" square baking dish with nonstick cooking spray and place chicken inside.

3 In a medium bowl, mix dressing and sour cream until fully blended, then add broccoli florets and toss to coat. Pour broccoli mixture over chicken.

4 Bake 40 minutes, or until the internal temperature reaches 165°F. Remove from the oven and turn on broiler.

5 Top chicken and broccoli with cheese and broil 1–2 minutes until cheese is melted.

6 Remove, allow to slightly cool, and serve.

SERVES 4

Per Serving:

Calories	630
Fat	48g
Sodium	820mg
Carbohydrates	6g
Fiber	2g
Sugar	3g
Protein	44g

MACROS AND HEALTHY HABITS

On days you don't track your macros, focus on patterns and habits that you see. Did you eat enough vegetables? Snack between meals? Are you giving your body consistency in the amount of food it gets every day? Pay attention and see how these habits fit into your health goals.

Instant Pot® Honey Garlic Chicken

SERVES 4	
Per Serving:	
Calories	325
Fat	2g
Sodium	1,327mg
Carbohydrates	42g
Fiber	0g
Sugar	24g
Protein	37g

Using just five ingredients, this chicken dish is so simple and always turns out perfectly. Pair it with broccoli florets, cauliflower rice, and avocado slices for a macro-friendly and delicious meal.

1½ pounds boneless, skinless chicken breasts
½ cup ketchup
¼ cup low-sodium soy sauce or coconut aminos
¼ cup honey
2 tablespoons minced garlic

1 Place chicken, ketchup, soy sauce, honey, and garlic in an Instant Pot®.
2 Close lid, set steam release to Sealing, press the Manual button, and set time to 9 minutes.
3 When the timer beeps, let pressure release naturally for 5 minutes, then quick-release any remaining pressure until the float valve drops.
4 Open lid, remove chicken from liquid, and set aside to cool for 10 minutes.
5 Transfer ½ cup of the liquid in the Instant Pot® to a large bowl. Add chicken to bowl.
6 Shred chicken using two forks or a hand mixer.
7 Serve immediately or cool to room temperature and refrigerate in an airtight container for up to 5 days. Chicken can also be frozen for up to 3 months.

Instant Pot® Lemon Artichoke Chicken

Meal prep chicken doesn't get much easier or more delicious than this. It's a versatile source of protein you can keep in the refrigerator at all times.

3 pounds boneless, skinless chicken breasts

½ cup low-sodium chicken broth

1 (12-ounce) jar Trader Joe's Artichoke Antipasto, undrained

1 medium lemon, sliced

½ teaspoon salt

1 Place chicken, broth, artichokes, lemon, and salt in an Instant Pot®.

2 Close lid, set steam release to Sealing, press the Manual button, and set time to 14 minutes.

3 When the timer beeps, let pressure release naturally for 5 minutes, then quick-release any remaining pressure until the float valve drops.

4 Open lid, remove chicken from liquid and set aside to cool for 10 minutes.

5 Use a slotted spoon to transfer the artichoke mixture left in the pot to a large bowl. Measure ½ cup of the cooking liquid and add it to the bowl. Add chicken to bowl.

6 Shred chicken using two forks or a hand mixer.

7 Serve immediately or cool to room temperature and refrigerate in an airtight container for up to 5 days. Chicken can also be frozen for up to 3 months.

Chicken Sausage with Butternut Squash and Apples

Per Serving:

Calories	279
Fat	11g
Sodium	1,041mg
Carbohydrates	21g
Fiber	2g
Sugar	13g
Protein	26g

BUTTERNUT SQUASH: UNDERRATED SUPERFOOD

Butternut squash is a low-fat, high-fiber, delicious food. It's excellent for overall health, and the fiber will keep you full between meals and keep your digestive system happy. It's very high in vitamin A, which is a potent fighter against breast cancer, as well as eye degeneration and the negative effects of aging.

This comforting, easy, and healthy weeknight meal requires a minimal number of ingredients and just one pan.

½ tablespoon coconut oil

1 (11-ounce) package precooked apple and maple chicken sausage, sliced

1 cup diced butternut squash

1 medium apple, peeled, cored, and diced

1 teaspoon ground cinnamon

¼ teaspoon ground nutmeg

½ teaspoon salt

1 Heat coconut oil in a large skillet over medium-high heat. Add sausage, squash, apple, cinnamon, nutmeg, and salt.

2 Sauté until apple is soft and butternut squash is lightly browned on the edges, about 7 to 8 minutes. Serve immediately.

One Pan BBQ Chicken and Vegetables

SERVES 3	
Per Serving:	
Calories	505
Fat	20g
Sodium	1,214mg
Carbohydrates	29g
Fiber	5g
Sugar	19g
Protein	48g

Serve this dish over rice, pasta, mashed potatoes, or roasted root vegetables.

6 slices thick-cut bacon, chopped

6 (4-ounce) boneless, skinless chicken thighs

1 (16-ounce) bag frozen pepper and onion strips

1 (14.5-ounce) can diced tomatoes

½ cup barbecue sauce

1 In a large skillet over medium-high heat, cook bacon until crisp, about 10 minutes. Add chicken to the skillet and cook 8–10 minutes per side until browned and cooked through.

2 Add pepper and onion strips and tomatoes. Cook, stirring occasionally, until mixture begins to boil. Reduce heat to low, stir in barbecue sauce, and simmer 5 minutes until sauce is heated through. Serve immediately.

Cheesy Brussels Sprouts with Chicken Sausage

SERVES 4	
Per Serving:	
Calories	213
Fat	10g
Sodium	939mg
Carbohydrates	10g
Fiber	3g
Sugar	4g
Protein	20g

Brussels sprouts can be shredded by hand, but you can also find them pre-shredded in the produce department of your grocery store. Once you have all of the ingredients on hand, this satisfying meal comes together in a matter of minutes.

½ tablespoon olive oil

1 (11-ounce) package precooked chicken sausage, sliced

10 ounces Brussels sprouts, shredded

5 (.75-ounce) wedges creamy Swiss spreadable cheese

1 Heat oil in a large skillet over medium heat. Add sausage and sauté until lightly browned, about 5 minutes.

2 Add Brussels sprouts to the skillet and sauté for 5–7 minutes until Brussels sprouts are bright green and a little brown on the edges.

3 Transfer Brussels sprouts and sausage to a large bowl and add cheese wedges. Toss together until cheese is melted. Serve immediately.

Slow Cooker Chicken Olé

This is one of the easiest versions of the popular Chicken Olé casserole. Make it your own by adding your favorite vegetables, torn corn tortillas, or canned beans.

1 (16-ounce) jar mild or medium salsa

¼ cup Dijon mustard

2 tablespoons lime juice

2 pounds boneless, skinless chicken breasts

SERVES 4	
Per Serving:	
Calories	295
Fat	7g
Sodium	1,210mg
Carbohydrates	8g
Fiber	4g
Sugar	4g
Protein	48g

1 In a small bowl, combine salsa, mustard, and lime juice. Stir well.
2 Place chicken in a 4- to 6-quart slow cooker and cover with salsa mixture.
3 Cover and cook on high for 4 hours or on low for 6 hours or until chicken is cooked all the way through.
4 Serve chicken with sauce from slow cooker.

Garlic Mustard Drumsticks

Make these drumsticks for a quick family-friendly dinner or as a simple party appetizer to serve to guests.

12 chicken drumsticks (3 pounds total weight)

4 tablespoons salted butter or ghee, melted

2 tablespoons whole-grain mustard

½ teaspoon garlic powder

¼ teaspoon salt

⅛ teaspoon ground black pepper

SERVES 6	
Per Serving:	
Calories	310
Fat	16g
Sodium	341mg
Carbohydrates	0g
Fiber	0g
Sugar	0g
Protein	42g

1 Preheat oven to 425°F. Line a large baking sheet with parchment paper. Place drumsticks on the prepared baking sheet.
2 In a small bowl, mix together butter, mustard, garlic powder, salt, and pepper. Brush the butter mixture over the tops of the drumsticks.
3 Bake for 45–50 minutes or until the internal temperature reaches 165°F.
4 Serve hot or at room temperature.

Meal Prep Sweet Potato and Chicken Casserole

Serve this sweet casserole with a green salad for a complete macro-balanced meal. This recipe freezes well, so you can always have a satisfying starchy, protein-packed meal in the freezer when you need it.

SERVES 4	
Per Serving:	
Calories	400
Fat	8g
Sodium	979mg
Carbohydrates	35g
Fiber	3g
Sugar	20g
Protein	46g

FEEL-GOOD SWEET POTATOES

Sweet potatoes are a great source of complex carbohydrates, which are important for the production of the feel-good hormone serotonin. Who knew sweet potatoes could make you happy?

1½ pounds sweet potatoes, peeled and cut into 1" cubes
2 tablespoons salted butter
½ teaspoon salt
¼ teaspoon ground black pepper
2 cups Instant Pot® Shredded Chicken (see recipe in this chapter)
¾ cup barbecue sauce, divided
1½ teaspoons apple cider vinegar

1 Place sweet potatoes in a large pot and cover with water. Bring to a boil over high heat. Reduce heat to low and simmer 20–30 minutes until sweet potatoes are easily pierced with a fork.

2 Drain water and return sweet potatoes to the pot. Using a potato masher, mash the potatoes. Stir in butter, salt, and pepper. Spread mashed sweet potatoes in a 9" square baking dish.

3 Preheat oven to 350°F.

4 In a medium bowl, toss chicken with ½ cup barbecue sauce. Spread chicken mixture over sweet potatoes in the baking pan.

5 In a small bowl, mix the remaining ¼ cup barbecue sauce with vinegar and drizzle over the casserole.

6 Bake for 30 minutes until the top just starts to brown.

7 Cool completely, then divide casserole among four covered containers and store in the refrigerator for up to 1 week.

Game Day Party Wings

Sticky, messy, and super tasty—these chicken wings will be the first to run out at your next casual party.

1 cup honey

1 cup olive oil

1 cup low-sodium soy sauce or coconut aminos

1 teaspoon ground ginger

3 pounds chicken wing sections

1 Preheat oven to 300°F.
2 In a small bowl, mix together honey, oil, soy sauce, and ginger.
3 Place wings in a 9" × 13" baking dish and pour honey mixture over them.
4 Bake for 1 hour, then remove baking dish from oven. Turn on broiler.
5 Spoon off three-quarters of the liquid from dish and discard.
6 Return baking dish to oven and broil wings for 10 minutes until lightly browned. Allow to cool slightly before serving.

SERVES 8	
Per Serving:	
Calories	476
Fat	43g
Sodium	1,624mg
Carbohydrates	3g
Fiber	0g
Sugar	1g
Protein	21g

Healthy Baked Popcorn Chicken

Crispy popcorn chicken doesn't have to be a guilty pleasure. Enjoy this lighter baked version for a game day snack or as a fun and easy weeknight dinner.

1 cup low-fat plain Greek yogurt

½ teaspoon salt, divided

8 ounces boneless, skinless chicken breasts, cut into large cubes

¼ cup dried bread crumbs

½ teaspoon garlic powder

1 Preheat oven to 450°F. Line a baking sheet with parchment paper.
2 In a large bowl, combine yogurt and ¼ teaspoon salt. Add chicken and toss to coat. In a separate bowl, combine bread crumbs, garlic powder, and remaining ¼ teaspoon salt.
3 Dredge coated chicken in the bread crumb mixture until evenly coated. Place chicken on the prepared baking sheet and bake for 12–15 minutes or until cooked through. Serve hot.

SERVES 2	
Per Serving:	
Calories	253
Fat	5g
Sodium	911mg
Carbohydrates	16g
Fiber	1g
Sugar	4g
Protein	36g

Maple Turkey Burgers

SERVES 4	
Per Serving:	
Calories	220
Fat	12g
Sodium	651mg
Carbohydrates	7g
Fiber	0g
Sugar	6g
Protein	20g

Made with just a few ingredients, these turkey burgers come together in no time and take a typical turkey burger up a notch with sweet and savory flavors of maple, sage, and thyme.

1 pound ground turkey breast

2 tablespoons maple syrup

1½ teaspoons ground sage

1 teaspoon dried thyme

1 teaspoon salt

1 tablespoon coconut oil

1 In a large mixing bowl, combine ground turkey, maple syrup, sage, thyme, and salt.

2 Shape mixture into four (½"-thick) patties.

3 Heat coconut oil in a large skillet over medium heat. Add patties to the skillet and heat until cooked through, about 5–6 minutes per side. Serve immediately.

Masala Chicken Bowls

SERVES 4	
Per Serving:	
Calories	245
Fat	11g
Sodium	452mg
Carbohydrates	11g
Fiber	4g
Sugar	6g
Protein	24g

When you use prepared cauliflower rice, frozen vegetables, and jarred masala sauce, this one pan dish is ready in less than 20 minutes.

1 pound ground chicken breast

1 (16-ounce) bag frozen pepper and onion strips

1 cup jarred tikka masala simmer sauce

1 (16-ounce) bag frozen cauliflower rice, thawed

1 Spray a large skillet with nonstick cooking spray and heat over medium heat. Add ground chicken and sauté for 7–8 minutes, breaking it up with a wooden spoon as it cooks.

2 Add pepper and onion strips and tikka masala sauce. Heat, stirring, for 5 minutes. Transfer to a bowl and set aside.

3 In the same skillet, sauté cauliflower rice for 3 to 4 minutes until translucent. Divide cauliflower rice among four bowls and top with chicken mixture.

Mango Chicken Bowls

Refreshing and sweet mango livens up this macro-balanced dish. If you're watching your carbs, swap the brown rice for cauliflower rice.

4 (4-ounce) boneless, skinless chicken breasts

1 tablespoon olive oil

¼ teaspoon salt

¼ teaspoon ground black pepper

2 large mangos, peeled, pitted, and diced

1 medium green bell pepper, seeded and chopped

1 cup low-sodium chicken broth

2 scallions, chopped

1 tablespoon lime juice

1 teaspoon minced garlic

½ teaspoon ground ginger

2 cups cooked brown rice

SERVES 4	
Per Serving:	
Calories	240
Fat	5g
Sodium	151mg
Carbohydrates	46g
Fiber	4g
Sugar	24g
Protein	5g

1 Preheat oven to 400°F. Spray a baking sheet with nonstick cooking spray.

2 Brush chicken with oil and season with salt and pepper. Place on the prepared baking sheet.

3 Bake for 25–28 minutes or until the internal temperature reaches 165°F.

4 Remove from oven and set aside.

5 In a large skillet over medium-high heat, add mangos, bell pepper, broth, scallions, lime juice, garlic, and ginger, and bring to a boil. Reduce heat to medium.

6 Add rice to skillet and stir to combine. Cook for 1 minute to heat through.

7 Cut chicken into slices.

8 Divide rice mixture among four plates and serve immediately with chicken.

Lazy Cook's Cheese-Stuffed Turkey Meatloaf

Cheese-stuffed meatloaf might seem intimidating, especially for a weeknight dinner, but this recipe is anything but difficult. With only a few basic steps and a minimal number of ingredients, it's quite a simple recipe.

3 tablespoons plus ⅓ cup ketchup, divided

1½ teaspoons light brown sugar

1½ teaspoons Dijon mustard

3 teaspoons Worcestershire sauce

2 pounds extra-lean ground turkey breast

¾ cup Italian bread crumbs

2 large eggs

¼ teaspoon salt

⅛ teaspoon ground black pepper

1 cup shredded Cheddar cheese

SERVES 8	
Per Serving:	
Calories	260
Fat	8g
Sodium	612mg
Carbohydrates	13g
Fiber	0g
Sugar	5g
Protein	33g

1 Preheat oven to 350°F. Spray a 9" × 5" loaf pan with nonstick cooking spray or line it with parchment paper.

2 In a small bowl, combine 3 tablespoons ketchup, brown sugar, mustard, and Worcestershire sauce. Mix well.

3 In a large bowl, combine ground turkey, bread crumbs, remaining ⅔ cup ketchup, eggs, salt, and pepper. Mix with your hands until well blended.

4 Place mixture on a 12" × 16" piece of plastic wrap or parchment paper and pat firmly into a 10" × 12" rectangle.

5 Sprinkle cheese evenly over turkey mixture. Roll up jelly roll–style, starting from a short end, by lifting the plastic wrap and removing it as you roll. Seal ends of roll. Place meatloaf seam side down in prepared pan.

6 Bake 45 minutes. Remove from oven, brush ketchup mixture over the top of the meatloaf and return to oven. Bake for 20 minutes more. Remove from oven and set aside for 10 minutes.

7 Serve warm.

GROUND TURKEY: PROTEIN AT THE READY

It can be hard to reach your protein goal, especially if you have to cook fresh protein every time you eat. A useful trick is to simply cook a lot of ground turkey in a pan with minimal seasoning. Keep it in the refrigerator and add it to pasta, eggs, burritos, or any other dish that needs a protein boost. It's a versatile addition that doesn't add an overpowering flavor.

Turkey Meatloaf Muffins

These mini meatloaves are high in protein and great for a quick meal or snack. Individual muffins make it easy to consider portion control when calculating your daily macros.

1 pound ground turkey breast

1 small yellow onion, peeled and minced

1 tablespoon Dijon mustard

1 teaspoon Italian seasoning

½ teaspoon salt

1 cup Cauliflower Mash (see recipe in Chapter 10)

¼ cup marinara sauce

1 Preheat oven to 350°F. Spray a muffin tin with nonstick cooking spray.

2 In a large mixing bowl, combine turkey, onion, mustard, seasoning, and salt. Divide among muffin cups and smooth tops. Bake for 30 minutes.

3 Remove from oven and take individual meatloaf muffins out of tin, then top with Cauliflower Mash and marinara sauce. Serve immediately.

Spicy Avocado Turkey Burgers

Sriracha sauce, onion, lime juice, and pepper jack cheese add intensity to traditional turkey burgers.

4 (4-ounce) turkey burger patties

1 teaspoon salt

1 teaspoon ground black pepper

4 (1-ounce) slices pepper jack cheese

2 medium avocados, peeled, pitted, and diced

½ medium onion, peeled and chopped

2 teaspoons minced garlic

3 tablespoons lime juice

3 tablespoons sriracha sauce

1 Preheat a gas or charcoal grill.

2 Sprinkle burgers with salt and pepper. Grill for 5–6 minutes per side until fully cooked. Top with a slice of cheese, cover grill, and cook 1 minute.

3 In a medium bowl, mash avocados, onion, garlic, and lime juice.

4 Top each burger with avocado mixture and sriracha.

CHAPTER 6

Beef and Pork

Steak House Blue Cheeseburgers

SERVES 4	
Per Serving:	
Calories	232
Fat	15g
Sodium	391mg
Carbohydrates	4g
Fiber	0g
Sugar	1g
Protein	21g

Recreate your favorite steak house experience in your own kitchen. These juicy burgers combine the rich taste of beef with the sharp kick of blue cheese, reminiscent of a blue cheese-crusted filet mignon. Serve the burger on a potato bun with a green salad for a complete meal.

1 pound 90% lean ground beef

1 large egg

¼ cup dried bread crumbs

1 tablespoon steak seasoning

½ cup crumbled blue cheese

1 Preheat a gas or charcoal grill and lightly oil the grate.

2 In a large bowl, combine ground beef, egg, bread crumbs, and seasoning. Form mixture into four evenly sized patties.

3 Grill patties for 3–4 minutes on one side, then flip patties over. Top patties with cheese and cook another 3–4 minutes.

Hearty Beef Stew

SERVES 4	
Per Serving:	
Calories	490
Fat	19g
Sodium	799mg
Carbohydrates	49g
Fiber	8g
Sugar	11g
Protein	30g

Prep this stew in the morning for the perfect Sunday night dinner and leftovers for the week. Or just add everything to your slow cooker before you leave for work, and you'll come home to a fresh dinner.

4 medium red potatoes, cut into quarters

¼ cup all-purpose flour

1 pound beef stew meat

1 (14.5-ounce) can diced tomatoes, undrained

1 medium onion, peeled and chopped

5 medium carrots, peeled and sliced

16 ounces sliced mushrooms

½ teaspoon dried thyme

½ teaspoon salt

¼ teaspoon ground black pepper

2 cups beef broth (low-sodium canned) or water

1 Add all ingredients to a slow cooker and mix well.

2 Cook on low 7–8 hours until beef and potatoes are tender.

3 Serve hot.

Swedish-Style Meatballs

These homemade meatballs are much healthier than the frozen meatballs you can buy at the store. While they're not smothered in rich, creamy gravy, they're still packed with delicious flavor, so you'll feel good about eating this healthier version.

1 teaspoon olive oil

1 small onion, peeled and minced

1 clove garlic, peeled and minced

1 stalk celery, minced

¼ cup minced fresh parsley

1 pound 90% lean ground beef

1 large egg

¼ cup dried bread crumbs

½ teaspoon salt

¼ teaspoon ground black pepper

½ teaspoon allspice

2 cups low-sodium beef broth

1 Heat oil in a large skillet over medium heat and sauté onion and garlic 5 minutes.

2 Add celery and parsley and cook 3 more minutes or until celery softens, then set aside.

3 In a large bowl, combine onion mixture, ground beef, egg, bread crumbs, salt, pepper, and allspice, mixing well. Form into roughly 20 balls, using about 2 tablespoons of meat mixture for each.

4 Add broth to the same skillet and bring to a boil over medium-high heat. Add meatballs, cover, and cook 20 minutes, stirring occasionally.

5 Serve warm.

MAKES 20 MEATBALLS	
Per Serving (5 meatballs):	
Calories	265
Fat	15g
Sodium	430mg
Carbohydrates	5g
Fiber	0g
Sugar	0g
Protein	25g

REASONS WHY THE SCALE FLUCTUATES

The scale is not always the best measure of fat loss, because it doesn't tell the whole picture. You may be frustrated by weight fluctuations if you weigh yourself often. These fluctuations are common, normal, and likely temporary. Several everyday factors can influence weight, including changing hormone levels due to ovulation or menstruation, lack of sleep, inflammation from a tough workout, stress, and sodium or alcohol consumption. Remember, these fluctuations don't necessarily correlate to your progress.

Balsamic Grilled Steak

SERVES 6	
Per Serving:	
Calories	207
Fat	11g
Sodium	187mg
Carbohydrates	2g
Fiber	0g
Sugar	2g
Protein	24g

Thanks to a delicious marinade of balsamic vinegar, garlic, and rosemary, this steak is so tender, it will nearly melt in your mouth. Add this steak to a big garden salad or pair with your favorite starch, such as roasted potatoes or rice, for a complete and well-balanced meal.

1 teaspoon kosher salt

¼ cup balsamic vinegar

1 tablespoon olive oil

1 clove garlic, peeled and minced

1 tablespoon dried rosemary

1 (1½-pound) flank steak

1 In a large zip-top plastic bag, combine salt, vinegar, oil, garlic, and rosemary. Add steak, turn to coat in marinade, seal bag, and refrigerate overnight.

2 Preheat a gas or charcoal grill and lightly oil the grate.

3 Remove steak from marinade and grill 3–5 minutes per side. Transfer steak to a cutting board and let rest 5 minutes.

4 Slice steak across the grain and serve.

Cowboy Caviar Cauliflower Rice Bowls

SERVES 4	
Per Serving:	
Calories	455
Fat	22g
Sodium	447mg
Carbohydrates	31g
Fiber	10g
Sugar	9g
Protein	28g

You can make this meal ahead of time and reheat it, which makes a super fast weeknight dinner.

1 pound 85% lean ground beef

1½ cups Cowboy Caviar (see recipe in Chapter 8)

4 cups riced cauliflower

½ cup guacamole

1 Place beef in a large skillet over medium-high heat. Sauté until no longer pink, about 8 minutes, using a wooden spoon to break up meat as it cooks. Add Cowboy Caviar and bring to a boil.

2 Reduce heat to medium-low and simmer for 5 minutes. Transfer to a large bowl.

3 In the same skillet, sauté riced cauliflower until translucent and lightly browned, about 5 minutes.

4 Divide cauliflower among four plates. Top with ground beef mixture and guacamole. Serve immediately.

Orange Beef Stir-Fry

This low-fat spin on a classic Chinese dish is a healthy alternative that's easy to prepare at home. Orange marmalade and a frozen stir-fry vegetable medley are the secret ingredients that cut down prep time without losing out on flavor. For an extra-spicy kick, try adding some hot sauce or chili peppers. Serve over white rice or cauliflower rice for a low-carb option.

¼ cup orange marmalade

2 tablespoons low-sodium soy sauce or coconut aminos

1 tablespoon olive oil

½ pound lean sirloin steak, cut into thin strips

2 teaspoons minced garlic

1 (14.4-ounce) bag frozen stir-fry vegetables (with broccoli), defrosted

1 In a small bowl, combine marmalade and soy sauce. Set aside.

2 Heat oil in large skillet over medium-high heat. Add steak to skillet and sauté for 2 minutes.

3 Add garlic, stir-fry vegetables, and marmalade mixture. Bring to a boil, stirring frequently.

4 Reduce heat to medium-low and simmer for 2–3 minutes until sauce thickens slightly.

5 Serve hot.

SERVES 2	
Per Serving:	
Calories	392
Fat	13g
Sodium	137mg
Carbohydrates	40g
Fiber	5g
Sugar	29g
Protein	32g

THE FOURTH MACRONUTRIENT

Alcohol is the fourth macronutrient. It's not typically included with the others because it provides no nutrients. Even so, you should track these calories and macros because they add up quickly.

Beef and Broccoli Kebabs

Your favorite beef and broccoli combo found its way to the grill. These juicy kebabs are bursting with flavor, thanks to a simple marinade and nutrient-dense broccoli florets. They're quick and easy to throw on the grill for summer parties and other get-togethers.

SERVES 4

Per Serving:

Calories	331
Fat	13g
Sodium	575mg
Carbohydrates	23g
Fiber	3g
Sugar	14g
Protein	32g

WHO KNEW?

Broccoli contains more protein per calorie than steak. Of course, you would need to eat a lot of broccoli to get the same amount of calories that you do from the meat.

⅓ cup low-sodium soy sauce or coconut aminos

¼ cup maple syrup

2 tablespoons lime juice

1 tablespoon ground ginger

1 pound lean sirloin steak, cut into cubes

1 head broccoli, cut into large florets

2 tablespoons olive oil

3 tablespoons ground black pepper

1 In a large bowl, mix soy sauce, maple syrup, lime juice, and ginger. Add steak and toss until coated. Cover bowl and marinate in the refrigerator at least 30 minutes.

2 Preheat a gas or charcoal grill and lightly oil the grate.

3 Place broccoli and oil in a large bowl and toss to coat. Remove steak from marinade and discard marinade.

4 Alternate steak and broccoli on eight metal grilling skewers. Season with pepper.

5 Grill 6–8 minutes for medium-rare, turning often. Serve immediately.

Sirloin Chopped Salad

SERVES 1	
Per Serving:	
Calories	400
Fat	21g
Sodium	640mg
Carbohydrates	13g
Fiber	2g
Sugar	6g
Protein	42g

This simple, low-carb salad is much more interesting than the standard grilled chicken salad. Plus, this one contains a variety of healthy fats to keep you full for longer. Cook the steak in advance, and you'll have healthy protein ready to go whenever you need it.

2 cups mixed salad greens
4 ounces cooked sirloin steak, cut into strips
¼ cup crumbled blue cheese
¼ cup balsamic vinaigrette

Place greens, steak, and cheese in a large bowl. Top with dressing and toss to coat. Serve immediately.

Grilled Sirloin with No-Fail Chimichurri

SERVES 2	
Per Serving:	
Calories	400
Fat	28g
Sodium	230mg
Carbohydrates	5g
Fiber	1g
Sugar	0g
Protein	31g

A delicious twist on a traditional sirloin, this minimalist recipe allows the flavor of the steak to come through while providing a little kick from the fresh seasonings. Serve with roasted potatoes and steamed green vegetables for the perfect macro-friendly meal.

2 (4-ounce) sirloin steaks
½ cup No-Fail Chimichurri (see recipe in Chapter 10)

1 Preheat a gas or charcoal grill and lightly oil the grate.
2 Grill steaks about 4 minutes per side.
3 Transfer steaks to a cutting board and let stand 10 minutes. Thinly slice steaks across the grain. Serve with chimichurri.

Asian Grilled Flank Steak

When it comes to steak marinades, it's hard to beat the classic combination of soy sauce and honey. But toss in garlic, ginger, and a splash of rice wine vinegar, and you've just made the best steak marinade you've ever tasted. Be sure to allow the marinade to intensify overnight before cooking. It's worth the wait!

¼ cup low-sodium soy sauce or coconut aminos

½ cup olive oil

2 tablespoons honey

2 tablespoons rice wine vinegar

1 tablespoon ground ginger

1 tablespoon minced garlic

1 (2-pound) flank steak

SERVES 4	
Per Serving:	
Calories	621
Fat	41g
Sodium	691mg
Carbohydrates	10g
Fiber	0g
Sugar	9g
Protein	49g

1 In a large gallon-sized zip-top plastic bag, combine soy sauce, oil, honey, vinegar, ginger, and garlic. Add steak to bag. Seal bag and turn to coat steak with marinade. Refrigerate for up to 24 hours, turning the bag occasionally.

2 Preheat a gas or charcoal grill and lightly oil the grate.

3 Remove steak from marinade and discard marinade. Grill 8–10 minutes per side.

4 Remove from grill and slice thinly across the grain. Serve warm or at room temperature.

Skinny Meatballs

SERVES 5

Per Serving:

Calories	213
Fat	13g
Sodium	225mg
Carbohydrates	3g
Fiber	1g
Sugar	0g
Protein	22g

JUST ADD SAUCE FOR MAXIMUM FLAVOR

Anytime you're eating precooked meat, mix up your flavor game with a variety of sauces. Barbecue sauce, Buffalo wing sauce, hot sauce, honey mustard, ranch or blue cheese salad dressing, pesto, salsa, hummus... the options are endless, so there is no excuse to eat dry, boring food.

These healthier meatballs have been lightened up using extra-lean beef to minimize the fat content. Though considered a "skinny" recipe, these meatballs don't lack flavor. Even the pickiest of eaters will love them. In fact, these meatballs are the perfect family-friendly meal for any night of the week. If you prefer a different low-fat meat, this recipe also works well with ground turkey, bison, or chicken.

1 pound 92% lean ground beef

½ cup minced onion

2 large egg whites

1 large egg

¼ cup oat bran

2 tablespoons grated Parmesan cheese

1 teaspoon dried oregano

½ teaspoon garlic powder

2 tablespoons unsweetened almond milk

¼ teaspoon salt

¼ teaspoon ground black pepper

2 tablespoons olive oil

1 Preheat oven to 375°F. Spray a rimmed baking sheet with non-stick cooking spray.
2 In a large bowl, mix all ingredients together.
3 Shape mixture into twenty balls.
4 Place meatballs on the prepared baking sheet and bake 30–35 minutes, turning halfway through to ensure even browning.
5 Serve warm.

Bean-Free Chili

This quick and easy Bean-Free Chili recipe is a satisfying meal on a chilly day and ready in just over 30 minutes. If you have a little more time, simmering the chili longer will really deepen the flavors. For a spicy kick, add hot sauce, sriracha, or sliced jalapeño peppers.

1 pound 90% lean ground beef

1 tablespoon salted butter or ghee

1 (16-ounce) bag frozen pepper and onion strips

3 teaspoons minced garlic

2 tablespoons tomato paste

2 tablespoons chili powder

1 tablespoon ground cumin

½ teaspoon salt

1 large tomato, chopped

1 cup low-sodium beef broth

1 Place ground beef in a large pot or Dutch oven. Sauté over medium heat, using a wooden spoon to break it up, until no longer pink, about 8–10 minutes. Use a slotted spoon to transfer beef to a plate. Discard any fat left in the pot.

2 Melt butter in the same pot over medium heat. Add pepper and onion strips and sauté for 3–5 minutes or until warmed. Add garlic and sauté 30 seconds.

3 Stir in tomato paste, chili powder, cumin, and salt. Cook, stirring, for another minute. Add tomato, broth, and ground beef. Bring to a boil.

4 Reduce heat to low, cover pot, and simmer for 20 minutes.

5 Serve warm.

SERVES 4	
Per Serving:	
Calories	255
Fat	15g
Sodium	393mg
Carbohydrates	4g
Fiber	2g
Sugar	3g
Protein	23g

USE SUNDAY TO GET BACK ON TRACK

If you lived it up on Friday and Saturday, use Sunday as the day to get back to your healthy habits. Don't let the weekend merriment roll into the next week, and don't wait until Monday to get back on track. Start Sunday morning with a nutritious meal and some food prep. Getting yourself organized on Sunday sets you up for a healthy week ahead.

Meal Prep Salsa Rice Bowls

SERVES 4	
Per Serving:	
Calories	253
Fat	11g
Sodium	623mg
Carbohydrates	11g
Fiber	6g
Sugar	6g
Protein	26g

This bowl recipe is so easy, you'll likely want to add this meal to your regular rotation. Lean ground beef works best, but ground turkey or chicken also make a tasty protein choice. Get creative with your salsa choices as well—any flavor or variety will work. Top it with a scoop of guacamole or shredded Cheddar cheese if your daily fat goal allows for it.

2 (10-ounce) packages frozen cauliflower rice

1 pound 90% lean ground beef

1 cup salsa

1　Cook cauliflower rice as directed on the package and set aside.
2　In a large skillet over medium-high heat, sauté ground beef until no longer pink, about 8 minutes. Break up meat with a wooden spoon as it cooks. Drain off any extra drippings in the skillet.
3　Add salsa to beef, stir to combine, and heat for 5 minutes.
4　Divide cauliflower rice between four containers with lids and top with beef mixture.
5　Store in the refrigerator for up to a week. Reheat in the microwave on high for 2–3 minutes.

Pizza Cottage Pie

Pizza and cottage pie is a match made in comfort food heaven. Use pre-made mashed potatoes (fresh or frozen) to speed up the prep time for this recipe.

2 pounds russet potatoes, peeled and quartered

1½ teaspoons salt, divided

2 tablespoons salted butter, melted

½ cup unsweetened almond milk

½ teaspoon ground black pepper

1 pound 90% lean ground beef

1 small onion, peeled and diced

½ medium red bell pepper, seeded and diced

2 tablespoons pizza seasoning (or 4 teaspoons Italian seasoning and 2 teaspoons each garlic powder and onion salt)

½ cup shredded low-fat mozzarella cheese

SERVES 4	
Per Serving:	
Calories	448
Fat	19g
Sodium	424mg
Carbohydrates	41g
Fiber	5g
Sugar	5g
Protein	32g

1 Place potatoes and 1 teaspoon salt in a large pot. Add water to cover potatoes. Bring to a boil over high heat and cook uncovered 15 minutes or until fork-tender. Drain and transfer to a large bowl.

2 Add butter and almond milk to potatoes and mash using a potato masher. Season with remaining salt and black pepper. Set aside.

3 Preheat oven 350°F.

4 Place ground beef in a large skillet over medium-high heat. Sauté until no longer pink, about 8 minutes, using a wooden spoon to break up meat as it cooks. Add onion, bell pepper, and pizza seasoning. Reduce heat to medium and cook for another 5 minutes, stirring often.

5 Transfer to a 6" × 9" baking dish. Top with mashed potatoes and smooth top with a spatula. Sprinkle cheese over potatoes.

6 Bake for 25 minutes, then set oven to broil.

7 Broil casserole for 3–5 minutes until the top is lightly browned.

8 Cool 5 minutes before serving.

Spaghetti Squash Taco Boats

This is one of the tastiest ways to eat spaghetti squash. A delicious low-carb alternative to taco pasta, these "boats" make for a fun presentation and can be made ahead of time and kept in the refrigerator until you need them. Steaming the squash in the microwave cuts out at least 30 minutes of cook time.

2 (3-pound) spaghetti squash

1 tablespoon olive oil

½ small yellow onion, peeled and minced

1 teaspoon minced garlic

1 pound 90% lean ground beef

1 (15-ounce) can black beans, drained and rinsed

1 (14.5-ounce) can diced tomatoes, undrained

3 tablespoons taco seasoning

¼ cup water

½ cup shredded Cheddar cheese

¼ cup finely chopped fresh cilantro

SERVES 4	
Per Serving:	
Calories	617
Fat	23g
Sodium	676mg
Carbohydrates	69g
Fiber	17g
Sugar	21g
Protein	37g

INSTANT POT° SPAGHETTI SQUASH

It doesn't get easier than this! Slice a 3-pound spaghetti squash in half and scoop out the seeds. Add a cup of water to the Instant Pot° along with the spaghetti squash. Close lid, set the steam release to Sealing, press the Manual button, and set time to 7 minutes. When the timer beeps, quick-release the pressure until the float valve drops and open the lid. You now have perfectly cooked squash to use in a recipe or as a replacement for pasta.

1 Cut spaghetti squash lengthwise and remove seeds. Place halves cut side down in a microwave-safe dish filled with 1" of water. Microwave on high for 10 minutes. Continue to cook for 1-minute intervals until squash is tender when pierced with a knife. Cook time will be about 12–15 minutes total. Remove from microwave, flip halves over, and let cool for 10 minutes.

2 Use a fork to scrape the flesh into strands. Set halves aside.

3 Heat oil in a large skillet over medium-high heat. Sauté onion until slightly softened, about 5 minutes. Add garlic and sauté 30 seconds. Add ground beef and cook 8–10 minutes, using a wooden spoon to break up the meat, until no longer pink. Drain excess fat from skillet.

4 Stir in beans, tomatoes, taco seasoning, and water. Bring to a boil, then reduce heat to medium-low and simmer until thickened, about 5 minutes.

5 Preheat oven to 400°F.

6 Place spaghetti squash halves on a large baking sheet. Top each half with ground beef mixture. Sprinkle with cheese.

7 Bake for 6–8 minutes or until cheese is melted.

8 Garnish with cilantro and serve immediately.

Deconstructed Cheeseburger Salad

SERVES 4

Per Serving:

Calories	412
Fat	29g
Sodium	520mg
Carbohydrates	9g
Fiber	1g
Sugar	3g
Protein	29g

THE POWER OF PROGRESS PHOTOS

Progress photos show true signs of body composition changes. (Have you taken your "before" photos yet? If not, make sure you do it ASAP!) Try to keep the lighting, camera angle, and clothing the same across all the photos for consistency and to be able to easily compare. While the scale can sometimes stall or plateau, photos may show composition changes that are very motivating to see. Photos let you measure progress *off* the scale.

This salad tastes like a big, juicy cheeseburger, but without all of the carbs from the bun. The homemade salad dressing is the star of this meal. You might even want to make extra for other salads.

1 pound 90% lean ground beef

¼ cup mayonnaise

1 teaspoon yellow mustard

1 teaspoon dill pickle juice

1 tablespoon ketchup

¼ teaspoon onion powder

2 romaine hearts, chopped

4 dill pickle spears, chopped

1 cup diced red onion

1 cup halved cherry tomatoes

¾ cup shredded Cheddar cheese

1 Place ground beef in a large skillet over medium-high heat. Sauté until no longer pink, about 8 minutes, using a wooden spoon to break up meat as it cooks. Drain excess fat from skillet.

2 In a small bowl, whisk together mayonnaise, mustard, pickle juice, ketchup, and onion powder.

3 In a large bowl, toss together romaine, pickles, onion, and tomatoes. Divide mixture among four plates. Top with meat mixture and sprinkle with cheese.

4 Drizzle with dressing and serve immediately.

Three-Ingredient Cottage Pie

If you're in a comfort food mood, dinner doesn't get easier than this. Prep this meal at the beginning of the week and store in the refrigerator—just reheat it when it's time to eat.

1 (24-ounce) bag steam and mash frozen potatoes
1 pound 90% lean ground beef
1 (16-ounce) bag frozen mixed vegetables (peas, corn, and carrots)

1 Cook and mash frozen potatoes as instructed on package. Set aside and keep warm.

2 Place ground beef in a large skillet over medium-high heat. Sauté until no longer pink, about 8 minutes, using a wooden spoon to break up meat as it cooks.

3 Add vegetables to the skillet and stir to combine. Reduce heat to medium-low, cover, and cook for 10 minutes, stirring occasionally.

4 Preheat broiler.

5 Transfer mixture to an 11" × 7" baking dish. Top with mashed potatoes and use a spatula to smooth the top. Place baking dish under broiler and broil until lightly browned, 3–5 minutes. Serve immediately.

SERVES 6	
Per Serving:	
Calories	203
Fat	8g
Sodium	271mg
Carbohydrates	15g
Fiber	2g
Sugar	3g
Protein	17g

One Pan Kale Marinara

SERVES 4	
Per Serving:	
Calories	344
Fat	19g
Sodium	133mg
Carbohydrates	10g
Fiber	4g
Sugar	3g
Protein	33g

This simple main dish is high in protein, nutrients, and fiber. Prep this meal at the beginning of the week for a quick grab-and-go lunch or dinner that you just need to reheat.

1 tablespoon olive oil

½ medium yellow onion, peeled and diced

1 tablespoon minced garlic

1 pound 90% lean ground beef

1¼ cups no-sugar-added marinara sauce

4 cups baby kale

1 Heat oil in a large skillet over medium-high heat. Sauté onion until slightly softened, about 5 minutes. Add garlic and sauté 30 seconds. Add ground beef and cook 8–10 minutes, using a wooden spoon to break up the meat, until no longer pink. Drain excess fat from skillet.

2 Stir in marinara sauce and heat for 3 minutes.

3 Add kale and cook, stirring, for 2 minutes until wilted.

4 Serve warm.

Sweet Potato Hash

SERVES 4	
Per Serving:	
Calories	327
Fat	15g
Sodium	363mg
Carbohydrates	21g
Fiber	4g
Sugar	6g
Protein	27g

This one pan dish is great for breakfast, lunch, or dinner. It can be made with ground chicken or turkey if you're looking for a lower fat option.

2 large sweet potatoes, peeled and diced

1 tablespoon olive oil

1 tablespoon minced garlic

¼ teaspoon ground cinnamon

½ teaspoon salt

1 pound 90% lean ground beef

4 cups baby spinach

1 Place sweet potatoes in a large bowl. Add oil, garlic, cinnamon, and salt and toss to coat. Transfer to a large skillet.

2 Cover skillet and cook over medium heat for 15 minutes, stirring occasionally.

3 Add ground beef to the skillet and sauté until no longer pink, about 8 minutes, using a wooden spoon to break up meat as it cooks.

4 Add spinach and stir until wilted. Serve immediately.

Pizza Meatballs

When you're in the mood for pizza, reach for these meatballs instead. They're packed with the same great flavor and cheesy goodness of traditional pizza with fewer refined carbs. Double the batch and freeze some for a quick and healthy dinner that just needs reheating.

1½ pounds 90% lean ground beef

⅓ cup Italian bread crumbs

¼ cup grated Parmesan cheese

1 large egg

1 tablespoon pizza seasoning (or 2 teaspoons Italian seasoning and 1 teaspoon each garlic powder and onion salt)

½ teaspoon salt

⅛ teaspoon ground black pepper

1 pound mozzarella cheese, cut into 18 small cubes

2 (24-ounce) jars marinara sauce

1 Preheat oven to 375°F. Line a large baking sheet with parchment paper.
2 In a large bowl, combine ground beef, bread crumbs, Parmesan, egg, pizza seasoning, salt, and pepper. Mix well. Shape mixture into eighteen meatballs (1½"–2" in diameter) and place them on the prepared baking sheet.
3 Push a cube of mozzarella into the center of each meatball and reshape to completely enclose cheese.
4 Bake for 20 minutes.
5 Pour marinara sauce into a large saucepan and add meatballs. Bring to a boil over medium-high heat. Reduce heat to simmer 10–15 minutes until sauce is warm and meatballs are cooked all the way through.
6 Serve immediately, or store in an airtight container in the refrigerator for up to 1 week.

SERVES 6	
Per Serving:	
Calories	620
Fat	35g
Sodium	1,561mg
Carbohydrates	28g
Fiber	6g
Sugar	7g
Protein	47g

TRACKING A DAY WHEN DINING OUT

Leave yourself a calorie "buffer" for dining out. This buffer could be one-third to one-half of your total calories for the day, depending on how much you'd like to splurge. Fill your breakfast and lunch with protein and non-starchy vegetables. Most restaurant meals are loaded with carbs and fat and skimpy on protein, so it's in your best interest to front-load your protein (and fiber) the best you can. This will also keep your blood sugar steady, so you're not going to dinner starving.

Pork Fried Cauliflower Rice

Pork Fried Cauliflower Rice is an easy low-carb meal that is chock-full of vegetables and fiber, both of which are important for overall health and weight loss goals. This recipe is so tasty, flavorful, and satisfying, you won't even miss the rice.

SERVES 4	
Per Serving:	
Calories	265
Fat	10g
Sodium	864mg
Carbohydrates	12g
Fiber	4g
Sugar	3g
Protein	28g

HOMEMADE LOW-CARB "RICE"

Cauliflower is fairly neutral in flavor, particularly when you add other flavors and seasonings to it. If you're unable to find riced cauliflower at your local store, it's quite easy to make at home. Simply take a head of cauliflower, core and chop it, and pulse it in a food processor until the pieces are as small as grains of rice. Steam or sauté these little bits as a low-carb rice substitute.

¼ cup low-sodium soy sauce or coconut aminos

2 tablespoons lime juice

2 tablespoons water

1 tablespoon minced garlic

1 tablespoon ground ginger

1 pound lean ground pork

¼ teaspoon salt

1 medium yellow onion, peeled and chopped

3 cups riced cauliflower

6 cups roughly chopped baby spinach

½ cup chopped fresh cilantro

1 In a small bowl, whisk together soy sauce, lime juice, water, garlic, and ginger. Set aside.

2 Place ground pork in a large skillet over medium-high heat. Sauté until no longer pink, about 8 minutes, using a wooden spoon to break up meat as it cooks. Season with salt.

3 Use a slotted spoon to transfer pork to a plate and set aside. Drain all but 1 tablespoon fat from the skillet.

4 Heat skillet over medium-high heat again and add onion. Sauté until slightly softened, about 5 minutes. Return pork to the skillet and add riced cauliflower. Cook, stirring, for 2 minutes.

5 Stir in soy sauce mixture and bring to a boil. Reduce heat to medium-low and simmer for 3 minutes. Add spinach and stir until wilted.

6 Top with cilantro before serving.

Slow Cooker Barbecue Pulled Pork

Pulled pork is tender, flavorful, and easy to make in your slow cooker.

1 (4-pound) pork shoulder roast

1 cup barbecue sauce

½ cup apple cider vinegar

½ cup low-sodium chicken broth

2 tablespoons maple syrup

1½ tablespoons Worcestershire sauce

1 tablespoon chili powder

1 large onion, peeled and chopped

2 cloves garlic, peeled and crushed

SERVES 8	
Per Serving:	
Calories	477
Fat	28g
Sodium	152mg
Carbohydrates	15g
Fiber	0g
Sugar	12g
Protein	40g

1 Place pork in a 4- to 6-quart slow cooker. Combine the remaining ingredients in a small bowl. Pour mixture over pork.

2 Cover and cook on high until pork shreds easily with a fork, 4–6 hours.

3 Transfer pork to a large rimmed platter and shred meat using two forks. Return shredded pork to the slow cooker and stir to combine with the sauce. Serve warm.

One Pan Garlic Herb Pork

This tender and juicy pork roast is a healthy and easy dinner. Best of all, it's made in just one dish with only 10 minutes of prep.

1 (2-pound) boneless pork roast

4 teaspoons minced garlic

2 teaspoons salt

1 tablespoon ground sage

2 teaspoons dried rosemary

¼ teaspoon ground black pepper

1 tablespoon extra-virgin olive oil

SERVES 6	
Per Serving:	
Calories	339
Fat	25g
Sodium	1,516mg
Carbohydrates	0g
Fiber	0g
Sugar	0g
Protein	27g

1 Preheat oven to 450°F.

2 Pat pork roast dry with a paper towel and place it in a shallow roasting pan.

3 In a small bowl, mix together garlic, salt, sage, rosemary, pepper, and oil. Rub mixture all over pork roast.

4 Roast for 15 minutes. Reduce oven temperature to 300°F and roast for another 20 minutes or until a meat thermometer inserted into the center of the roast registers 145°F.

Sheet Pan Italian Sausage and Peppers

SERVES 4

Per Serving:

Calories	252
Fat	14g
Sodium	892mg
Carbohydrates	14g
Fiber	3g
Sugar	7g
Protein	17g

LEARN FROM YOUR MISTAKES

When it comes to sticking with your plan, give yourself some grace. Rather than blame yourself or your lack of willpower, think about what tripped you up. If you can identify the challenge, you can make tweaks to help you keep moving forward with your goals.

Sheet pan dinners are endlessly versatile, healthy, and one of the easiest ways to nail multiple food groups with only one dish. This Italian sausage and pepper meal is guaranteed to become a go-to weeknight dinner. It's loaded with Italian flavors, and it's filling and enjoyable either on its own or as an easy add-on to pasta, sandwiches, and more.

2 medium red bell peppers, seeded and sliced

2 medium yellow bell peppers, seeded and sliced

1 medium yellow onion, peeled and sliced

1 tablespoon olive oil

2 teaspoons Italian seasoning

¼ teaspoon salt

1 pound pork sausage, sliced

1 Preheat oven to 400°F. Line a baking sheet with parchment paper.

2 In a large bowl, combine peppers, onion, oil, Italian seasoning, and salt. Pour mixture onto prepared baking sheet and spread out into a single layer.

3 Place sausage slices on top of the vegetable mixture. Roast for 30–35 minutes until sausage slices are cooked through. Serve immediately.

Dijon-Roasted Pork Tenderloin

SERVES 8	
Per Serving:	
Calories	447
Fat	21g
Sodium	585mg
Carbohydrates	6g
Fiber	0g
Sugar	6g
Protein	57g

This juicy and delicious pork tenderloin is simple to prepare and uses only a few common ingredients, but the end result is irresistible. It's the perfect way to spice up your dinner rotation if you're feeling stuck in a rut.

1 (4-pound) pork loin roast, trimmed

1 teaspoon salt

½ teaspoon ground black pepper

¼ cup whole-grain Dijon mustard

¼ cup light brown sugar

1 Preheat oven to 425°F.

2 Place pork roast in a roasting pan and season roast with salt and pepper. Roast for 30 minutes, then remove from the oven. Reduce oven heat to 375°F.

3 Brush mustard over roast and sprinkle it with brown sugar. Press sugar into mustard with a basting brush.

4 Return roast to the oven and roast for an additional 30 minutes, occasionally basting with the drippings. Cook until a meat thermometer inserted into the center of the roast registers 145°F.

5 Remove pan from oven, cover with foil and allow to rest 10 minutes.

6 Slice pork and serve with a spoonful of drippings from the pan.

Mashed Potato and Chorizo Quesadillas

The flavor combination of mashed potatoes and chorizo is both comforting and satisfying. These quesadillas make a great weeknight dinner or appetizers for a party. Serve with shredded lettuce, sour cream, and salsa if you like.

2 medium russet potatoes, peeled and quartered

1½ teaspoons salt, divided

½ cup whole milk

2 tablespoons salted butter

½ teaspoon ground black pepper

1 (12-ounce) package ground Mexican chorizo sausage

8 (7") whole-grain tortillas

2 cups shredded Cheddar cheese

2 tablespoons vegetable oil

SERVES 8	
Per Serving:	
Calories	429
Fat	27g
Sodium	687mg
Carbohydrates	30g
Fiber	2g
Sugar	1g
Protein	17g

1 Place potatoes and 1 teaspoon salt in a medium saucepan. Add water to cover potatoes and bring to a boil over high heat. Reduce heat to medium and simmer until potatoes are tender, about 20 minutes; drain.

2 Transfer potatoes to a large bowl along with milk, butter, pepper, and remaining ½ teaspoon salt. Mash with a potato masher and set aside.

3 In a large skillet over medium-high heat, sauté chorizo 10 minutes; drain.

4 Add cooked chorizo to mashed potatoes and stir well.

5 Place tortillas on a flat work surface. Add ½ cup potato mixture and ¼ cup cheese to a tortilla and fold it in half. Repeat with the remaining filling and tortillas.

6 In a large skillet, heat 1 tablespoon oil over medium heat. Add 2 tortillas to the skillet. Cook 3–4 minutes, or until crisp and golden brown, turning once. Repeat with remaining tortillas, adding the remaining 1 tablespoon oil as needed. Serve.

Sausage and Kale Soup

SERVES 4

Per Serving:

Calories	626
Fat	39g
Sodium	1,198mg
Carbohydrates	35g
Fiber	19g
Sugar	6g
Protein	32g

Full of sausage and plenty of vegetables, this soup is healthy, hearty, and satisfying. It's a great family-friendly meal to keep on hand in the refrigerator—just reheat and eat!

12 ounces pork sausage, sliced

1 medium yellow onion, peeled and diced

2 medium carrots, peeled and diced

2 stalks celery, diced

8 cups chopped kale leaves

8 cups low-sodium chicken broth

1 tablespoon salt

¾ cup brown rice

Combine all ingredients in a 6- to 8-quart slow cooker and cook on high for 4 hours or on low for 8 hours. Serve hot.

Sheet Pan Kielbasa and Roasted Vegetables

SERVES 4

Per Serving:

Calories	618
Fat	38g
Sodium	1,106mg
Carbohydrates	42g
Fiber	11g
Sugar	7g
Protein	28g

This recipe works with just about any vegetables. Feel free to try out your family's favorites.

1 pound Brussels sprouts, halved

1 pound baby potatoes, halved

1 large head of broccoli, cut into florets

3 large carrots, peeled and sliced

½ large yellow onion, peeled and sliced

1½ tablespoons olive oil

½ teaspoon salt

¼ teaspoon ground black pepper

1 pound kielbasa sausage, sliced

1 Preheat oven to 425°F. Line a large baking sheet with parchment paper or a silicone mat.

2 In a large bowl, toss Brussels sprouts, potatoes, broccoli, carrots, onion, oil, salt, and pepper. Pour onto the prepared baking sheet and top with kielbasa.

3 Bake for 20–30 minutes, stirring once. Remove from oven and cool slightly before serving.

CHAPTER 7

Fish and Seafood

Bourbon Lime Salmon

SERVES 8

Per Serving:

Calories	476
Fat	20g
Sodium	255mg
Carbohydrates	27g
Fiber	0g
Sugar	0g
Protein	44g

Salmon gets sassy with a kick from bourbon and lime juice. Salmon is one of the best natural sources of omega-3 fatty acids, which can lower your chances of developing cardiovascular disease and some types of cancer.

1 cup packed brown sugar

6 tablespoons bourbon

¼ cup low-sodium soy sauce or coconut aminos

2 tablespoons lime juice

2 teaspoons grated fresh ginger

½ teaspoon salt

¼ teaspoon ground black pepper

2 cloves garlic, peeled and crushed

8 (6-ounce) salmon fillets

4 teaspoons sesame seeds

½ cup sliced scallions

1 Combine brown sugar, bourbon, soy sauce, lime juice, ginger, salt, pepper, and garlic in a large resealable plastic bag. Marinate salmon fillets in the bag at least 30 minutes in the refrigerator.

2 Preheat broiler.

3 Transfer fish to a broiler pan and discard marinade. Broil fish 10–12 minutes until it flakes easily.

4 Sprinkle fish with sesame seeds and scallions and serve.

Grilled Tuna Teriyaki

Tuna steaks are easy to find at most stores. They provide a healthy dose of protein and omega-3 fatty acids, as well as potassium, magnesium, iron, and vitamins A, B_6, and B_{12}.

2 tablespoons low-sodium soy sauce or coconut aminos

1 tablespoon rice wine vinegar

1 tablespoon minced fresh ginger

1 clove garlic, peeled and minced

1 tablespoon vegetable oil

4 (6-ounce) tuna steaks

SERVES 4	
Per Serving:	
Calories	267
Fat	5g
Sodium	519mg
Carbohydrates	1g
Fiber	0g
Sugar	0g
Protein	55g

1. In a small bowl, whisk together soy sauce, vinegar, ginger, garlic, and oil.
2. Place tuna in a shallow baking dish and pour three-quarters of the marinade over it. Set aside to marinate for 30 minutes, flipping tuna to marinate the other side after 15 minutes.
3. Preheat a gas or charcoal grill.
4. Place tuna steaks on the grill and cook for 4–5 minutes for rare or 6–8 minutes for medium-rare. Carefully flip, brush with remaining marinade, and grill another 4 minutes for rare or 5–6 minutes for medium-rare.
5. Remove from grill and serve.

Garlic and Herb Seared Salmon

Pan-seared salmon is crispy on the outside and tender and flaky on the inside. Get ready to fall in love with the fresh-tasting garlic sauce—you'll want to use it on every type of seafood.

4 teaspoons minced garlic

1 teaspoon dried herbes de Provence

1 teaspoon red wine vinegar

1 teaspoon plus 2 tablespoons olive oil, divided

2 tablespoons Dijon mustard

4 (6-ounce) wild-caught salmon fillets

4 lemon wedges

1 Combine garlic, herbs, vinegar, 1 teaspoon oil, and mustard in a small bowl. Set aside.

2 Heat remaining 2 tablespoons oil in a large nonstick skillet over medium-high heat. Add salmon and cook 5 minutes.

3 Flip fillets and cook 3 minutes, spooning half the garlic sauce on the cooked side of each fillet.

4 Flip fillets again, cooking 1 more minute and spreading the remaining sauce on the other side of fillets. Flip fillets one last time and cook 1 minute.

5 Remove and serve each fillet with a lemon wedge.

SERVES 4

Per Serving:	
Calories	227
Fat	9g
Sodium	405mg
Carbohydrates	0g
Fiber	0g
Sugar	0g
Protein	36g

WILD-CAUGHT VERSUS FARM-RAISED FISH

Whenever possible, buy wild-caught fish. It's a bit more expensive, but the quality is significantly better than farm-raised fish. Fish raised on a farm are often kept in small tanks, consume low-quality food, and are sometimes fed food dye to make the meat look more appetizing. Wild-caught fish eat a natural diet, so they are much higher in healthy fats and nutrients.

Healthy Fish and Chips

BAKE YOUR WAY TO BETTER HEALTH

French fries are traditionally, well, fried. The frying process can add trans fats and omega-6 fatty acids, which can cause inflammation and should be avoided. When you slice fresh potatoes and crisp them in the oven instead, you have a healthy side dish that's still delicious. Try mixing up your seasonings for variety—spicy seasonings, garlic salt, and ranch seasonings all work very well with homemade French fries.

Baking fish and chips is not only healthier and neater than frying; it also allows you to cook both fish and potatoes at the same time. So you can get a family-favorite dinner on the table faster.

1 medium sweet potato, peeled and cut crosswise into ⅛" slices

1 medium russet potato, cut crosswise into ⅛" slices

2 tablespoons olive oil, divided

¼ teaspoon dried rosemary

1 teaspoon salt, divided

½ teaspoon ground black pepper, divided

1 large egg white, beaten

2 tablespoons unsweetened almond milk

¼ cup almond flour

¼ cup dried bread crumbs

4 (4-ounce) cod fillets

1 Preheat oven to 450°F. Line a large baking sheet with parchment paper. Spray a 9" × 9" baking pan lightly with nonstick cooking spray.

2 In a large bowl, toss sweet potato, potato, 1 tablespoon oil, rosemary, ½ teaspoon salt, and ¼ teaspoon pepper.

3 Arrange slices in a single layer on the prepared baking sheet. Bake for 18–20 minutes until browned and crisp, tossing at the halfway mark.

4 Meanwhile, combine egg white and almond milk in a shallow bowl. In another shallow bowl, combine almond flour, bread crumbs, remaining ½ teaspoon salt, and remaining ¼ teaspoon pepper.

5 Dip each piece of fish into egg mixture, then in the bread crumb mixture. Place fillets in the prepared baking dish and drizzle with the remaining 1 tablespoon oil.

6 Bake fish for 8–10 minutes until fish flakes easily when tested with a fork.

7 Serve fish with sweet potatoes and potatoes.

Lemon Dill Salmon

This speedy recipe requires just 10 minutes of prep and virtually no cleanup. Try this simple method with any firm-fleshed fish.

1 (1½-pound) salmon fillet

1 tablespoon salted butter or ghee, melted

2 teaspoons minced garlic

2 tablespoons chopped fresh dill

2 tablespoons lemon juice

1 tablespoon lemon zest

½ teaspoon salt

SERVES 4	
Per Serving:	
Calories	200
Fat	7g
Sodium	471mg
Carbohydrates	0g
Fiber	0g
Sugar	0g
Protein	35g

1 Preheat oven to 375°F.

2 Line a baking sheet with foil and center salmon on the foil.

3 In a small bowl, mix together butter, garlic, dill, lemon juice, lemon zest, and salt.

4 Pour mixture over salmon. Fold up the ends of the foil so that salmon is sealed in a pouch. Bake for 15–20 minutes until fish flakes with a fork. Serve immediately.

Parmesan-Crusted Salmon

One bite of this luscious salmon will convince you to make this recipe part of your regular dinner repertoire. Try the Parmesan crust on other types of fish, like cod, haddock, or catfish.

1 (4-ounce) salmon fillet

1 teaspoon Dijon mustard

1½ teaspoons mayonnaise

⅛ teaspoon salt

⅛ teaspoon ground black pepper

1½ tablespoons grated Parmesan cheese

SERVES 1	
Per Serving:	
Calories	238
Fat	13g
Sodium	721mg
Carbohydrates	1g
Fiber	0g
Sugar	0g
Protein	30g

1 Preheat broiler. Line a small baking sheet with parchment paper.

2 Place fillet on prepared baking sheet.

3 In a small bowl, stir together mustard and mayonnaise. Brush mustard mixture on one side of fillet. Season with salt and pepper, then top with cheese.

4 Broil for 8–10 minutes until cheese is lightly browned and fillet flakes easily with a fork. Serve hot.

Cod with Bacon, Red Onion, and Kale

Per Serving:

Calories	358
Fat	18g
Sodium	1,156mg
Carbohydrates	20g
Fiber	2g
Sugar	5g
Protein	30g

This good-for-you recipe contains lean protein, lots of fibrous vegetables, and bacon, which is a truly winning combination. It's a nutritious and delicious one pan meal that comes together in no time.

4 slices thick-cut bacon, chopped

2 (6-ounce) cod fillets

1 medium red onion, peeled and sliced

4 cups roughly chopped kale leaves

¼ teaspoon salt

1　In a large skillet, cook bacon for 5–7 minutes over medium-high heat until slightly crisp. Remove bacon and set aside, leaving the remaining fat in the pan.

2　Add fillets to the pan and sear for 4 minutes, then remove and set aside. (Fillets won't be fully cooked at this point.)

3　Add onion to the pan and sauté for 2 minutes. Add kale and salt. Sauté for another 1–2 minutes until onion is soft and kale begins to wilt.

4　Return fillets to the skillet and cover with a lid. Cook for 7–8 minutes until cod flakes easily with a fork.

5　Divide cod, onion, and kale between two plates. Top with bacon and serve immediately.

Baked Coconut-Crusted Cod

This baked cod combines slightly sweet toasted coconut with tangy lime and a hit of cayenne pepper for a wonderful balanced flavor.

2 tablespoons honey

1 tablespoon lime juice

½ cup unsweetened shredded coconut

½ cup panko bread crumbs

½ teaspoon salt

½ teaspoon cayenne pepper

2 (6-ounce) cod fillets

SERVES 2	
Per Serving:	
Calories	439
Fat	24g
Sodium	707mg
Carbohydrates	37g
Fiber	6g
Sugar	22g
Protein	24g

1 Preheat oven to 425°F. Line a baking sheet with parchment paper.
2 In a shallow bowl, combine honey and lime juice. In another shallow bowl, combine coconut, bread crumbs, salt, and pepper.
3 Dip fillets in honey mixture and then dredge in coconut and bread crumb mixture.
4 Place fillets on the prepared baking sheet and bake for 18–20 minutes until coconut turns a golden brown and fish flakes easily with a fork. Serve immediately.

Pecan-Crusted Salmon

Tangy mustard, sweet maple syrup, and crunchy pecans combine to make an appetizing crust for baked salmon.

2 tablespoons Dijon mustard

2 tablespoons maple syrup

4 (6-ounce) salmon fillets

½ cup finely chopped pecans

SERVES 4	
Per Serving:	
Calories	446
Fat	25g
Sodium	276mg
Carbohydrates	9g
Fiber	2g
Sugar	7g
Protein	45g

1 Preheat oven to 425°F. Spray a 9" × 13" baking dish with nonstick cooking spray.
2 In a small bowl, mix together mustard and maple syrup.
3 Place fillets in a single layer in the prepared baking dish. Spread mustard mixture over fillets. Sprinkle with pecans, pressing them into the mustard mixture.
4 Bake for 12–15 minutes until salmon is cooked through and flakes easily with a fork. Serve immediately.

Maple Mustard Tuna Steaks

SERVES 4

Per Serving:

Calories	218
Fat	4g
Sodium	347mg
Carbohydrates	10g
Fiber	0g
Sugar	9g
Protein	35g

Maple syrup adds a wonderful sweetness and a beautiful caramelized crust to meaty tuna steaks, and zesty Dijon mustard balances the flavors.

3 tablespoons maple syrup

1½ tablespoons Dijon mustard

1½ tablespoons lemon juice

2 teaspoons extra-virgin olive oil

4 (5-ounce, 1"-thick) tuna steaks

½ teaspoon salt

¼ teaspoon ground black pepper

1 In a shallow bowl, combine maple syrup, mustard, lemon juice, and oil. Reserve 2 tablespoons of maple and mustard mixture and set aside.

2 Add tuna to remaining maple and mustard mixture and turn to coat. Set aside to marinate for 10 minutes, turning once after 5 minutes.

3 Coat a large stainless steel or cast iron skillet with nonstick cooking spray and heat over medium-high heat.

4 Remove tuna from marinade and season with salt and pepper.

5 Place tuna in pan and cook for 1–2 minutes on each side until lightly seared on the outside.

6 Remove tuna from pan. Drizzle with reserved maple and mustard mixture and serve.

Homemade Fish Sticks

Crunchy and delicious, these Homemade Fish Sticks will get rave reviews all around. Because they're made with wholesome ingredients, you don't have to worry about artificial ingredients and additives found in the packaged ones.

1½ cups dried bread crumbs

½ cup grated Parmesan cheese

½ tablespoon onion salt

¼ teaspoon salt

⅓ cup almond flour

1 large egg

1 tablespoon water

2 (6-ounce) flounder fillets

2 tablespoons olive oil

1 In a shallow bowl, combine bread crumbs, cheese, onion salt, and salt. Place almond flour in a second shallow bowl. In a third shallow bowl, whisk egg with water.

2 Remove skin and cut fillets into eight strips of equal size.

3 Dust fish with almond flour, then dip in egg mixture. Finally, dredge fish in the bread crumb mixture.

4 Heat oil in a large skillet. In two batches, fry fish for 2 minutes per side until golden brown. Serve hot.

SERVES 4	
Per Serving:	
Calories	331
Fat	16g
Sodium	1,180mg
Carbohydrates	25g
Fiber	1g
Sugar	0g
Protein	22g

GLASS IS BETTER THAN PLASTIC

When you use glass storage containers, you don't have to worry about harmful plastics getting into your food when you reheat it. Glass containers resist stains and odors, can be washed in the dishwasher, and are safe for use in the oven or freezer. Plus, you can see exactly what's inside, and they look nice and neat in your refrigerator after a Sunday meal prep.

Spicy Grilled Shrimp Skewers

SERVES 4

Per Serving:

Calories	153
Fat	5g
Sodium	283mg
Carbohydrates	4g
Fiber	0g
Sugar	3g
Protein	23g

Shrimp is a mild-flavored food, but the spicy Asian sauce in this recipe really brings the heat. When served warm and fresh off the grill, these skewers are the perfect pairing for a summer salad.

2 tablespoons minced scallions

1 teaspoon sriracha hot sauce

1½ tablespoons Thai sweet chili sauce

2½ tablespoons light mayonnaise

40 large raw shrimp, peeled and deveined

2 teaspoons ground black pepper

1 Preheat grill to medium.

2 In a small bowl, mix scallions, hot sauce, chili sauce, and mayonnaise, stirring well.

3 Thread 5 shrimp on each of 8 metal skewers and sprinkle with pepper.

4 Grill shrimp skewers 6–8 minutes per side. Remove from grill, coat with sauce, and serve warm.

Margarita Shrimp

SERVES 4

Per Serving:

Calories	114
Fat	2g
Sodium	156mg
Carbohydrates	0g
Fiber	0g
Sugar	0g
Protein	24g

Serve these flavorful shrimp with grilled vegetables, on a green salad, or stuffed in a tortilla with avocado, shredded cabbage, and Mexican crema.

½ tablespoon olive oil

1 pound large shrimp, peeled and deveined

¼ teaspoon ground cumin

4 cloves garlic, peeled and minced

¼ teaspoon crushed red pepper flakes

¼ teaspoon salt

¼ teaspoon ground black pepper

2 ounces tequila

2 tablespoons lime juice

1 Heat oil in a large skillet or wok over medium-high heat.

2 Season shrimp with cumin, garlic, red pepper flakes, salt, and black pepper, then add to hot oil and cook about 2 minutes per side.

3 Add tequila and cook another 30–40 seconds. Remove and drizzle with lime juice before serving.

Tropical Shrimp Skewers

The combination of grilled shrimp, pineapple, and coconut will make you feel like you're on vacation—even on a Tuesday in February! Either fresh or canned pineapple will work in the recipe, so use whatever is most convenient for you.

3 teaspoons minced garlic

2 tablespoons extra-virgin olive oil

2 tablespoons red wine vinegar

2 tablespoons chopped fresh parsley

½ teaspoon salt

2 pounds large shrimp, peeled and deveined

4 cups pineapple chunks

3 tablespoons shredded coconut

1 Preheat a gas or charcoal grill.

2 In a large bowl, combine garlic, oil, vinegar, parsley, and salt. Add shrimp and toss to coat.

3 Thread shrimp and pineapple alternately onto metal or wooden skewers. Transfer skewers to the grill and cook for 3–5 minutes per side until shrimp are pink.

4 Remove skewers from grill and sprinkle with coconut flakes before serving.

SERVES 4	
Per Serving:	
Calories	297
Fat	10g
Sodium	282mg
Carbohydrates	25g
Fiber	3g
Sugar	18g
Protein	28g

SHRIMP FOR THYROID HEALTH

Shrimp is one of the best food sources of iodine, an important mineral that plays a role in proper thyroid function and brain health. Many people don't get enough iodine in their diet, but shrimp is an easy way to remedy that deficiency.

Zoodle Shrimp Scampi

CHOOSE SHRIMP MORE OFTEN

Shrimp is low in calories, but it provides a high amount of protein, healthy fats, and nutrients. A 3-ounce serving has 84 calories, 18 grams of protein, and no carbs. This serving size provides more than twenty different vitamins and minerals, including 50 percent of your daily needs for selenium, a mineral that may help reduce inflammation and promote heart health.

This lightened-up version of shrimp scampi comes together in just 15 minutes and uses nutritious and fiber-rich zucchini noodles instead of pasta.

1 tablespoon olive oil

1 pound large shrimp, peeled and deveined

4 teaspoons minced garlic

1 teaspoon salt

½ teaspoon ground black pepper

¼ cup low-sodium chicken broth

¼ cup lemon juice

2 large zucchini, trimmed and spiralized

3 tablespoons grated Parmesan cheese

¼ cup chopped fresh Italian parsley

1 Heat oil in a large skillet over medium-low heat.
2 Add shrimp, garlic, salt, and pepper. Sauté for 4–6 minutes until shrimp start to turn pink.
3 Add broth, lemon juice, and zucchini noodles to the skillet. Increase heat to medium-high and bring to a boil. Cook for 1 minute or until shrimp are completely cooked and zucchini noodles are softened.
4 Sprinkle with cheese and parsley and serve immediately.

Foolproof Pan-Seared Scallops

SERVES 2	
Per Serving:	
Calories	275
Fat	17g
Sodium	879mg
Carbohydrates	6g
Fiber	0g
Sugar	0g
Protein	23g

If not cooked correctly, scallops can be chewy and bland. But with this easy recipe, you're guaranteed to get perfectly buttery and seared scallops every time.

½ pound sea scallops
¼ teaspoon salt
⅛ teaspoon ground black pepper
3 tablespoons salted butter, divided
1½ tablespoons lemon juice
¼ cup dry white wine

1 Rinse scallops with water and then lay them on a paper towel. Season with salt and pepper.
2 In a large stainless steel or cast iron skillet, melt 2 tablespoons butter over medium-high heat.
3 Once the butter is melted and sizzling, place scallops into skillet.
4 Allow scallops to cook for about 5 minutes. Wait to flip them until they freely pull away from the pan.
5 Cook for another 3 minutes on the other side. Transfer scallops to a plate, drizzle with lemon juice, and keep warm.
6 Add wine to the pan with remaining 1 tablespoon butter. Cook, stirring occasionally, until reduced by half, about 3 minutes. Drizzle sauce over scallops and serve immediately.

Tuna Salad Plate

When you're short on time, this high-protein, low-carb tasting plate comes together in no time, especially if you have some hard-cooked eggs in your refrigerator already.

1 (5-ounce) can solid white tuna, drained

1 teaspoon mayonnaise

2 teaspoons sweet relish

1 large hard-cooked egg, peeled and sliced

½ medium avocado, peeled, pitted, and sliced

½ medium cucumber, sliced

¼ teaspoon salt

⅛ teaspoon ground black pepper

SERVES 1	
Per Serving:	
Calories	307
Fat	16g
Sodium	1,122mg
Carbohydrates	5g
Fiber	3g
Sugar	0g
Protein	40g

1 In a small bowl, combine tuna, mayonnaise, and sweet relish. Place tuna mixture on a plate.

2 Arrange egg, avocado, and cucumber slices around tuna mixture. Season with salt and pepper and serve.

Smoked Salmon Salad

This low-carb salad is rich and savory with the satisfying flavors of smoked salmon, eggs, and avocado, while fresh greens and lemon lighten everything up.

4 large eggs

6 cups mixed salad greens

8 ounces smoked salmon, sliced

1 medium avocado, peeled, pitted, and sliced

2 tablespoons extra-virgin olive oil

3 tablespoons lemon juice

¼ teaspoon salt

½ teaspoon ground black pepper

SERVES 4	
Per Serving:	
Calories	345
Fat	25g
Sodium	655mg
Carbohydrates	9g
Fiber	4g
Sugar	3g
Protein	23g

1 Place eggs in a small saucepan and cover with water. Bring to a boil over high heat. Boil for 7 minutes, then remove from heat. Transfer eggs to a bowl of ice water to cool for 5 minutes.

2 Peel eggs and slice into halves.

3 In a large bowl, combine greens, eggs, salmon, and avocado. Drizzle oil and lemon on top and season with salt and pepper. Toss gently before serving. Serve immediately.

Tuna "Ceviche"

Transform an ordinary can of tuna into a flavorful and protein-packed meal by adding just a handful of fresh ingredients.

2 (5-ounce) cans water-packed white tuna, drained

½ teaspoon extra-virgin olive oil

1 small jalapeño pepper, seeded and minced

1 small red onion, peeled and finely chopped

1 medium tomato, diced

1½ tablespoons chopped fresh cilantro

1 medium avocado, peeled, pitted, and diced

¼ teaspoon salt

¼ teaspoon ground black pepper

3 tablespoons lime juice

1 Place tuna in a medium bowl. Add oil, jalapeño, onion, tomato, cilantro, avocado, salt, and pepper. Carefully mix together.

2 Drizzle lime juice over mixture and serve immediately.

Asian Salmon Salad

This Asian-inspired salad is infused with the tasty bold flavors of sesame and ginger, and it's an excellent source of healthy fats.

2 tablespoons low-sodium soy sauce

1 (1") piece ginger, peeled and chopped

1 clove garlic, peeled and minced

2 tablespoons chopped scallions

¼ cup vegetable oil

3 tablespoons white vinegar

1 tablespoon sesame oil

1 tablespoon olive oil

4 (6-ounce) salmon fillets

2 teaspoons salt

2 teaspoons ground black pepper

4 cups mixed salad greens

1 Combine soy sauce, ginger, garlic, scallions, vegetable oil, vinegar, and sesame oil in a food processor and pulse until smooth.

2 Heat olive oil in a large skillet over medium heat. Season salmon with salt and pepper and cook 5 minutes per side.

3 Divide greens among four bowls. Top with salmon and drizzle with dressing before serving.

Pineapple Shrimp Fried Rice

It's so easy to make your own nutritious and macro-friendly version of takeout fried rice. You'll love this combination of savory, sweet, and spicy flavors.

1 teaspoon olive oil

1½ pounds medium shrimp, peeled and deveined

1½ cups riced cauliflower

4 scallions, chopped

1 small jalapeño pepper, seeded and chopped

3 teaspoons minced garlic

2 cups cold cooked brown rice

1½ cups diced pineapple

2 tablespoons low-sodium soy sauce or coconut aminos

1 teaspoon fish sauce

1 Heat oil in a large skillet over medium heat.
2 Add shrimp and cook for 3–5 minutes until just opaque; set aside.
3 Add riced cauliflower, scallions, jalapeño, and garlic to the skillet. Sauté 2 minutes, then add brown rice and pineapple.
4 Stir in soy sauce and fish sauce. Return shrimp to the skillet and cook, stirring constantly, for 2 minutes.
5 Serve hot or at room temperature.

SERVES 6

Per Serving:

Calories	210
Fat	3g
Sodium	526mg
Carbohydrates	19g
Fiber	3g
Sugar	1g
Protein	26g

WHICH RICE IS THE HEALTHIEST?

It actually doesn't matter what sort of rice you use. White rice, brown rice, jasmine rice, and wild rice all have very similar nutritional content. You may have heard that brown rice is healthier, but the only real difference is its speed of absorption. Brown rice absorbs slower, which is why some have issues digesting it, so it's really a personal preference.

Ahi Tuna Poke Bowls

It may seem intimidating, but you can make your own poke bowl at home. It's super easy to make, and the only thing you need to cook is the rice.

2 cups cooked and cooled brown rice

¼ cup rice wine vinegar

¼ cup low-sodium soy sauce or coconut aminos

2 cups mixed salad greens

1 pound sushi-grade ahi tuna, thinly sliced

1 medium cucumber, diced

2 medium avocados, peeled, pitted, and sliced

⅓ cup thinly sliced scallions

1 tablespoon black or white sesame seeds

1 In a large bowl, combine rice, vinegar, and soy sauce.

2 Place ½ cup salad greens and ½ cup rice mixture in each of four bowls.

3 Top with tuna, cucumber, avocados, scallions, and sesame seeds. Serve immediately.

SERVES 4	
Per Serving:	
Calories	305
Fat	4g
Sodium	927mg
Carbohydrates	34g
Fiber	3g
Sugar	2g
Protein	31g

POKE—WHAT?

Poke is pronounced *poh-KAY* and rhymes with *okay*. The word *poke* simply means "chunk" in Hawaiian. Poke is typically any seafood that is cut into small chunks and marinated.

Open-Faced Salmon Melts

SERVES 2	
Per Serving:	
Calories	402
Fat	13g
Sodium	822mg
Carbohydrates	37g
Fiber	3g
Sugar	7g
Protein	36g

Canned salmon is a convenient source of protein that you can keep on hand for quick and easy meals. These open-faced sandwiches are not only tasty; they also let you get all of your macros in one meal.

1 (5-ounce) can wild pink salmon, drained and flaked

2 stalks celery, thinly sliced

½ cup full-fat plain Greek yogurt

1 tablespoon Dijon mustard

1 teaspoon garlic powder

2 (1-ounce) slices whole-grain bread

1½ ounces Swiss cheese, shredded

1 Preheat broiler.

2 In a small bowl, combine salmon, celery, yogurt, mustard, and garlic powder. Mix well.

3 Scoop salmon mixture onto bread and spread evenly. Top with cheese.

4 Place sandwiches on a baking sheet and broil for about 3 minutes until cheese is slightly browned. Serve immediately.

Shrimp Tacos

SERVES 4	
Per Serving:	
Calories	178
Fat	9g
Sodium	511mg
Carbohydrates	9g
Fiber	3g
Sugar	0g
Protein	16g

Shrimp Tacos make a healthy, protein-packed, and flavorful meal for Taco Tuesday or any time when you're craving Mexican food.

1 large avocado, peeled and pitted

1 tablespoon lime juice

¼ teaspoon salt

1 pound large shrimp, peeled and deveined

1 tablespoon avocado oil

1½ tablespoons taco seasoning

4 (7") corn tortillas

1 cup shredded red cabbage

1 Preheat broiler.

2 In a small bowl, mash avocado with lime juice and salt. Set aside.

3 Place shrimp in a large bowl and pat dry with paper towels. Add oil and taco seasoning and toss until evenly coated.

4 Transfer shrimp to a large baking sheet and arrange in a single layer. Broil for 2–3 minutes until shrimp are bright pink.

5 Place tortillas on a flat surface. Spread with avocado mixture and top with shrimp and cabbage. Serve immediately.

Sweet Potato and Salmon Tots

Sweet Potato and Salmon Tots will win over even the pickiest eaters. Serve them as a snack with ketchup or honey mustard or as a side dish or use them to top a salad for lunch.

2 (5-ounce) cans wild pink salmon, drained and flaked

⅓ cup mashed sweet potato

1 large egg

2 tablespoons almond flour

2 tablespoons mayonnaise

1½ tablespoons lemon juice

½ teaspoon salt

¼ teaspoon ground black pepper

SERVES 4	
Per Serving:	
Calories	209
Fat	13g
Sodium	557mg
Carbohydrates	6g
Fiber	1g
Sugar	2g
Protein	17g

1 Preheat oven to 350°F. Line a baking sheet with parchment paper.
2 Combine all ingredients in a medium bowl. Stir until fully combined.
3 Scoop tablespoonfuls of the mixture and roll them into 1" cylinders. Place on the prepared baking sheet.
4 Bake for 30 minutes, flipping halfway through. Serve hot.

Curried Tuna Cakes

These quick and easy tuna cakes are perfect for quick lunches or dinners, and they take less than 10 minutes to make. They're a great high-protein, low-carb option.

1 (5-ounce) can white tuna, drained and flaked

1 large egg

1½ teaspoons almond flour

½ teaspoon curry powder

½ teaspoon garlic powder

2 scallions, finely chopped

⅛ teaspoon salt

⅛ teaspoon ground black pepper

1½ teaspoons avocado oil

SERVES 2	
Per Serving:	
Calories	123
Fat	6g
Sodium	373mg
Carbohydrates	0g
Fiber	0g
Sugar	0g
Protein	18g

1 In a medium bowl, combine tuna, egg, almond flour, curry powder, garlic powder, scallions, salt, and pepper. Mix well.
2 Divide tuna mixture in half and form each half into a patty.
3 Heat oil in a medium skillet over medium-low heat.
4 Add tuna cakes to the skillet and slowly cook on each side until lightly browned, about 8 minutes per side.
5 Remove from skillet and serve immediately.

Asian Shrimp Noodles

Per Serving:

Calories	441
Fat	8g
Sodium	738mg
Carbohydrates	70g
Fiber	4g
Sugar	4g
Protein	21g

YOU DON'T HAVE TO BE PERFECT TO SEE RESULTS

Here's a quick rule of thumb for macro goals: Try to be within 5–10 grams for each macronutrient (protein, carbs, and fat). Don't worry about being "perfect" and give yourself some wiggle room with your numbers. At the end of the day, even if you're 10 grams over or under your goal, you're still doing okay. Just be sure to keep an eye on your overall calories and keep them as consistent as possible.

This noodle recipe provides protein, fiber, and a delicious Asian-inspired flavor to top it all off. It's a quick-fix dinner that needs only a handful of ingredients (mostly pantry staples) and is ready in under 20 minutes.

1 (16-ounce) package dry rice noodles

3 tablespoons olive oil

6 scallions, chopped

1 tablespoon finely chopped fresh ginger

1 pound shrimp, peeled and deveined

1 teaspoon salt

1 teaspoon ground black pepper

¾ cup water

⅓ cup low-sodium soy sauce or coconut aminos

2 (12-ounce) bags shredded cabbage mix for coleslaw

1 Cook noodles according to package directions and drain, rinsing under cold water. Transfer to a large bowl and set aside.

2 Heat oil in a large skillet over medium heat. Sauté scallions and ginger for 2 minutes.

3 Add shrimp to skillet in a single layer and sprinkle with salt and pepper. Cook 3–4 minutes until shrimp just begin to turn opaque, stirring frequently. Remove shrimp and set aside.

4 Add water and soy sauce to the skillet, scraping up browned bits. Stir in cabbage mix, cover, and cook 6 minutes over medium heat, stirring often. Uncover and return shrimp to the skillet. Cook, stirring, until heated through, about 2 minutes.

5 Transfer cabbage and shrimp mixture to the bowl with noodles. Mix well. Serve immediately.

CHAPTER 8

Vegetarian and Vegan

Quinoa and Mushroom Protein Burgers

Not only are mushrooms full of important vitamins and minerals, but they also generally have more protein than other vegetables. Enjoy these burgers as is or serve inside a lettuce wrap or on a bun with your favorite toppings.

SERVES 4

Per Serving:

Calories	201
Fat	8g
Sodium	323mg
Carbohydrates	25g
Fiber	2g
Sugar	2g
Protein	7g

4 medium portobello mushroom caps, chopped

1 clove garlic, peeled and minced

2 tablespoons canola oil, divided

1 teaspoon salt

¼ teaspoon ground black pepper

¼ cup chopped red onion

3 scallions, chopped

2 teaspoons rice wine vinegar

1 cup cooked quinoa

¼ cup cornstarch

1 Preheat oven to 375°F.

2 In a 9" × 9" baking dish, combine mushrooms, garlic, 1 tablespoon oil, salt, and pepper, mixing well.

3 Bake 20 minutes. Remove from oven and allow to cool for 15 minutes. Transfer to a blender or food processor.

4 Add onion, scallions, and vinegar to the blender and pulse until smooth.

5 Transfer mixture to a large bowl and stir in quinoa and cornstarch. Cover bowl and refrigerate at least 2 hours.

6 Heat remaining 1 tablespoon oil in a large nonstick skillet over medium heat. Form mixture into four patties and cook in the skillet for 5–7 minutes per side. Serve immediately.

Lemon Dill Chickpea Salad

This simple, lemony chickpea salad can be enjoyed on a sandwich, in a wrap, or on top of a salad.

2 (15-ounce) cans chickpeas, drained and rinsed

2 stalks celery, chopped

½ medium red onion, peeled and chopped

2 tablespoons mayonnaise

2 tablespoons lemon juice

2 teaspoons minced fresh dill

¼ teaspoon salt

SERVES 4	
Per Serving:	
Calories	296
Fat	10g
Sodium	238mg
Carbohydrates	36g
Fiber	11g
Sugar	1g
Protein	15g

1 In a medium bowl, mash chickpeas with a fork.
2 Add remaining ingredients, mix well, and refrigerate at least 1 hour before serving.

Mediterranean Chickpea Pita Sandwiches

Canned chickpeas can stand in for a variety of different ingredients—everything from ground meat to pasta. They're also packed with protein, fiber, and nutrients, which will keep you satisfied long after your meal.

1 (15-ounce) can chickpeas, drained and rinsed

1 cup quartered grape tomatoes

½ medium cucumber, peeled and chopped

¼ teaspoon salt

2 tablespoons Italian salad dressing

¼ cup low-fat plain Greek yogurt

2 (8") whole-grain pitas, halved

SERVES 4	
Per Serving:	
Calories	234
Fat	5g
Sodium	481mg
Carbohydrates	37g
Fiber	8g
Sugar	3g
Protein	11g

1 In a medium bowl, combine chickpeas, tomatoes, cucumber, and salt. In a small bowl, stir together salad dressing and yogurt.
2 Open each pita half to create a pocket. Spread a thin layer of yogurt mixture inside each pita pocket. Stuff pita pockets with chickpea mixture. Serve immediately.

Broiled Tomato Sandwiches

SERVES 2

Per Serving:

Calories	466
Fat	31g
Sodium	487mg
Carbohydrates	40g
Fiber	5g
Sugar	9g
Protein	8g

These broiled sandwiches combine fresh tomato slices and a seasoned herb spread for a delicious, nontraditional, healthy lunch. It's a perfect match for soup, and can be made in a matter of minutes.

2 tablespoons olive oil

2 tablespoons balsamic vinegar

1 large tomato, sliced

3 tablespoons mayonnaise

½ teaspoon dried parsley

¼ teaspoon dried oregano

¼ teaspoon ground black pepper

3 tablespoons grated Parmesan cheese

4 slices whole-grain bread

1 Preheat broiler.
2 In a small bowl, whisk oil and vinegar together. Add tomato, cover, and set aside to marinate for 30–60 minutes.
3 In a separate small bowl, mix mayonnaise, parsley, oregano, pepper, and cheese.
4 Place bread slices on a baking sheet and spread with mayonnaise mixture. Top 2 of the slices with marinated tomatoes. Place remaining 2 bread slices on top of tomatoes, mayonnaise side down.
5 Broil 5 minutes or until bread is toasted and golden brown. Serve immediately.

Baked Mozzarella Sticks

This healthy version of a popular appetizer is easy to prepare at home and makes a great snack or side dish. They're made with lower-fat cheese, coated with crispy seasoned bread crumbs, and baked (not fried) until crispy and golden brown.

12 sticks reduced-fat mozzarella string cheese, cut in half horizontally

½ cup egg whites

2 tablespoons all-purpose flour

½ cup Italian bread crumbs

½ cup panko bread crumbs

2 teaspoons grated Parmesan cheese

1 tablespoon dried parsley

SERVES 12	
Per Serving:	
Calories	138
Fat	7g
Sodium	432mg
Carbohydrates	7g
Fiber	0g
Sugar	1g
Protein	12g

1 Freeze mozzarella pieces for at least 1 hour. Line a large baking sheet with parchment paper.

2 Place egg whites in a shallow bowl and flour in another shallow bowl.

3 In a third shallow bowl, mix Italian and panko bread crumbs, Parmesan, and parsley.

4 Dip frozen mozzarella pieces in flour, roll in egg whites, then cover well with bread crumb mix.

5 Place the sticks on the prepared baking sheet and freeze for 1 hour.

6 Preheat oven to 400°F.

7 Bake for 10 minutes, turning halfway through. Serve hot.

Roasted Chickpea Tacos

SLIGHTLY INCREASE YOUR PORTIONS

Hitting your protein goal can be as simple as adding an extra ounce of chicken to your dinner plate, another ¼ cup of beans to a lunchtime salad, or an additional egg at breakfast. Small tweaks at each meal can add up quickly!

A filling of roasted chickpeas makes these tacos a tasty meat-free option for Taco Tuesday (or any day of the week). Full of fiber and plant protein, these tacos are both healthy and delicious.

1 (15-ounce) can chickpeas, drained, rinsed, and dried

1 medium red bell pepper, seeded and sliced

1 tablespoon extra-virgin olive oil

1½ tablespoons taco seasoning

½ teaspoon salt, divided

1 medium avocado, peeled and pitted

1 tablespoon lime juice

4 (7") corn tortillas

1 Preheat oven to 425°F and line a baking sheet with parchment paper.

2 Place chickpeas and bell pepper on the prepared baking sheet. Drizzle with oil and toss to coat. Sprinkle with taco seasoning and ¼ teaspoon salt. Bake for 15–20 minutes.

3 Remove from the oven, toss chickpeas and pepper slices, and bake for an additional 10–15 minutes.

4 Meanwhile, in a small bowl, mash avocado with a fork until smooth. Stir in lime juice and remaining ¼ teaspoon salt.

5 Lay tortillas on a flat work surface. Spread avocado mixture on tortillas and top with chickpea mixture. Serve immediately.

Lentil Taco Lettuce Wraps

SERVES 4	
Per Serving:	
Calories	225
Fat	6g
Sodium	424mg
Carbohydrates	31g
Fiber	13g
Sugar	6g
Protein	12g

The seasoning and chewy texture of the lentil mixture create a "meaty" taco base that even regular meat eaters will enjoy. If your daily carb goal allows, use flour or corn tortillas instead of lettuce wraps. If you don't have a batch of Cowboy Caviar made, jarred salsa works as an excellent substitute.

1 (16.9-ounce) package ready-to-eat lentils

1 tablespoon taco seasoning

¾ cup Cowboy Caviar (see recipe in this chapter)

8 large leaves Bibb or romaine lettuce

1 medium avocado, peeled, pitted, and diced

1 In a medium bowl, combine lentils, taco seasoning, and Cowboy Caviar. Mix well.

2 Spoon ¼ cup lentil mixture onto each lettuce leaf and top with avocado. Serve immediately.

Barbecue Lentil and Walnut Kale Wraps

SERVES 4	
Per Serving:	
Calories	238
Fat	4g
Sodium	341mg
Carbohydrates	35g
Fiber	9g
Sugar	4g
Protein	16g

It doesn't take all that much effort to make these delicious and satisfying wraps. The lentil and walnut filling is high in protein and fiber-rich. Wraps make a perfect light summer dinner or grab-and-go lunch.

1 (16.9-ounce) package ready-to-eat lentils

1 tablespoon chopped walnuts

2 tablespoons barbecue sauce

8 large leaves lacinato or Tuscan kale

2 tablespoons ranch salad dressing

1 In a medium bowl, combine lentils, walnuts, and barbecue sauce. Mix well.

2 Spoon ¼ cup of lentil mixture onto each kale leaf and drizzle with salad dressing. Serve immediately.

Crispy Peanut Tofu with Cauliflower Rice

Savory and sweet, this peanutty tofu and cauliflower dish is loaded with flavor. Best of all, it can be made ahead of time for a quick reheatable weeknight dinner.

1½ teaspoons sesame oil

1½ tablespoons low-sodium soy sauce or coconut aminos

2 teaspoons maple syrup

1½ tablespoons creamy peanut butter

8 ounces extra-firm tofu, drained, cut into cubes, and patted dry

2 teaspoons olive oil

2 teaspoons cornstarch

½ teaspoon salt

2 cups riced cauliflower

½ small lime, sliced into wedges

SERVES 2	
Per Serving:	
Calories	353
Fat	25g
Sodium	520mg
Carbohydrates	16g
Fiber	5g
Sugar	8g
Protein	16g

1 Preheat oven to 400°F. Line a baking sheet with parchment paper.
2 In a large mixing bowl, whisk together sesame oil, soy sauce, maple syrup, and peanut butter. Set aside.
3 Place tofu in a large mixing bowl and toss with olive oil, cornstarch, and salt. Transfer to the prepared baking sheet.
4 Bake for 15–20 minutes until edges begin to brown and crisp.
5 Add tofu to the mixing bowl with the peanut butter mixture and toss to coat.
6 Heat a medium nonstick skillet over medium heat. Add riced cauliflower and cook for 5–6 minutes until warm.
7 Top with tofu and serve immediately with lime wedges.

Roasted Balsamic Tempeh and Vegetables

SERVES 4	
Per Serving:	
Calories	452
Fat	22g
Sodium	231mg
Carbohydrates	33g
Fiber	12g
Sugar	14g
Protein	31g

Sheet pan meals are the best when you're short on time (or motivation). Toss everything in a bowl, throw it on a sheet pan, and pop it in the oven. You'll have tasty tempeh and a rainbow of vegetables just bursting with nutrients and flavor in no time.

¼ **cup olive oil**

¼ **cup balsamic vinegar**

3 **teaspoons minced garlic**

1 **tablespoon dried Italian seasoning**

¼ **teaspoon salt**

⅛ **teaspoon ground black pepper**

1 **pound tempeh, cut into ½" chunks**

5 **medium carrots, peeled and chopped**

1 **medium red onion, peeled and chopped**

3 **cups broccoli florets**

3 **cups quartered button mushrooms**

2 **medium zucchini, trimmed and sliced**

1 Preheat oven to 350°F. Line a large baking sheet with parchment paper.

2 In a small bowl, combine oil, vinegar, garlic, Italian seasoning, salt, and pepper and mix well.

3 Place tempeh, carrots, onion, broccoli, mushrooms, and zucchini in a large bowl. Drizzle with the dressing and toss to coat.

4 Transfer to the prepared baking sheet and spread out in a single layer. Roast for 45 minutes, tossing halfway, until vegetables are tender.

5 Serve warm.

Pesto Tofu Scramble

Loaded with protein-packed tofu and a variety of tender vegetables and tied together with pesto sauce, this meal is warm, satisfying, and highly nutritious. It makes a great healthy breakfast or lunch.

9 ounces extra-firm tofu, drained

½ tablespoon avocado oil

½ medium yellow onion, peeled and diced

¾ cup halved grape tomatoes

1 teaspoon minced garlic

2 cups baby spinach

2 tablespoons pesto

½ teaspoon onion salt

2 tablespoons crumbled feta cheese

SERVES 2	
Per Serving:	
Calories	234
Fat	12g
Sodium	912mg
Carbohydrates	15g
Fiber	5g
Sugar	5g
Protein	17g

1 Place tofu in a small bowl and break it up into chunks using a fork. (The texture should be similar to that of scrambled eggs.)

2 Heat oil in a large nonstick skillet over medium heat. Sauté onion, tomatoes, and garlic for 4–5 minutes until onion is soft.

3 Add crumbled tofu, spinach, pesto, and onion salt to the pan. Sauté 1–2 minutes until spinach wilts and tofu is warm.

4 Divide mixture between two plates, top with cheese, and serve immediately.

Thai Veggie Burgers

Who doesn't love a good burger? These are crispy on the outside and bursting with the fragrant flavors of ginger and sesame. Serve them wrapped in lettuce leaves with fresh guacamole or on whole-grain buns with slices of pineapple if your daily macro goals allow it.

⅓ cup rolled oats

1 (15-ounce) can chickpeas, drained and rinsed

2 teaspoons low-sodium soy sauce or coconut aminos

2 teaspoons lime juice

2 teaspoons sesame oil

2 teaspoons minced garlic

2 teaspoons dried ginger

2 tablespoons creamy peanut butter

2 tablespoons minced fresh cilantro

½ tablespoon olive oil

1 In a food processor or blender, combine oats, chickpeas, soy sauce, lime juice, sesame oil, garlic, ginger, peanut butter, and cilantro. Pulse until mixture is fully combined yet slightly chunky. Refrigerate mixture for 30 minutes.

2 Heat olive oil in a large skillet over medium heat.

3 Divide bean mixture into four equal portions and form each one into a patty. Fry patties for 5–6 minutes on each side. Serve immediately.

MAKE EACH MEAL A BALANCED ONE

To make sure you're getting enough protein, consume some at *every* meal and snack. That way you're not eating a big bowl of egg whites at night because you haven't met your goal. Same goes for fat—don't be afraid of it! Your meals and snacks should include at least a little bit to make you feel full and satisfied.

Cauliflower "Mac" and Cheese

You don't have to give up the creamy, decadent tastes of macaroni and cheese when you're counting macros. Low in carbohydrates and loaded with nutrients, this dish has all of the cheesiness and comfort-food feel of the classic dish without all of the calories and fat.

2 tablespoons olive oil

1 teaspoon salt

½ teaspoon ground black pepper

1 teaspoon garlic powder

1 large head cauliflower, cored, outer leaves removed, and cut into florets

1 cup shredded sharp Cheddar cheese

½ cup shredded Gruyère cheese

½ cup unsweetened almond milk

1 tablespoon salted butter

⅛ teaspoon ground nutmeg

⅓ cup grated Parmesan cheese

1 Preheat oven to 450°F. Line a baking sheet with parchment paper.

2 In a medium mixing bowl, combine oil, salt, pepper, and garlic powder. Add cauliflower and toss to coat.

3 Pour cauliflower onto prepared baking sheet and arrange in a single layer. Roast for 15 minutes or until lightly browned and crispy. Transfer cauliflower to a 9" × 9" baking dish.

4 In a medium saucepan, combine Cheddar, Gruyère, milk, butter, and nutmeg over medium heat. Cook, stirring constantly, for 5 minutes.

5 Pour cheese mixture over cauliflower and toss to coat. Sprinkle with Parmesan.

6 Bake for 10–15 minutes until the top begins to brown. Remove from oven and cool for 10 minutes before serving.

SERVES 6

Per Serving:	
Calories	239
Fat	18g
Sodium	660mg
Carbohydrates	6g
Fiber	2g
Sugar	2g
Protein	13g

COLORFUL CAULIFLOWER

The most common type of cauliflower is white. But did you know that there are purple, green, and orange varieties? Each one has more or less the same nutrients, but the plant pigments are different. Try a different variety of cauliflower to brighten up your meals.

Buffalo Baked Potatoes

Baking potatoes can take up to an hour—who has that much time on a busy weeknight? However, if you bake them on the weekend or whenever you're using your oven for something else, this dish will be more than halfway done. Just make sure to let them cool completely, then keep them wrapped in foil in the refrigerator.

2 large russet potatoes

½ tablespoon olive oil

¼ teaspoon salt

¼ teaspoon ground black pepper

2 tablespoons Frank's RedHot Original Cayenne Pepper Sauce

½ cup shredded Cheddar cheese

1 small tomato, diced

1 scallion, sliced

½ medium avocado, peeled, pitted, and diced

2 teaspoons ranch-style salad dressing

1 Preheat oven to 400°F and line a baking sheet with parchment paper.

2 Pierce potatoes all over with a fork, then rub oil over the outside. Place on the prepared baking sheet.

3 Bake for 50–55 minutes until tender when pierced with a knife. Remove potatoes from the oven and set aside to cool for 10 minutes.

4 Make a lengthwise incision in each potato and gently squeeze edges to open up the incision. Using a fork, fluff up the insides of each potato. Season with salt and pepper. Drizzle pepper sauce over potatoes and top with cheese.

5 Return potatoes to the oven and cook for an additional 5–8 minutes until cheese melts.

6 Remove potatoes from oven. Top with tomato, scallion, avocado, and ranch dressing. Serve immediately.

SERVES 2	
Per Serving:	
Calories	284
Fat	14g
Sodium	927mg
Carbohydrates	30g
Fiber	4g
Sugar	3g
Protein	9g

WHAT'S THE BEST POTATO?

All potatoes are very good for you and are easy-to-prepare carb sources, but dark-colored potatoes tend to be richer in vitamins and minerals. Sweet potatoes are full of fiber, vitamin C, and beta-carotene, making them both delicious and very healthy. If you want to mix things up, another healthy potato is the Japanese potato, or purple potato, which has a rich, nutty flavor.

Cheesy Cauliflower-Stuffed Peppers

These stuffed peppers are loaded with nutrients. The taste is cheesy without being heavy or high in calories. Pair them with your favorite protein as a side dish or enjoy them alone as a main dish.

1 tablespoon salted butter

2½ cups riced cauliflower

½ teaspoon garlic powder

¼ teaspoon salt

4 cups baby spinach

¾ cup crushed tomatoes

3 wedges creamy Swiss cheese spread

½ cup shredded Cheddar cheese

⅓ cup grated Parmesan cheese

3 large red, yellow, orange, or green bell peppers, halved horizontally and seeded

½ cup water

1 Preheat oven to 350°F.

2 Melt butter in a large skillet over medium-high heat. Add cauliflower, garlic powder, and salt and sauté for about 5 minutes until cauliflower rice softens and becomes translucent.

3 Add spinach and crushed tomatoes. Continue to cook for 2 minutes until spinach wilts and cauliflower rice is lightly browned. Transfer cauliflower mixture to a large mixing bowl. Add Swiss cheese spread and stir until fully combined.

4 In a small bowl, mix together Cheddar and Parmesan cheeses. Set aside.

5 Place peppers in a 9" × 13" baking dish. Pour water into the bottom of the baking dish.

6 Divide cauliflower mixture among the pepper halves and top them with the Cheddar and Parmesan mixture.

7 Cover the baking dish with foil and bake for 45 minutes.

8 Remove baking dish from the oven and turn on the broiler. Uncover baking dish and broil for 4–5 minutes until cheese is golden brown. Serve immediately.

Meal Prep Roasted Sweet Potatoes with Black Beans and Eggs

This simple make-ahead lunch or dinner is ready when you are thanks to just a few key ingredients that can be prepared easily ahead of time. Loaded with protein, fiber, and nutrients, this dish will fill you up and give you long-lasting energy for hours.

2 medium sweet potatoes, peeled and cubed

1 teaspoon olive oil

¼ teaspoon salt

⅛ teaspoon ground black pepper

4 large eggs

1 (15-ounce) can black beans, drained and rinsed

SERVES 2	
Per Serving:	
Calories	478
Fat	13g
Sodium	615mg
Carbohydrates	65g
Fiber	13g
Sugar	7g
Protein	25g

1 Preheat oven to 400°F. Line a baking sheet with parchment paper.

2 In a large bowl, toss sweet potatoes with oil, salt, and pepper. Transfer to the prepared baking sheet and spread out in a single layer. Bake for 25–30 minutes until tender.

3 Cover eggs with water in a medium saucepan. Bring to a boil over high heat. Remove from heat, cover, and set aside for 10 minutes. Drain eggs, run under cold water, and peel eggs.

4 Divide sweet potato and black beans between two containers. Add 2 eggs to each, cover, and refrigerate for up to 5 days.

Sheet Pan Sesame Tofu and Vegetables

SERVES 4	
Per Serving:	
Calories	255
Fat	12g
Sodium	340mg
Carbohydrates	24g
Fiber	4g
Sugar	5g
Protein	12g

The variety of vegetables in this easy one pan meal will help you hit both your macro- and micronutrient goals for the day.

2 tablespoons tahini

2 tablespoons lemon juice

1 tablespoon low-sodium soy sauce or coconut aminos

1 teaspoon minced garlic

12 ounces extra-firm tofu, drained, patted dry, and cut into ½" cubes

2 medium sweet potatoes, peeled and diced into ½" pieces

1 tablespoon olive oil, divided

½ teaspoon salt, divided

2 cups cauliflower florets

2 cups chopped kale

1 Preheat oven to 400°F. Line two baking sheets with parchment paper.

2 Combine tahini, lemon juice, soy sauce, and garlic in a small bowl. Set aside.

3 Place tofu and sweet potatoes on one of the baking sheets. Drizzle with ½ tablespoon oil and sprinkle with ¼ teaspoon salt. Toss gently to coat. On the other baking sheet, toss cauliflower and kale with the remaining ½ tablespoon oil and ¼ teaspoon salt.

4 Place both baking sheets in the oven and roast 20–25 minutes until cauliflower begins to lightly brown. Remove cauliflower and kale from oven. Gently toss tofu and sweet potatoes and roast for 20 minutes longer.

5 Transfer the contents of both baking sheets to a large bowl. Drizzle with tahini mixture and toss to coat.

6 Serve hot or at room temperature.

Green Goddess Bowls

These nutritious and protein-packed bowls are loaded with vegetables, greens, and grains, and topped with a creamy tahini dressing. Ready in just about 20 minutes, this healthy meal will have you glowing from the inside out!

¾ cup white or red quinoa

1½ cups water

½ tablespoon avocado oil

½ medium onion, peeled and chopped

1 teaspoon minced garlic

1 cup frozen shelled edamame, thawed

1 small zucchini, trimmed and chopped

2 cups roughly chopped kale

⅛ teaspoon salt

⅛ teaspoon ground black pepper

¼ cup Lemon Tahini Dressing (see recipe in Chapter 10)

1 Place quinoa and water in a medium saucepan and bring to a boil over high heat. Reduce heat to low, cover, and simmer 12–15 minutes until water is fully absorbed.

2 Heat oil in a large skillet over medium-high heat. Sauté onion and garlic for 2–3 minutes. Add edamame and zucchini and cook for another 5 minutes.

3 Stir in kale and cook for about 2 minutes until wilted. Season with salt and pepper.

4 Divide quinoa between two bowls, top with vegetable mixture, and drizzle with dressing. Serve immediately.

SERVES 2	
Per Serving:	
Calories	464
Fat	13g
Sodium	325mg
Carbohydrates	64g
Fiber	12g
Sugar	6g
Protein	23g

VEGETABLES, VEGETABLES, AND MORE VEGETABLES!

Aim to eat 6–8 servings of non-starchy vegetables per day. Vegetables (and some fruit) are where the majority of your carbs should come from. If going over your carb goal is a common occurrence, you might not be getting enough vegetables.

Nourish Bowls

ADD SOME VOLUME TO YOUR DIET

The best way to combat hunger without adding a lot of calories is to mix in some vegetables with your protein sources. But this doesn't always mean you have to have another boring salad. Instead of a cup of spaghetti with marinara sauce, fill your plate with a half cup of spaghetti and a full cup of zucchini noodles. Vegetables, loaded with micronutrients, fiber, and water, can help you to feel full.

Brown rice, white beans, and dried cranberries in a sweet and savory tahini dressing combine to make comforting warm bowls that are nourishing for both body and soul. With a balanced ratio of protein, fiber, fat, and carbohydrates, it's the perfect meal in a bowl.

½ tablespoon avocado oil

½ medium sweet onion, peeled and chopped

1 cup white beans, drained and rinsed

2 cups baby spinach

⅛ teaspoon salt

⅛ teaspoon ground black pepper

2 cups cooked brown rice

2 tablespoons dried cranberries

2 tablespoons pumpkin seeds

¼ cup Cinnamon Tahini Dressing (see recipe in Chapter 10)

1 Heat oil in a large skillet over medium-high heat and sauté onion for 2–3 minutes until slightly softened.

2 Add beans and spinach and heat for 1 minute until spinach is wilted. Season with salt and pepper. Remove from heat and stir in rice.

3 Add cranberries, pumpkin seeds, and dressing. Gently stir to combine. Serve immediately.

Cilantro Rice and Beans

Eating rice and beans in combination creates a complete plant-based protein in addition to supplying you with a significant amount of fiber, carbohydrates, and other nutrients.

2 cups cooked white or basmati rice

1 tablespoon lime juice

1 teaspoon salt

3 tablespoons chopped fresh cilantro

1 teaspoon avocado oil

1 (15-ounce) can black beans, drained and rinsed

Combine all ingredients in a medium bowl and toss to combine. Serve immediately.

SERVES 4	
Per Serving:	
Calories	197
Fat	4g
Sodium	783mg
Carbohydrates	31g
Fiber	2g
Sugar	2g
Protein	10g

Spicy Cabbage Bowls

This one pan dinner is made quickly in just 10 minutes flat. Just add eggs and hot sauce to coleslaw mix, and you'll have a low-carb meal that's packed with protein and flavor.

1 tablespoon olive oil, divided

6 cups coleslaw mix

¼ teaspoon salt

⅛ teaspoon cayenne pepper

4 large eggs

1 teaspoon hot sauce or sriracha

SERVES 2	
Per Serving:	
Calories	230
Fat	16g
Sodium	480mg
Carbohydrates	8g
Fiber	4g
Sugar	5g
Protein	14g

1 In a large skillet, heat ½ tablespoon oil over medium-high heat. Add coleslaw mix and sauté for 5 minutes until mixture begins to soften.

2 Season with salt and cayenne pepper, then divide mixture between two bowls.

3 Heat the remaining ½ tablespoon oil in the skillet over medium-high heat. Fry eggs for 2–3 minutes, flipping after 2 minutes if desired.

4 Top cabbage bowls with eggs and hot sauce, and serve.

Slow Cooker Moroccan Lentils

SERVES 6

Per Serving:

Calories	89
Fat	1g
Sodium	538mg
Carbohydrates	13g
Fiber	6g
Sugar	2g
Protein	7g

LENTILS FOR PROTEIN POWER

Lentils are loaded with potassium, folate, iron, and fiber. One ½-cup serving of lentils contains about half as much protein as a 3-ounce serving of chicken, and three times as much protein as a serving of quinoa.

Lentils are high in protein and fiber, and they take on just about any flavor you add to them. This dish is inspired by the flavors of Morocco—cumin, paprika, peppers, tomato, and fresh herbs. It makes a great plant-based side dish or a filling addition to bowls or salads.

1½ cups dried brown or green lentils

1 large tomato, diced

1 small yellow onion, peeled and diced

1 medium red bell pepper, seeded and diced

2 teaspoons minced garlic

½ cup chopped fresh parsley or cilantro, divided

2 teaspoons ground cumin

2½ teaspoons paprika

1½ teaspoons salt

¼ teaspoon cayenne pepper

6 cups vegetable stock

1 Combine lentils, tomato, onion, bell pepper, garlic, ¼ cup parsley, cumin, paprika, salt, cayenne pepper, and stock in a 4- to 6-quart slow cooker.

2 Cook on high for 4 hours, or on low for 8 hours.

3 Top with remaining parsley before serving.

Butternut Squash Gratin

This spin on a traditional dish replaces potatoes with squash for a meal that has a bit more fiber and fewer total carbs. Panko bread crumbs form the crusty top, but you can also add additional Parmesan cheese for more flavor and a bit more fat.

1 large butternut squash, peeled and thinly sliced

½ cup whole milk

2 cloves garlic, peeled and minced

½ cup freshly grated Parmesan cheese, divided

½ teaspoon ground black pepper

¾ teaspoon salt, divided

2 tablespoons salted butter, melted

½ cup panko bread crumbs

1 Preheat oven to 400°F. Spray a 10" × 13" baking dish with non-stick cooking spray.

2 In a large bowl, combine squash, milk, garlic, ¼ cup cheese, pepper, and ½ teaspoon salt.

3 Transfer mixture to the prepared baking dish, spreading evenly.

4 In a small bowl, combine butter, bread crumbs, remaining ¼ cup cheese, and remaining ¼ teaspoon salt.

5 Spread bread crumb mixture over the casserole and bake 30–35 minutes until hot and bubbling. Remove from oven and turn on the broiler.

6 Broil for 2 minutes under the broiler to crisp the top before serving.

SERVES 6	
Per Serving:	
Calories	213
Fat	6g
Sodium	518mg
Carbohydrates	35g
Fiber	9g
Sugar	7g
Protein	7g

Zucchini and Potato Bake

SERVES 4	
Per Serving:	
Calories	370
Fat	16g
Sodium	740mg
Carbohydrates	48g
Fiber	7g
Sugar	7g
Protein	8g

Potatoes are full of important nutrients and are a very filling source of carbohydrates. Combined with zucchini, this nutritious and tasty recipe will keep you full for hours.

2 medium zucchini, trimmed and sliced

4 medium potatoes, peeled and cut into large chunks

1 medium red bell pepper, seeded and chopped

1 clove garlic, peeled and minced

½ cup dried bread crumbs

¼ cup olive oil

1 teaspoon paprika

1 teaspoon salt

1 teaspoon ground black pepper

1 Preheat oven to 400°F.

2 In a medium baking pan, toss all ingredients together. Bake 1 hour or until potatoes are tender, stirring occasionally. Serve hot.

Cowboy Caviar

SERVES 6	
Per Serving:	
Calories	236
Fat	12g
Sodium	642mg
Carbohydrates	26g
Fiber	5g
Sugar	4g
Protein	6g

Colorful Cowboy Caviar never disappoints. Serve it as a side dish for a weeknight meal or as a dip for a party.

1 cup canned black beans, drained and rinsed

1 small red onion, peeled and finely chopped

1 cup corn kernels

1 cup quartered cherry tomatoes

1 cup canned black-eyed peas, drained and rinsed

1 medium red bell pepper, seeded and chopped

⅓ cup olive oil

⅓ cup lime juice

3 tablespoons chopped fresh cilantro

1 teaspoon salt

1 In a large bowl, combine black beans, onion, corn, tomatoes, black-eyed peas, and bell pepper.

2 In a small bowl, whisk together oil, lime juice, cilantro, and salt. Drizzle over bean mixture and toss to combine.

3 Serve immediately or refrigerate for up to 3 days.

Instant Pot® Barbecue Lentils

Use whatever variety of lentils you have on hand as well as your favorite brand of barbecue sauce. Be sure to check the ingredients in the sauce—many are high in sugar.

1 cup green, red, or brown dried lentils

1 cup water

¼ cup barbecue sauce

1 medium yellow onion, peeled and chopped

¼ teaspoon salt

SERVES 4	
Per Serving:	
Calories	242
Fat	1g
Sodium	302mg
Carbohydrates	43g
Fiber	18g
Sugar	9g
Protein	15g

1 Place all ingredients in an Instant Pot®. Close lid, set steam release to Sealing, press the Manual button, and set time to 7 minutes.

2 When the timer beeps, let pressure release naturally for 5 minutes, then quick-release any remaining pressure until the float valve drops. Open lid.

3 Serve warm or at room temperature.

Vegetable Couscous with Peanut Sauce

Couscous is great for quick weeknight dinners because it cooks up in the blink of an eye and is a versatile addition to sides or main dishes. For added protein, serve this couscous with Crispy Peanut Tofu with Cauliflower Rice (see recipe in this chapter).

1 cup water

1 tablespoon salted butter or ghee

1 cup couscous

½ teaspoon salt

2 cups frozen mixed vegetables (peas, corn, carrots, and green beans), thawed

1 tablespoon Easy Peanut Sauce (see recipe in Chapter 10)

SERVES 2	
Per Serving:	
Calories	471
Fat	10g
Sodium	671mg
Carbohydrates	79g
Fiber	6g
Sugar	7g
Protein	13g

1 In a medium saucepan, bring water and butter to a boil over high heat. Remove pan from the heat and stir in couscous and salt. Cover and set aside for 15 minutes.

2 Add vegetables to couscous in the pan and stir to combine.

3 Drizzle with Easy Peanut Sauce and serve immediately.

Sweet Potato Quesadillas

SERVES 4

Per Serving:

Calories	320
Fat	14g
Sodium	574mg
Carbohydrates	36g
Fiber	5g
Sugar	3g
Protein	14g

HOW TO HIT YOUR VEGETARIAN PROTEIN GOAL

Adding a bit of cheese to scrambled eggs, shelled edamame to a green salad, or hemp hearts to your morning oatmeal are a few ways you can increase your daily intake of protein. They all add up!

Mashed sweet potatoes combine with cheese, black beans, and spinach in these warm, comforting quesadillas. Top them with salsa, sour cream, guacamole, or whatever else your taste buds desire.

1 large sweet potato, peeled and sliced
¼ teaspoon salt
¼ teaspoon ground black pepper
4 (7") whole-grain tortillas
⅔ cup canned black beans, drained and rinsed
1 cup chopped baby spinach
1½ cups shredded Cheddar cheese

1 Preheat oven to 400°F. Line a baking sheet with parchment paper.
2 Fill a medium saucepan with 1" of water and bring to a boil over high heat. Place sweet potato in a steaming basket and place basket in the saucepan. Cover and steam for 10–12 minutes until tender. Transfer sweet potatoes to a bowl and mash with a fork. Season with salt and pepper.
3 Lay 2 tortillas on the prepared baking sheet and spread with mashed sweet potato. Top with black beans, spinach, and cheese. Cover with the remaining tortillas and bake for 10–15 minutes until golden brown and crispy.
4 Slice into wedges and serve.

CHAPTER 9

Pasta and Pizza

Spicy Buffalo Macaroni and Cheese

SERVES 2	
Per Serving:	
Calories	595
Fat	29g
Sodium	1,435mg
Carbohydrates	40g
Fiber	4g
Sugar	2g
Protein	44g

This recipe combines two classic American flavors—Buffalo chicken and macaroni and cheese. It contains significantly less fat than the traditional dish that you'd order at a restaurant, so you can enjoy this meal guilt-free.

2 cups elbow macaroni

1 tablespoon salted butter

½ cup fat-free shredded Cheddar cheese

6 ounces grilled chicken, cut into strips

2 tablespoons Frank's RedHot Original Cayenne Pepper Sauce

½ cup crumbled blue cheese

1 Fill a large pot with water and bring to a boil over high heat. Add macaroni and cook for 9 minutes. Drain and return to pot.

2 Stir in butter and Cheddar cheese until melted.

3 Top with chicken, pepper sauce, and blue cheese. Serve hot.

Chicken and Pesto Farfalle

SERVES 4	
Per Serving:	
Calories	339
Fat	10g
Sodium	611mg
Carbohydrates	25g
Fiber	2g
Sugar	3g
Protein	37g

This is a low-fat and high-protein dish with minimal ingredients for an easy preparation. It's one of those easy weeknight meals that tastes amazing yet doesn't take a ton of time to pull together.

8 ounces dried farfalle

1 cup frozen chopped green beans

½ cup reduced-fat pesto sauce

2 cups grilled chicken, cut into bite-sized pieces

½ cup crumbled feta or goat cheese

1 Fill a large pot with water and bring to a boil over high heat. Add pasta and cook for 11 minutes. Drain pasta, reserving ½ cup pasta cooking water.

2 Place green beans in a small skillet with enough water to cover them. Cover skillet and heat over medium heat for 5 minutes; drain.

3 Combine pasta, pesto, reserved water, chicken, green beans, and cheese in a large bowl and stir to combine. Serve hot or cold.

High-Protein Italian Pasta Bake

This dish is ridiculously quick to prepare and requires just a few ingredients—but you would never know it. It's delicious and nutritious, and it tastes even better the next day.

4 ounces chickpea penne pasta

1 pound 90% lean ground beef

1 (16-ounce) bag frozen pepper and onion strips, thawed

2 tablespoons Italian seasoning

1 cup marinara sauce

1 large egg

1 cup shredded mozzarella cheese

1 Preheat oven to 350°F.

2 Fill a large pot with water and bring to a boil over high heat. Add pasta and cook for 6 minutes. Drain and transfer to a large bowl.

3 Meanwhile, in a large skillet over medium-high heat, cook ground beef, breaking it up with a wooden spoon while it cooks. Sauté for 7–8 minutes until no longer pink. Add pepper and onion strips and Italian seasoning to the skillet and sauté 2 minutes.

4 Transfer ground beef mixture to the bowl with pasta. Add marinara sauce and egg. Mix ingredients well.

5 Pour ingredients into a 9" × 13" baking dish and top with cheese.

6 Bake for 10 minutes until cheese is melted. Serve immediately.

SERVES 4	
Per Serving:	
Calories	438
Fat	21g
Sodium	348mg
Carbohydrates	24g
Fiber	6g
Sugar	5g
Protein	40g

HOW MUCH PROTEIN SHOULD YOU EAT PER MEAL?

Take your total protein goal for the day and divide it among your meals and snacks. For instance, if your goal is 120 grams of protein per day and you typically eat four meals, you'll need to get around 30 grams of protein per meal.

Mediterranean Shrimp Penne

TOMATOES FOR HEALTH

Tomatoes are a very powerful and nutritious food that should be included in your diet on a regular basis. In addition to being loaded with micronutrients, tomatoes can improve your heart health and vision health, and can act as an anticarcinogen, which means they reduce the risk of developing cancer from environmental toxins.

This garlicky shrimp and pasta dish provides healthy carbohydrates and protein with a lot less fat than many traditional shrimp dishes, like scampi.

12 ounces whole-grain penne

2 tablespoons olive oil

¼ cup chopped red onion

1 tablespoon chopped garlic

¼ cup white wine

2 (14.5-ounce) cans diced tomatoes

1 pound large shrimp, peeled and deveined

½ cup grated Parmesan cheese

1 Fill a large pot with water and bring to a boil over high heat. Add pasta and cook for 13 minutes. Drain and keep warm.
2 Heat oil in a medium nonstick skillet over medium-high heat. Add onion and garlic and sauté about 5 minutes until tender.
3 Add wine and tomatoes and cook 10 more minutes, stirring frequently. Add shrimp to sauce and cook an additional 5 minutes.
4 Toss shrimp with pasta and serve with Parmesan sprinkled on top.

Light Fettuccine Alfredo

Fettuccine Alfredo is one of the heaviest, fattiest, cream-based pasta dishes around. It's delicious, but it's tough to fit into your daily macro goals. But that was before this lower-calorie version existed. Let's just say it's going to become your new favorite for pasta night!

8 ounces fettuccine

1 cup nonfat milk

6 (.75-ounce) wedges creamy mozzarella spreadable cheese

1 teaspoon garlic powder

1½ tablespoons grated Parmesan cheese

1 tablespoon salted butter or ghee

⅛ teaspoon salt

⅛ teaspoon ground black pepper

1 Fill a large pot with water and bring to a boil over high heat. Add pasta and cook for 12 minutes. Drain and place pasta in a large bowl.

2 In a medium saucepan over medium heat, combine spreadable cheese, garlic powder, Parmesan cheese, butter, salt, and pepper. Cook, stirring often, until everything is melted and the sauce is smooth, about 15 to 20 minutes.

3 Pour sauce over pasta and toss to combine. Serve immediately.

SERVES 4

Per Serving:

Calories	785
Fat	30g
Sodium	1,520mg
Carbohydrates	95g
Fiber	4g
Sugar	12g
Protein	37g

WHOLE-GRAIN VERSUS REGULAR PASTA

In terms of total calories, there really isn't much of a difference between whole-grain and regular pastas. However, many whole-grain pastas are higher in fiber and protein, so that alone is a good enough reason to use them. Check the nutrition labels before buying.

Instant Pot® Chicken Pasta

This easy meal—made with just five ingredients—takes less than 10 minutes to throw together. It's a simple recipe to add to your weekend meal prep, and makes a delicious and filling lunch or dinner during the week. It's high in protein and fiber, low in fat, gluten- and dairy-free, and macro-friendly.

1½ pounds boneless, skinless chicken thighs

4 organic chicken stock cubes

2 cups low-sodium chicken stock, divided

8 ounces high-protein chickpea pasta

1 (16-ounce) bag frozen mixed vegetables (corn, carrots, green beans, and peas), thawed

SERVES 6	
Per Serving:	
Calories	409
Fat	16g
Sodium	1,211mg
Carbohydrates	33g
Fiber	2g
Sugar	8g
Protein	33g

1 Place chicken, stock cubes, and 1 cup stock in an Instant Pot®. Close lid, set steam release to Sealing, press the Manual button, and set time to 10 minutes. When the timer beeps, quick-release the pressure until the float valve drops and open the lid.

2 Remove chicken from the pot. Shred with two forks and return to the pot with pasta and the remaining 1 cup stock. Be sure pasta is fully submerged in the liquid.

3 Close lid, set steam release to Sealing, press the Manual button, and set time to 5 minutes. When the timer beeps, quick-release the pressure until the float valve drops and open the lid. Stir in mixed vegetables. Serve immediately.

Buffalo Blue Chicken Pasta

SERVES 4	
Per Serving:	
Calories	325
Fat	9g
Sodium	1,134mg
Carbohydrates	44g
Fiber	11g
Sugar	3g
Protein	19g

Blue cheese and Buffalo sauce may just be the greatest flavor combination ever. It's so delicious, this pasta dish will likely become a staple for a quick dinner in your house.

8 ounces chickpea rotini pasta

1 teaspoon salted butter or ghee

½ cup diced onion

⅓ cup Frank's RedHot Original Cayenne Pepper Sauce

8 ounces Instant Pot® Shredded Chicken (see recipe in Chapter 5)

4 ounces crumbled blue cheese

1 Fill a large pot with water and bring to a boil over high heat. Add pasta and cook for 7 minutes. Drain, transfer to a large bowl, and set aside.

2 Melt butter in a large skillet over medium heat. Sauté onion 5–7 minutes until soft and translucent. Add pasta, pepper sauce, and chicken. Mix well, then top with cheese. Serve immediately.

Garlic Parmesan Pasta

SERVES 4	
Per Serving:	
Calories	383
Fat	18g
Sodium	331mg
Carbohydrates	42g
Fiber	2g
Sugar	2g
Protein	12g

This simple yet elegant pasta can be served as a main meal or a side dish. Add chicken or shrimp to make it a well-rounded meal.

8 ounces angel hair pasta

¼ cup olive oil

1 tablespoon minced fresh oregano

¼ cup minced fresh parsley

3 teaspoons minced garlic

⅛ teaspoon crushed red pepper flakes

¼ teaspoon salt

¼ teaspoon ground black pepper

½ cup grated Parmesan cheese

1 Fill a large pot with water and bring to a boil over high heat. Add pasta and cook for 4 minutes. Drain and transfer to a large bowl.

2 Meanwhile, heat oil in a small saucepan over medium heat. Add oregano, parsley, garlic, red pepper, and salt. Sauté for 1 minute.

3 Remove from heat and pour over pasta. Toss gently to combine. Sprinkle with black pepper and cheese. Serve immediately.

Artichoke Parmesan Pasta

This creamy and comforting dish is loaded with plant-based protein, so you won't need to add an additional source. The whole family will love it.

8 ounces chickpea penne

1 (12-ounce) jar marinated artichoke hearts, undrained

¾ cup grated Parmesan cheese

2 cups baby spinach

½ teaspoon salt

1 Fill a large pot with water and bring to a boil over high heat. Add pasta and cook for 7 minutes. Drain and transfer to a large bowl.
2 Place artichoke hearts and liquid, cheese, spinach, and salt in a food processor and pulse until smooth. Pour sauce over pasta and stir to mix. Serve immediately.

SERVES 4	
Per Serving:	
Calories	353
Fat	14g
Sodium	892mg
Carbohydrates	36g
Fiber	10g
Sugar	5g
Protein	23g

Creamy Bacon Pistachio Pasta

Unlike a lot of cheesy pasta dishes, this one is macro-friendly with a balanced ratio of protein, carbs, and fat.

8 ounces ziti

4 slices thick-cut bacon

¼ cup fat-free ricotta cheese

½ cup grated Parmesan cheese

¼ cup 1% milk

½ tablespoon extra-virgin olive oil

¼ teaspoon salt

¼ teaspoon ground black pepper

¼ cup shelled pistachios

1 Fill a large pot with water and bring to a boil over high heat. Add pasta and cook for 9 minutes. Drain and transfer to a large bowl.
2 In a medium skillet over medium heat, cook bacon for 8–10 minutes or until crisp. Drain on paper towels and chop coarsely.
3 In a small bowl, combine ricotta, Parmesan, milk, oil, salt, and pepper; blend well. Add cheese mixture to pasta and mix well.
4 Stir in bacon and pistachios. Serve immediately.

SERVES 4	
Per Serving:	
Calories	394
Fat	14g
Sodium	716mg
Carbohydrates	46g
Fiber	2g
Sugar	5g
Protein	20g

Ravioli Lasagna

A homemade lasagna is a beautiful sight to see, but sometimes you don't have time to make one from scratch. This simple version will become a family favorite.

1 pound pork sausage, casings removed

1 (26-ounce) jar pasta sauce, divided

2 (30-ounce) bags frozen large cheese ravioli, divided

1 (10-ounce) package frozen chopped spinach, thawed and drained

1½ cups shredded mozzarella cheese, divided

½ cup grated Parmesan cheese, divided

1 Preheat oven to 350°F. Spray a 9" × 13" baking dish with nonstick cooking spray.

2 Place sausage in a large skillet over medium-high heat. Sauté until no longer pink, about 8 minutes, using a wooden spoon to break up meat as it cooks. Drain excess fat from skillet.

3 Spread one-third of pasta sauce on the bottom of the prepared dish.

4 Arrange one-half of ravioli on top of sauce. Top with sausage and spinach. Layer one-third of pasta sauce, ¾ cup mozzarella, and ¼ cup Parmesan over sausage and spinach, then arrange remaining ravioli on top.

5 Cover with the remaining sauce, mozzarella, and Parmesan. Tightly cover the baking dish with foil.

6 Bake 45 minutes. Uncover and bake for an additional 12–15 minutes or until cheese is melted and lightly browned. Serve immediately.

SERVES 8	
Per Serving:	
Calories	694
Fat	38g
Sodium	1,635mg
Carbohydrates	56g
Fiber	19g
Sugar	17g
Protein	33g

SCHEDULE DAYS *OFF* FROM TRACKING

Once you get the hang of counting macros, you can schedule days off from tracking. If it makes sense for your social life, track meals from Sunday through Thursday and then take a break from tracking on Friday and Saturday. Or try tracking Monday, Tuesday, and Thursday and then just do your thing on the other days. Of course, you should be mindful of your choices on your off days, but you don't have to track every single day to see results.

Pumpkin Mac and "Cheese"

SERVES 4

Per Serving:

Calories	257
Fat	3g
Sodium	247mg
Carbohydrates	50g
Fiber	5g
Sugar	7g
Protein	8g

ARE NUTS A GOOD SOURCE OF PROTEIN?

The short answer is no. It's a common misconception that nuts are a good source of protein. They're actually a better source of healthy fats. A 1-ounce serving of almonds contains 14 grams of fat and only 6 grams of protein.

Ultra-creamy and dairy-free, this pasta dish is a comforting meal that's perfect for fall. If you're following a gluten-free diet, use your favorite gluten-free pasta.

8 ounces elbow macaroni

1 cup unsweetened almond milk

1 teaspoon garlic powder

½ cup nutritional yeast

¼ teaspoon dried thyme

1½ teaspoons Dijon mustard

1 cup canned pumpkin purée

1 tablespoon maple syrup

¼ teaspoon salt

¼ teaspoon ground black pepper

1 Fill a large pot with water and bring to a boil over high heat. Add pasta and cook for 9 minutes. Drain and transfer to a large bowl.

2 Meanwhile, heat milk in a small saucepan over medium heat for 2 minutes. Add garlic powder, nutritional yeast, thyme, mustard, pumpkin, maple syrup, salt, and pepper and whisk until thoroughly combined. Reduce heat to low and cook until the sauce has thickened, about 5 minutes.

3 Pour the pumpkin sauce over the macaroni and mix well. Serve hot.

Cheesy Edamame Spaghetti

This isn't your traditional bowl of spaghetti! Roasted cashews combine with Parmesan and garlic powder for a nutty and cheesy seasoning that will knock your socks off.

4 ounces brown rice spaghetti

1 cup unsalted roasted cashews

⅓ cup grated Parmesan cheese

1 teaspoon garlic powder

½ teaspoon salt

3 cups frozen edamame, thawed

2 cups finely chopped fresh parsley

2 teaspoons extra-virgin olive oil

½ teaspoon ground black pepper

SERVES 4	
Per Serving:	
Calories	568
Fat	30g
Sodium	1,244mg
Carbohydrates	49g
Fiber	17g
Sugar	5g
Protein	25g

1 Fill a large pot with water and bring to a boil over high heat. Add pasta and cook for 10 minutes. Drain and transfer to a large bowl.

2 Add cashews, cheese, garlic powder, and salt to a food processor. Pulse until a coarse texture is achieved. Set aside.

3 Toss pasta with edamame, parsley, oil, and pepper. Top with cashew mixture, toss to combine, and serve.

Pesto Chicken Pizza

A store-bought crust, rotisserie (or leftover) chicken, and jarred pesto combine to make the absolute perfect weeknight meal that comes together in minutes. Pair a slice with a big salad or your favorite steamed vegetables for a macro-balanced meal.

1 (12", 10-ounce) thin pizza crust

¾ cup pesto

1 cup chopped rotisserie chicken breast

6 ounces fresh mozzarella cheese, sliced

1 medium tomato, sliced

¾ cup crumbled feta cheese

SERVES 6	
Per Serving:	
Calories	430
Fat	25g
Sodium	878mg
Carbohydrates	26g
Fiber	0g
Sugar	4g
Protein	26g

1 Preheat oven to 450°F.

2 Place pizza crust on a pizza pan or baking sheet.

3 Spread pesto evenly over crust. Top with chicken, mozzarella, tomato slices, and feta.

4 Bake for 8–10 minutes until cheese is fully melted. (For a crispier crust, bake the pizza directly on the oven rack.)

5 Remove from oven and cool for 5 minutes before cutting.

Mini Buffalo Chicken Pizzas

These mini pizzas can be served as an easy weeknight meal or a filling game day party snack.

SERVES 4	
Per Serving:	
Calories	463
Fat	19g
Sodium	2,034mg
Carbohydrates	36g
Fiber	5g
Sugar	5g
Protein	35g

4 English muffins, sliced in half

½ cup pizza sauce

½ cup Frank's RedHot Original Cayenne Pepper Sauce

2 teaspoons Tabasco sauce

½ teaspoon dried oregano

½ teaspoon garlic powder

2 cups Buffalo-Style Shredded Chicken (see recipe in Chapter 5)

2 cups shredded mozzarella cheese

2 tablespoons ranch salad dressing

2 scallions, finely chopped

1 Preheat oven to 350°F. Place English muffin halves on a large baking sheet, cut side up.

2 In a small bowl, combine pizza sauce, pepper sauce, Tabasco sauce, oregano, and garlic powder. Spread mixture on English muffins. Top with chicken and cheese.

3 Bake for 10 minutes until the cheese is melted. Remove from oven, drizzle with dressing, top with scallions, and serve.

Broccoli and Cheddar Pita Pizzas

Broccoli and Cheddar are undoubtedly a delicious flavor combination, but feel free to switch up your choice of vegetables, cheese, and hummus to personalize your pizzas.

SERVES 2	
Per Serving:	
Calories	319
Fat	19g
Sodium	634mg
Carbohydrates	25g
Fiber	7g
Sugar	4g
Protein	11g

1 teaspoon olive oil

¾ cup frozen broccoli florets, chopped

⅛ teaspoon salt

2 (8") whole-wheat pitas

½ cup hummus

2 (1-ounce) slices Cheddar cheese

1 Preheat oven to 375°F. Line a baking sheet with parchment paper.

2 In a small skillet, heat oil over medium-high heat. Sauté broccoli until thawed. Season with salt.

3 Place pitas on the prepared baking sheet. Spread hummus over pitas in a thick layer and top with broccoli and a slice of cheese.

4 Bake for 8–10 minutes until cheese is melted and the pita is lightly toasted. Cool slightly and slice into quarters before serving.

Portobello Pesto Pizzas

If you're watching your carbs and want to increase your nutrient intake, portobello mushroom caps make a great whole-food "crust" for pizza. Topped with pesto, tomato, onion, feta, and balsamic vinegar, these are all-star vegetarian pizzas.

2 teaspoons extra-virgin olive oil

1 small yellow onion, peeled and diced

1 medium Roma tomato, diced

2 teaspoons minced garlic

4 large portobello mushroom caps

⅛ teaspoon salt

⅛ teaspoon ground black pepper

3 tablespoons pesto

¼ cup crumbled feta cheese

1 tablespoon balsamic vinegar

SERVES 4	
Per Serving:	
Calories	99
Fat	7g
Sodium	545mg
Carbohydrates	6g
Fiber	1g
Sugar	2g
Protein	3g

1 Preheat oven to 425°F. Line a baking sheet with parchment paper.

2 In a medium skillet, heat oil over medium heat. Add onion and sauté for 5 minutes or until soft and translucent. Add tomato and garlic. Sauté for another 5 minutes, then remove from heat and set aside.

3 Place mushroom caps (stem side up) on the prepared baking sheet. Season with salt and pepper, then spread with pesto. Top with tomato mixture and sprinkle with feta cheese. Bake for 10–12 minutes.

4 Remove from oven and drizzle with vinegar. Slice into halves or quarters with a pizza cutter. Serve immediately.

Low-Carb Eggplant Pizzas

SERVES 4

Per Serving:

Calories	248
Fat	17g
Sodium	401mg
Carbohydrates	12g
Fiber	5g
Sugar	6g
Protein	11g

Using eggplant is a great way to add more vegetables to your diet, especially when it's used as a base for delicious pizza toppings.

1 large eggplant, cut into ½" slices

¼ cup extra-virgin olive oil

¼ teaspoon salt

¼ teaspoon ground black pepper

¾ cup tomato sauce

½ teaspoon Italian seasoning

4 ounces part-skim mozzarella cheese, thinly sliced

2 tablespoons minced fresh basil

PLAN LIKE A PRO

At the beginning of the week, use a meal tracking app to log 2 or 3 days of macro-balanced meals, then rotate them throughout the week. There's no need to plan out every day of the week with all-new meals and snacks. Double or triple recipes and save the leftovers for later meals. You can always make tweaks, but the base of your plan will be set for the week. This will save you time and help you stick to your macros.

1 Preheat broiler and line a baking sheet with parchment paper.
2 Brush each side of eggplant slices with oil and season with salt and pepper.
3 Heat a large nonstick skillet over medium heat. Cook eggplant slices in batches until tender and lightly browned, about 3–5 minutes per side.
4 Transfer eggplant slices to the prepared baking sheet and top each with tomato sauce, Italian seasoning, and cheese.
5 Broil for 3–5 minutes until cheese is melted and lightly browned.
6 Top with basil and serve.

Spinach, Sausage, and Provolone Pizza

SERVES 6

Per Serving:

Calories	225
Fat	6g
Sodium	202mg
Carbohydrates	34g
Fiber	1g
Sugar	0g
Protein	9g

Pizza is one of the few meals that rarely gets boring, especially when topped with flavorful (and nutritious!) ingredients like spinach, sausage, and provolone cheese. Make your own pizza dough or look for it in your grocery's bakery department.

1 tablespoon olive oil

8 ounces Italian sausage, casings removed

3 cups baby spinach

¼ teaspoon salt

⅛ teaspoon ground black pepper

1 pound pizza dough

4 ounces sharp provolone cheese, thinly sliced

1 Preheat oven to 425°F. Spray a baking sheet with nonstick cooking spray.

2 Heat oil in a large skillet over medium-high heat. Add sausage and cook, breaking it up with a spoon, until no longer pink, 4–5 minutes. Add spinach, salt, and pepper. Toss 1 minute until spinach is wilted.

3 Spread dough on the prepared baking sheet. Top with cheese, then sausage mixture.

4 Bake until crust is crisp and cheese has melted, 12–15 minutes.

5 Remove from oven. Cool for 5 minutes before slicing and serving.

CHAPTER 10

Sides and Sauces

Garlic Parmesan Fries

SERVES 2	
Per Serving:	
Calories	172
Fat	3g
Sodium	623mg
Carbohydrates	32g
Fiber	4g
Sugar	2g
Protein	4g

Homemade fries are a favorite quick and delicious weeknight side, especially when garlic and Parmesan are involved. This recipe makes enough to serve two people, but you can prepare it in bulk to have on hand for the rest of the week or to feed a large party.

1 teaspoon olive oil

1 clove garlic, peeled and crushed

1 large potato, cut into sticks

½ teaspoon salt

1 tablespoon grated Parmesan cheese

1 tablespoon chopped parsley

1 Preheat oven to 425°F.
2 In a medium bowl, combine oil and garlic and toss potato sticks in mixture, coating well.
3 Arrange fries on a baking sheet, spreading evenly, and sprinkle with salt. Bake for 10 minutes per side.
4 Remove from the oven, top with Parmesan and parsley, and serve.

Cilantro Lime Rice

SERVES 4	
Per Serving:	
Calories	16
Fat	0g
Sodium	44mg
Carbohydrates	3g
Fiber	1g
Sugar	0g
Protein	1g

Riced cauliflower is a great substitute for traditional rice when you need to lower your daily carb intake. This simple side is full of flavor and pairs perfectly with just about any Mexican or southwestern dish. It's also delicious in burritos or bowls!

1 (10-ounce) bag frozen riced cauliflower, thawed

3 tablespoons water

2 tablespoons lime juice

2 teaspoons grated lime zest

½ cup chopped fresh cilantro

1 Combine cauliflower and water in a large microwave-safe bowl and microwave on high 3–5 minutes until cauliflower is soft.
2 Stir in lime juice, zest, and cilantro. Mix well and serve immediately.

Sweet Potato Wedges

These oven-baked fries are nutritious, satisfying, and perfectly crispy. Baking them greatly reduces the amount of fat in a family favorite.

4 medium sweet potatoes, cut into thick wedges

2½ tablespoons olive oil

½ teaspoon paprika

½ teaspoon garlic powder

1 teaspoon salt

½ teaspoon ground black pepper

1 Preheat oven to 400°F.
2 Combine all ingredients in a large bowl, tossing until sweet potatoes are well coated. Arrange on a baking sheet.
3 Cook 30–35 minutes, turning halfway through, until fries reach desired level of crispness. Serve.

SERVES 4	
Per Serving:	
Calories	193
Fat	8g
Sodium	626mg
Carbohydrates	31g
Fiber	4g
Sugar	7g
Protein	1g

Buffalo Blue Brussels Sprouts

If you want a meat-free and low-fat version of Buffalo wings for the big game, these Brussels sprouts are a healthy alternative to fried wings.

2 tablespoons olive oil

1 pound Brussels sprouts, trimmed and halved

¼ cup Frank's RedHot Original Cayenne Pepper Sauce

2 tablespoons crumbled blue cheese

1 Preheat oven to 425°F.
2 Heat oil in a large skillet over medium heat. Sauté Brussels sprouts for 4–5 minutes until softened.
3 Spread sprouts on a large baking sheet and roast for 12–15 minutes until edges start to crisp.
4 Transfer to a large bowl, toss with pepper sauce until well coated, and top with cheese before serving.

SERVES 4	
Per Serving:	
Calories	137
Fat	8g
Sodium	656mg
Carbohydrates	11g
Fiber	4g
Sugar	3g
Protein	5g

Zucchini Fries

SERVES 4	
Per Serving:	
Calories	162
Fat	2g
Sodium	531mg
Carbohydrates	27g
Fiber	4g
Sugar	8g
Protein	10g

If you want a crispy fry recipe without the calories and carbs from potatoes, zucchini makes an excellent substitution.

1 cup dried bread crumbs

¼ teaspoon garlic powder

2 tablespoons grated Parmesan cheese

¼ teaspoon salt

3 large egg whites, beaten

4 medium zucchini, peeled and cut into 3" sticks

1 Preheat oven to 425°F. Line a baking sheet with parchment paper.
2 Combine bread crumbs, garlic powder, cheese, and salt in a large bowl. Place egg whites in a separate bowl.
3 Dip zucchini sticks into egg whites, toss in bread crumb mixture to coat, and arrange on the prepared baking sheet.
4 Bake 20–25 minutes or until fries begin to brown, turning halfway through.

Cabbage Slaw

SERVES 4	
Per Serving:	
Calories	104
Fat	6g
Sodium	169mg
Carbohydrates	10g
Fiber	4g
Sugar	6g
Protein	2g

This quick and simple slaw is perfect on its own as a low-calorie side or as a topping on a sandwich or burger. It's packed with healthy nutrients and fiber to keep you full and energized.

½ small head cabbage, shredded

½ medium red bell pepper, seeded and sliced

¼ small red onion, peeled and sliced

2 tablespoons olive oil

1½ tablespoons apple cider vinegar

¼ teaspoon salt

1 Toss all ingredients together in a large bowl.
2 Cover and refrigerate at least 1 hour before serving.

Buffalo Tahini

This is a versatile finishing sauce. It's great on roasted, grilled, or steamed vegetables and delicious stirred into pasta sauce, drizzled on a big bowl of salad greens, or tossed with grains or beans.

¾ cup tahini
¼ cup Frank's RedHot Original Cayenne Pepper Sauce
1 tablespoon sriracha sauce
½ cup warm water

1 Combine all ingredients in a medium bowl and whisk until smooth.
2 If the sauce seems too thick, add more water, 1 teaspoon at a time, until it reaches the desired consistency.

MAKES 1½ CUPS	
Per Serving (2 tablespoons):	
Calories	102
Fat	9g
Sodium	192mg
Carbohydrates	0g
Fiber	0g
Sugar	0g
Protein	5g

Lemon Tahini Dressing

This simple, all-purpose dressing is perfect for green salads, roasted vegetables, or meat dishes. You may need to double the recipe—it will go fast!

¼ cup tahini
¼ cup lemon juice
1 tablespoon maple syrup or agave nectar

In a small bowl, whisk all ingredients together. Use immediately or refrigerate for up to 3 days.

MAKES ½ CUP	
Per Serving (2 tablespoons):	
Calories	114
Fat	9g
Sodium	0mg
Carbohydrates	4g
Fiber	0g
Sugar	4g
Protein	4g

Bang Bang Cauliflower

Deep-fried, breaded cauliflower, doused in a sweet and spicy sauce, is a popular restaurant appetizer. This is a lightened-up and gluten-free version. It makes a great side dish or vegetarian entrée.

½ cup Frank's RedHot Original Cayenne Pepper Sauce

1 tablespoon mayonnaise

1 tablespoon honey

2 teaspoons rice wine vinegar

1 teaspoon sriracha sauce

⅓ cup liquid egg whites or 2 large egg whites

⅔ cup almond flour

12 ounces cauliflower florets

1 Combine pepper sauce, mayonnaise, honey, vinegar, and sriracha sauce in a large bowl. Set aside.

2 Preheat oven to 400°F. Line a large baking sheet with parchment paper. Place egg whites in a shallow bowl. Place almond flour in another shallow bowl.

3 Dip cauliflower florets in egg whites and then dredge in almond flour. Place on prepared baking sheet. Bake for 20 minutes.

4 Remove baking sheet from oven and set aside to cool for 5 minutes. Increase oven temperature to 450°F.

5 Transfer cauliflower to the sauce in the bowl and toss to coat.

6 Return sauce-covered cauliflower to the baking sheet and bake for 5–7 minutes until crispy and lightly browned.

7 Remove from oven and serve immediately.

Easy Peanut Sauce

Make a batch (or two) of this addicting sauce at the start of the week and use as a salad dressing or a dipping sauce for roasted vegetables. It's also great drizzled over grilled meat or a stir-fry.

½ cup powdered peanut butter

½ cup low-sodium soy sauce or coconut aminos

4 teaspoons ground ginger

1 Combine all ingredients in a small bowl and mix well.

2 Serve immediately or refrigerate, covered, for up to 5 days.

MAKES ½ CUP	
Per Serving (2 tablespoons):	
Calories	130
Fat	4g
Sodium	1,536mg
Carbohydrates	12g
Fiber	2g
Sugar	4g
Protein	12g

Roasted Broccoli with Peanut Sauce

Roasted broccoli paired with a simple peanut sauce makes a delicious side that's loaded with good-for-you fiber, vitamin C, and a surprising amount of protein too.

1 pound broccoli, cut into florets

2 tablespoons olive oil

¼ teaspoon salt

¼ teaspoon ground black pepper

½ cup Easy Peanut Sauce (see recipe in this chapter)

SERVES 4	
Per Serving:	
Calories	217
Fat	10g
Sodium	343mg
Carbohydrates	19g
Fiber	8g
Sugar	7g
Protein	13g

1 Preheat oven to 425°F. Line a large baking sheet with parchment paper.

2 On the baking sheet, toss broccoli with oil until lightly coated. Sprinkle with salt and pepper.

3 Bake for 18–22 minutes, tossing halfway, until florets are light golden brown on the edges.

4 Transfer broccoli to a large bowl. Drizzle with Easy Peanut Sauce and toss to coat. Serve immediately.

Cauliflower Steaks with Lemon Tahini Drizzle

Cauliflower is a versatile vegetable. There are many different ways to prepare it, and this one may be the most satisfying. Thick slabs of cauliflower steak are seasoned to perfection, roasted, and drizzled with a creamy, bright dressing.

2 medium heads cauliflower, cored and outer leaves removed

2 tablespoons olive oil

1 teaspoon salt

½ teaspoon ground black pepper

1 teaspoon garlic powder

½ teaspoon paprika

½ cup Lemon Tahini Dressing (see recipe in this chapter)

1 Preheat oven to 425°F and line a large baking sheet with parchment paper.

2 Slice each cauliflower head into ¾" slices. Each head should produce about three to four steaks. Slices from the edges will likely fall apart, but these can be roasted alongside the steaks.

3 Brush both sides of cauliflower slices with oil. Sprinkle with salt, pepper, garlic powder, and paprika. Place on the prepared baking sheet and bake 15 minutes.

4 Remove pan from oven. Flip steaks carefully using a spatula and return to oven to bake for an additional 15–20 minutes until lightly browned and fork-tender.

5 Remove from oven, set aside to cool for 5 minutes, and drizzle with dressing before serving.

SERVES 3

Per Serving:	
Calories	283
Fat	19g
Sodium	890mg
Carbohydrates	21g
Fiber	9g
Sugar	8g
Protein	7g

TAHINI

Tahini is made from ground sesame seeds, and its texture is similar to that of peanut butter. It provides a good amount of protein and various minerals to your diet. Additionally, about 50 percent of the fat in tahini comes from monounsaturated fatty acids, which have anti-inflammatory properties and have been linked to a decreased risk of chronic disease.

Bacon-Wrapped Sweet Potato Wedges

SERVES 8	
Per Serving:	
Calories	371
Fat	24g
Sodium	1,333mg
Carbohydrates	17g
Fiber	2g
Sugar	4g
Protein	22g

Only two ingredients and minimal prep time are required for a satisfying sweet and savory side or appetizer. These wedges are perfect for game day parties and other get-togethers. Serve them with barbecue sauce, blue cheese dressing, or another favorite dipping sauce.

1 pound sliced bacon

4 medium sweet potatoes, each cut into 8 wedges

1 Preheat oven to 375°F. Line a large baking sheet with a silicone mat or foil.
2 Wrap a slice of bacon around each sweet potato wedge and place on the prepared baking sheet.
3 Bake for 35–40 minutes until bacon is fully cooked and sweet potatoes are soft.
4 Allow to cool slightly before serving.

Parmesan Roasted Fennel

SERVES 3	
Per Serving:	
Calories	122
Fat	9g
Sodium	502mg
Carbohydrates	4g
Fiber	1g
Sugar	2g
Protein	6g

This savory side complements other roasted dishes for a well-balanced main, or it can simply be eaten alone as a snack or additional to a salad.

2 (10-ounce) fennel bulbs, trimmed

1 tablespoon olive oil

¼ cup grated Parmesan cheese

¼ teaspoon salt

⅛ teaspoon ground black pepper

1 teaspoon minced fresh parsley

1 Preheat oven to 375°F. Line a baking sheet with parchment paper.
2 Slice each fennel bulb into 3 thick slices. Place on the prepared baking sheet and brush slices with oil.
3 Sprinkle with cheese, salt, and pepper. Bake for 30 minutes or until tops are lightly browned.
4 Remove from oven, sprinkle with parsley, and serve.

Cinnamon Tahini Dressing

This tahini dressing can be drizzled on just about everything. It's smooth and satisfying with a slightly sweet flavor that's guaranteed to liven up any old side dish, salad, or your favorite starch. Try it drizzled over Sweet Potato Wedges (see recipe in this chapter).

3 tablespoons tahini

2 tablespoons apple cider vinegar

1 teaspoon maple syrup

1 tablespoon water

⅛ teaspoon ground cinnamon

Combine all ingredients in a small bowl. Serve immediately or refrigerate for up to 5 days.

MAKES ½ CUP	
Per Serving (2 tablespoons):	
Calories	80
Fat	7g
Sodium	0mg
Carbohydrates	2g
Fiber	0g
Sugar	2g
Protein	2g

Green Goddess Dressing

Each version of a green goddess dressing has its own spin. This one is packed with protein, healthy fats, and nutrients. It adds a little extra something to salads, vegetable platters, or grain bowls.

½ cup creamy almond butter

½ cup fresh parsley

½ cup fresh spinach

1 teaspoon minced garlic

¼ cup chopped yellow onion

2 tablespoons lemon juice

1 teaspoon apple cider vinegar

1 teaspoon salt

½ teaspoon ground black pepper

1 tablespoon water

1 Place all ingredients in a high-speed blender or food processor. Blend until smooth.

2 If the dressing is too thick, add more water in small increments as you blend until the desired consistency is reached.

MAKES 1½ CUPS	
Per Serving (2 tablespoons):	
Calories	64
Fat	5g
Sodium	230mg
Carbohydrates	2g
Fiber	2g
Sugar	2g
Protein	3g

Honey Dressing

MAKES ½ CUP

**Per Serving
(2 tablespoons):**

Calories	90
Fat	9g
Sodium	160mg
Carbohydrates	2g
Fiber	0g
Sugar	1g
Protein	0g

Honey adds just the right amount of sweetness to this homemade salad dressing.

5 tablespoons extra-virgin olive oil

2 tablespoons apple cider vinegar

2 tablespoons Dijon mustard

2 teaspoons honey

½ teaspoon minced garlic

¼ teaspoon salt

⅛ teaspoon ground black pepper

In a small bowl, whisk all ingredients together. Use immediately or refrigerate for up to 3 days.

No-Fail Chimichurri

MAKES ¾ CUP

**Per Serving
(2 tablespoons):**

Calories	80
Fat	8g
Sodium	46mg
Carbohydrates	2g
Fiber	0g
Sugar	0g
Protein	0g

Bursting with flavor, chimichurri can be used to liven up salads, roasted vegetables, and grilled meats and seafood. Mix it with Instant Pot® Shredded Chicken (see recipe in Chapter 5) for a light and flavorful chicken salad.

1 bunch fresh cilantro

¼ cup extra-virgin olive oil

¼ cup apple cider vinegar or red wine vinegar

1½ tablespoons lemon juice

1 tablespoon minced garlic

⅛ teaspoon salt

Add all ingredients to a food processor or high-speed blender and blend until fully combined. Serve immediately or refrigerate for up to 1 week.

Coconut Ginger Carrots

Slightly sweet with a kick of ginger, these carrots are a side that you will want to make again and again. Bring this dish to your next potluck or serve it alongside your choice of protein for a balanced weeknight meal.

1 tablespoon olive oil

1½ cups minced onion

1 tablespoon ground ginger

2 teaspoons minced garlic

½ teaspoon salt

2 pounds carrots, peeled and cut into ¼" rounds

2 tablespoons lemon juice

½ cup shredded unsweetened coconut

1 Preheat oven to 375°F. Spray a 9" × 13" baking dish with nonstick cooking spray and set aside.

2 Heat oil in a large skillet over medium heat. Sauté onion and ginger for 5 minutes. Add garlic and salt and sauté for another 30 seconds.

3 Add carrots and stir with a wooden spoon until carrots are coated with the onion mixture.

4 Reduce heat to medium-low, stir in lemon juice, cover, and cook for 10 minutes.

5 Transfer carrot mixture to the prepared baking dish. Cover tightly with foil and bake for 20–30 minutes until carrots are fork-tender.

6 Remove dish from the oven, uncover, and sprinkle with coconut.

7 Return to oven and bake, uncovered, for another 10–15 minutes until coconut starts to lightly brown, then serve.

SERVES 6

Per Serving:

Calories	165
Fat	8g
Sodium	296mg
Carbohydrates	21g
Fiber	7g
Sugar	10g
Protein	2g

DON'T BE AFRAID TO MIX IT UP

Just because you eat a lot of vegetables doesn't mean you're getting enough micronutrients. It's the quality that matters, not the quantity. Don't fall into the bad habit of only eating a few vegetables; make an effort to eat as many as possible.

One Pan Maple Mustard Brussels Sprouts

Per Serving:

Calories	156
Fat	8g
Sodium	670mg
Carbohydrates	17g
Fiber	4g
Sugar	8g
Protein	4g

KEEP VEGETABLES VISIBLE

Pour a few servings of your favorite frozen vegetables into glass storage containers and keep them in the refrigerator for easy access throughout the week. Seeing them every time you open the refrigerator will encourage you to eat them.

The combination of sharp mustard and sweet maple goes so well with Brussels sprouts, and the recipe couldn't be easier to make.

2 tablespoons extra-virgin olive oil

1 pound Brussels sprouts, halved

½ teaspoon salt

⅛ teaspoon ground black pepper

¼ cup water

¼ cup Dijon mustard

2 tablespoons maple syrup

1 Heat oil in a large skillet over medium-high heat. Add Brussels sprouts, salt, and pepper and sauté for 5 minutes.

2 Pour in water, gently shake pan, and cover with a lid. Reduce heat to medium.

3 Cook for 7–8 minutes, tossing at the halfway point, until Brussels sprouts are bright green and fork-tender. Remove from heat.

4 In a small bowl, whisk together mustard and maple syrup. Drizzle over Brussels sprouts and stir to coat. Serve immediately.

Broccoli, Apples, and Red Onion

SERVES 4	
Per Serving:	
Calories	157
Fat	4g
Sodium	267mg
Carbohydrates	25g
Fiber	8g
Sugar	10g
Protein	5g

VEGETABLE PROTEIN

Broccoli, peas, and potatoes have a surprisingly decent amount of protein per serving. They're also loaded with nutrients and fiber, which are important to weight loss.

You might be surprised at how tasty this simple side dish is. It's even better after spending a few hours in the refrigerator.

1 large head broccoli, cut into florets

2 teaspoons olive oil

¼ teaspoon salt

⅛ teaspoon ground black pepper

¾ cup thinly sliced red onion

1 medium apple, cored and thinly sliced

½ cup Honey Dressing (see recipe in this chapter)

1 Preheat oven to 425°F and line a large baking sheet with parchment paper.

2 Toss broccoli with oil on the prepared baking sheet until florets are lightly coated. Spread broccoli in an even layer and sprinkle with salt and pepper.

3 Bake for 18–22 minutes, tossing halfway, until florets are light golden brown on the edges.

4 Remove pan from oven and set aside to cool for 15 minutes. Transfer cooled broccoli to a large bowl. Add onion, apple, and dressing. Toss to coat.

5 Serve at room temperature or refrigerate overnight and serve cold.

Wicked Sauce

This "wicked good" sauce truly takes a run-of-the-mill meal to the next level. Its chipotle flavor gives it a kick while chickpeas, nutritional yeast, and extra-virgin olive oil combine to create a macro-balanced sauce that can be used on anything and everything from salad and vegetables to grilled chicken and fish. Cut the amount of water in half for a thick and flavorful dip to serve with crudités and crackers.

⅓ cup nutritional yeast

¼ cup cooked chickpeas

¼ cup extra-virgin olive oil

¼ cup water

3 tablespoons lemon juice

1 teaspoon minced garlic

½ teaspoon curry powder

¼ teaspoon salt

¼ teaspoon smoked paprika

¼ teaspoon chili powder

¼ teaspoon cayenne pepper

¼ teaspoon dried oregano

1 Place nutritional yeast, chickpeas, oil, water, and lemon juice in a high-speed blender or food processor. Pulse to combine.

2 Add garlic, curry powder, salt, paprika, chili powder, cayenne, and oregano and blend until smooth.

3 If the sauce is too thick, add more water in small increments as you blend until the desired consistency is reached.

4 Serve immediately or refrigerate for up to 3 days.

MAKES 1 CUP	
Per Serving (2 tablespoons):	
Calories	68
Fat	6g
Sodium	70mg
Carbohydrates	4g
Fiber	0g
Sugar	0g
Protein	0g

Cauliflower Mash

Mashed cauliflower makes a delicious low-carb alternative to potatoes.

SERVES 4	
Per Serving:	
Calories	93
Fat	9g
Sodium	221mg
Carbohydrates	2g
Fiber	2g
Sugar	0g
Protein	0g

1 large head cauliflower, cored, outer leaves removed, and cut into florets (4 cups)

2 teaspoons minced garlic

2 tablespoons salted butter or ghee

1 tablespoon fresh thyme leaves

¼ teaspoon salt

⅛ teaspoon ground black pepper

1 Heat 1" water in a large saucepan with a steamer insert over high heat. Bring to a boil.

2 Place cauliflower in the insert and cover pan. Steam cauliflower for 10–15 minutes until cauliflower is very soft.

3 Transfer cauliflower to a food processor or high-speed blender along with garlic, butter, thyme, salt, and pepper.

4 Process until smooth. Serve immediately.

Parsnip Mash

Once you try parsnip mash, you might agree that it's just as rich and satisfying as traditional mashed potatoes. It's a perfect side dish for broiled fish, roasted chicken, and more.

SERVES 4	
Per Serving:	
Calories	235
Fat	8g
Sodium	303mg
Carbohydrates	38g
Fiber	11g
Sugar	11g
Protein	3g

2 pounds parsnips, peeled and chopped

2 tablespoons extra-virgin olive oil

2 teaspoons balsamic vinegar

½ teaspoon salt

⅛ teaspoon ground black pepper

1 Fill a large saucepan with water and bring to a boil over high heat. Add parsnips and boil for 8–10 minutes until very soft.

2 Use a slotted spoon to remove parsnips and transfer to a food processor or high-speed blender. Add oil, vinegar, salt, and pepper and process until smooth. (If mixture seems a bit dry, add a little of the cooking water from the saucepan.) Serve immediately.

Oven "Fried" Green Beans

The breading on these healthy "fries" is made with Parmesan cheese and almond flour, so it's naturally gluten-free. Try them with a burger or grilled chicken.

1 large egg

2 tablespoons olive oil

1 pound fresh green beans, trimmed

¼ cup almond flour

¼ cup grated Parmesan cheese

1 teaspoon salt

1 teaspoon garlic powder

½ teaspoon paprika

1 Preheat oven to 425°F. Line two large baking sheets with parchment paper.

2 In a large bowl, beat together egg and oil. Add green beans and toss to coat.

3 In a separate large bowl, combine almond flour, cheese, salt, garlic powder, and paprika. Add coated green beans to mix well.

4 Transfer green beans to the prepared baking sheets and bake about 15 minutes or until crispy, then serve.

SERVES 6	
Per Serving:	
Calories	109
Fat	7g
Sodium	467mg
Carbohydrates	7g
Fiber	3g
Sugar	2g
Protein	5g

Crispy Prosciutto-Wrapped Asparagus

SERVES 4	
Per Serving:	
Calories	111
Fat	5g
Sodium	924mg
Carbohydrates	4g
Fiber	2g
Sugar	2g
Protein	12g

This elegant side dish is simple to make, and it can be assembled ahead of time and refrigerated until ready to bake.

1 pound asparagus, trimmed

5 ounces thinly sliced prosciutto

1 Preheat oven to 450°F. Line a baking sheet with foil.
2 Wrap each asparagus spear in prosciutto and place on prepared baking sheet.
3 Bake for 10 minutes, flipping halfway.
4 Remove from oven and serve.

Creamy Dijon Dressing with a Kick

MAKES 1 CUP	
Per Serving (2 tablespoons):	
Calories	24
Fat	1g
Sodium	166mg
Carbohydrates	2g
Fiber	0g
Sugar	2g
Protein	2g

This spicy dressing is creamy and low in fat—thanks to plain yogurt instead of mayonnaise.

1 cup low-fat plain yogurt

3 tablespoons Dijon mustard

2 teaspoons sriracha sauce

Combine all ingredients in a small bowl and mix well. Serve immediately or refrigerate for up to 1 week.

CHAPTER 11

Appetizers and Snacks

Healthy Taco Dip

SERVES 12

Per Serving:

Calories	114
Fat	8g
Sodium	513mg
Carbohydrates	5g
Fiber	1g
Sugar	3g
Protein	5g

Traditional taco dip is typically loaded with cheese, calories, and lots and lots of fat. Serve this "skinny" version of a crowd-pleasing favorite with tortilla chips, pita chips, crackers, or crudités.

8 ounces reduced-fat cream cheese

8 ounces reduced-fat sour cream

1 (16-ounce) jar mild salsa

2 tablespoons taco seasoning

1 cup shredded reduced-fat Cheddar cheese

2 scallions, chopped

1 Preheat oven to 375°F.
2 In a large bowl, combine cream cheese, sour cream, salsa, and taco seasoning; mix well.
3 Spread the mixture on the bottom of a 9" square baking dish. Top with cheese.
4 Bake for 25–30 minutes until cheese is fully melted.
5 Remove from oven and top with scallions. Serve warm.

Prosciutto and Goat Cheese Jalapeño Poppers

SERVES 12

Per Serving:

Calories	78
Fat	5g
Sodium	156mg
Carbohydrates	2g
Fiber	0g
Sugar	1g
Protein	6g

Salty prosciutto and creamy goat cheese are tucked into a roasted jalapeño to make a super simple flavor bomb.

12 small jalapeño peppers

1½ cups crumbled goat cheese

8 ounces prosciutto, thinly sliced into 24 pieces

1 Preheat oven to 400°F. Line a large baking sheet with parchment paper.
2 Cut jalapeños in half lengthwise and scoop out the seeds. Stuff each half with about 1 tablespoon goat cheese.
3 Wrap each half with prosciutto and place on the prepared baking sheet.
4 Bake for 15–17 minutes until the prosciutto is crispy and cheese is lightly browned. Cool 5 minutes before serving.

Edamame Guacamole

This dip is loaded with fresh ingredients and plenty of flavor as well as healthy fats and some protein. It makes a healthy afternoon snack served with raw vegetables or crackers as well as a crowd-pleasing appetizer at parties.

1 large ripe avocado, peeled and pitted

1 cup shelled edamame

1½ tablespoons lime juice

2 teaspoons minced garlic

½ cup chopped fresh cilantro

½ cup chopped tomato

¼ cup chopped onion

½ teaspoon salt

¼ teaspoon ground black pepper

1 Combine all ingredients in a food processor until smooth.
2 Refrigerate at least 2 hours before serving.

A VEGAN PROTEIN FAVORITE

A cup of cooked edamame has about 18 grams of protein. Unlike most plant proteins, edamame is considered a whole protein source—it provides all the essential amino acids your body needs.

Creamy Spinach Dip

This lower-fat alternative to a traditional spinach dip makes a great snack and can be served with crackers, celery, or toasted bread. It's quick and easy to prepare, making it a great last-minute appetizer that feels anything but last-minute.

1 (10-ounce) package frozen spinach, thawed and drained

½ cup light sour cream

5 tablespoons light mayonnaise

⅓ cup grated Parmesan cheese

1 clove garlic, peeled and minced

1 cup shredded Monterey jack cheese

2 teaspoons chopped fresh parsley

1 Preheat oven to 375°F.

2 Combine all ingredients in a medium bowl, mixing well.

3 Transfer to a 9" × 9" baking dish and bake 20–25 minutes until cheese is completely melted.

4 Remove from oven and sprinkle with parsley before serving.

SERVES 10	
Per Serving:	
Calories	82
Fat	6g
Sodium	207mg
Carbohydrates	2g
Fiber	0g
Sugar	1g
Protein	5g

A CONVENIENT NUTRIENT BOOST

Spinach is one of the healthiest vegetables you can eat, and it's very mild in flavor. You can add spinach to nearly anything for an added nutrient boost without negatively affecting the taste. It's best to buy spinach fresh whenever possible. Frozen spinach can add significant moisture to a meal as it thaws, throwing off your recipe and food texture.

Baked Pesto and Parmesan Hummus

SERVES 4

Per Serving:

Calories	317
Fat	23g
Sodium	816mg
Carbohydrates	18g
Fiber	8g
Sugar	4g
Protein	10g

Bursting with fresh basil flavor, garlicky goodness, and cheese, this hummus is rich, smooth, and satisfying. Pair with vegetable crudités, crackers, or pita chips. It also makes a great sandwich spread.

2 cups hummus

2 tablespoons pesto

¼ cup grated Parmesan cheese

1 Preheat oven to 400°F.

2 In a medium bowl, combine hummus and pesto. Transfer mixture to a small (4-cup) baking dish. Smooth with a spatula. Sprinkle with cheese.

3 Bake for 15–20 minutes or until fully heated through. Serve immediately.

Peanut Butter and Banana Roll-Ups

MAKES 12 ROLL-UPS

Per Serving (2 roll-ups):

Calories	76
Fat	3g
Sodium	69mg
Carbohydrates	10g
Fiber	1g
Sugar	4g
Protein	2g

Peanut butter and banana combine to make a healthy snack that's loved by kids as well as adults. Make these sweet, creamy, and satisfying roll-ups for a quick snack or breakfast. Or wrap one up and tuck it into a lunch box.

2 (8") whole-wheat flour tortillas

¼ cup creamy peanut butter

1 tablespoon honey

1 teaspoon ground cinnamon

2 medium bananas, peeled

1 Place tortillas on a flat work space. Spread peanut butter evenly over each tortilla. Drizzle honey over peanut butter and sprinkle with cinnamon.

2 Place a banana at one end of a tortilla and roll it up into a cylinder. Cut into six slices. Repeat with the remaining tortilla and banana. Serve immediately.

Not-a-Million-Calories Maple Granola

This "granola" recipe is similar to the traditional granola that we all know and love, but it's not loaded with calories or too much sugar.

1 cup Cheerios cereal

½ cup quick-cooking oats

2 tablespoons sliced almonds

¼ teaspoon ground cinnamon

1 tablespoon coconut oil, melted

1 tablespoon honey

2 teaspoons maple extract

1 Preheat oven to 250°F. Line a baking sheet with parchment paper. In a large bowl, combine Cheerios, oats, almonds, and cinnamon.

2 In a small bowl, combine coconut oil, honey, and maple extract. Pour over cereal mixture and stir until cereal mixture is coated with oil mixture.

3 Transfer to the prepared baking sheet and spread out evenly. Bake for 25 minutes, or until cereal starts to brown.

4 Remove from oven and cool on the baking sheet for 10 minutes.

5 Serve immediately or store in an airtight container at room temperature for up to 1 week.

SERVES 2	
Per Serving:	
Calories	140
Fat	6g
Sodium	75mg
Carbohydrates	20g
Fiber	2g
Sugar	8g
Protein	2g

CHOOSE SNACKS WISELY

It's easy to snack on carb-rich foods, especially when you're on the go. Try to include at least 10 grams of protein in your snacks to increase your daily total.

Prosciutto-Wrapped Cantaloupe with Balsamic Glaze

Prosciutto-wrapped cantaloupe is simple, flavorful, and just perfect for easy entertaining on hot summer nights. It also makes a satisfying afternoon snack.

½ medium cantaloupe, seeded, peeled, and cut into ¼" slices

6 ounces prosciutto, thinly sliced

2 tablespoons balsamic glaze

1 Gently wrap cantaloupe slices with prosciutto, then drizzle with balsamic glaze.

2 Serve immediately.

HEALTHY EATING IS NOT BLACK AND WHITE

Counting macros gives you the freedom to enjoy any food that you want as long as you balance the rest of your choices. But if you don't balance those choices perfectly, it's not the end of the world. Macros are not the end all, be all of what you should eat or not eat. They're simply a guide to help you make more informed choices and help you become more aware of what foods work and don't work for you. Tracking macros should be a helpful tool, not something that stresses you out and controls your life.

Mixed-Berry Protein Muffins

MAKES 12 MUFFINS

Per Serving (1 muffin):

Calories	126
Fat	3g
Sodium	69mg
Carbohydrates	20g
Fiber	3g
Sugar	6g
Protein	5g

SUPER BERRIES

There's so much to love about berries. They're packed with fiber, vitamin C, and anti-inflammatory antioxidants. Frozen berries are a convenient and affordable way to get all of the nutritional benefits year-round.

When it comes to health, not all muffins are created equal. Many are loaded with sugar and leave you hungry a short while later. These fruity muffins are packed with nutrients as well as protein, so you'll feel great about your choice. Pair one with a smoothie, piece of fruit, or cup of coffee, and you're good to go!

1 medium banana, peeled and mashed

2 large eggs

¼ cup maple syrup

½ cup unsweetened almond milk

1 tablespoon melted coconut oil

2½ cups quick-cooking oats

¼ cup vanilla protein powder

1 teaspoon ground cinnamon

1 teaspoon baking powder

¼ teaspoon salt

1½ cups frozen mixed berries (strawberries, blackberries, blueberries, and raspberries), thawed

1 Preheat oven to 350°F. Spray a twelve-cup muffin tin with non-stick cooking spray.

2 In a large bowl, combine banana, eggs, maple syrup, almond milk, and coconut oil. Mix well. Add oats, protein powder, cinnamon, baking powder, and salt. Stir until well combined.

3 Carefully fold in berries. Spoon batter into the prepared muffin tin and bake for 18–20 minutes.

4 Cool muffins in the tin for 5 minutes, then turn muffins out onto a wire rack and cool completely before serving.

Protein Pizza "Muffins"

These eat-with-one-hand muffins make snack time easy. They're low in carbs and packed with protein for a fast, filling snack without the afternoon sugar rush. Make a large batch and keep them in the refrigerator for up to 5 days, so they're ready to grab and go whenever you want pizza flavor without the pizza calories.

18 slices turkey pepperoni, chopped

9 large eggs

2 cloves garlic, peeled and minced

1 cup chopped sun-dried tomatoes

3 teaspoons Italian seasoning

1 teaspoon onion powder

½ teaspoon salt

1 Preheat oven to 400°F. Spray a twelve-cup muffin tin with non-stick cooking spray.
2 In a large bowl, whisk together all ingredients.
3 Spoon mixture into the muffin tin, filling each cup three-quarters full. Bake 15 minutes or until muffins are lightly browned.
4 Remove from oven, allow to cool 5 minutes, and serve.

MAKES 12 MUFFINS	
Per Serving (1 muffin):	
Calories	70
Fat	4g
Sodium	213mg
Carbohydrates	3g
Fiber	1g
Sugar	2g
Protein	6g

Cauliflower Toast

THINK OUTSIDE THE BOX WITH SNACKS

Try eating a smaller portion of your lunch or dinner as a snack. That way, you're more likely to nail your macro goals instead of relying on traditional snacks that are typically loaded with carbs and fat.

Cauliflower Toast is a great way to replace the bread in your diet. It's easy to make, and you can save the leftovers in the refrigerator for several days. Add your favorite toppings and enjoy it as a snack or as part of any meal of the day.

1 pound (about 5 cups) cauliflower florets

1 tablespoon olive oil

1 large egg, beaten

1 cup shredded Cheddar cheese

¼ teaspoon garlic salt

½ teaspoon salt

¼ teaspoon ground black pepper

1. Preheat oven to 425°F. Line a baking sheet with parchment paper.
2. Place cauliflower in a food processor and pulse until the mixture resembles rice.
3. Heat olive oil in a large skillet over medium heat. Add cauliflower rice and sauté for 5 minutes.
4. Remove from heat and set aside for 5 minutes to cool slightly. Transfer cauliflower to a clean kitchen towel and wring out excess moisture.
5. Place cauliflower rice in a large bowl. Add egg, cheese, garlic salt, salt, and pepper. Mix to combine.
6. Divide cauliflower mixture into eight even portions and spoon onto the prepared baking sheet. Form the mixture into ½"-thick squares.
7. Bake for 15 minutes. Remove from the oven and flip. Bake for an additional 8–10 minutes or until lightly browned and crispy.
8. Serve immediately or refrigerate for up to 3 days.

Turkey Apricot Roll-Ups

Keep sliced deli turkey on hand for a go-to protein source whenever you need it. These roll-ups are delicious and super easy to put together on a busy afternoon when you've got little time to spare.

1 tablespoon apricot preserves

1 tablespoon Dijon mustard

6 (1-ounce) slices deli roasted turkey

1   Combine preserves and mustard in a small bowl. Mix well.

2   Spread turkey slices on a flat work space. Spoon about 1 teaspoon preserves mixture onto each slice of turkey and spread evenly. Roll turkey into cylinders. Serve immediately.

SERVES 6	
Per Serving:	
Calories	26
Fat	0g
Sodium	158mg
Carbohydrates	3g
Fiber	0g
Sugar	2g
Protein	3g

Ham and Swiss Rice Cakes

Rice cakes are versatile, especially when it comes to making a quick and satisfying open-faced sandwich. These ones are macro-friendly with a balanced ratio of protein, carbs, and fat—guaranteed to keep you full for hours.

2 (.75-ounce) wedges creamy Swiss spreadable cheese

2 plain salted rice cakes

2 teaspoons honey mustard

2 ounces sliced deli ham

1   Spread one wedge of cheese on each rice cake. Top with honey mustard, then deli ham.

2   Serve immediately.

SERVES 1	
Per Serving:	
Calories	210
Fat	9g
Sodium	840mg
Carbohydrates	19g
Fiber	0g
Sugar	4g
Protein	14g

Sweet Potato Baked Egg

A sweet potato is hollowed out to make the perfect cavity for baked eggs. Full of protein and healthy fats, this snack will fill you up and keep you satisfied all afternoon long.

1 medium sweet potato

1 teaspoon extra-virgin olive oil

⅛ teaspoon salt

2 large eggs

1 Preheat oven to 425°F and line a baking sheet with parchment paper.

2 Slice sweet potato in half lengthwise and place cut side down on the prepared baking sheet. Brush with oil and sprinkle with salt. Bake for 30 minutes or until fork-tender.

3 Remove sweet potato halves from the oven and set aside to cool for 5–10 minutes until cool enough to handle. Use a spoon to scoop out some of the flesh from each half of the sweet potato to make room for the egg. Reserve scooped out sweet potato for another use.

4 Crack 1 egg into each hole and return sweet potato halves to the oven for 10–15 minutes. Bake for less time if you like your eggs runny, and bake longer if you like them firmer.

5 Remove from oven and serve immediately.

SERVES 1	
Per Serving:	
Calories	317
Fat	17g
Sodium	450mg
Carbohydrates	24g
Fiber	4g
Sugar	7g
Protein	16g

FEAR NOT THE EGG

Because egg yolks are high in cholesterol, many people believe that consuming eggs increases bad cholesterol. This is simply not true. Egg yolks contain cholesterol, but some cholesterol is necessary for proper hormonal functioning. The egg yolks are also the most nutritious part of the egg, containing many other beneficial nutrients your body will use.

Tuna Cucumber Bites

Here's a fun variation on protein-packed tuna salad. These bites are easy to make and customizable with your favorite spices, herbs, and toppings.

1 (5-ounce) can tuna, drained and flaked

1 tablespoon mayonnaise

1 tablespoon Dijon mustard

1 medium cucumber, sliced into rounds

1 Combine tuna, mayonnaise, and mustard in a small bowl. Mix together.

2 Place cucumber slices on a platter. Top each slice with a spoonful of the tuna mixture. Serve immediately.

Roasted Carrot Bites

These Roasted Carrot Bites satisfy a salty craving without loads of fat, calories, or artificial ingredients. While they're best enjoyed fresh out of the oven, they can be reheated in a toaster oven or eaten cold right out of the refrigerator for a quick snack.

1½ pounds carrots, peeled and cut into ¼" slices

1 tablespoon olive oil

½ teaspoon salt

1 Preheat oven to 425°F.

2 Combine carrots, oil, and salt in an oven-safe baking dish. Bake for 40–45 minutes, tossing carrots midway through cooking.

3 Turn off oven and leave carrots in the oven until they cool, about 90 minutes to 2 hours.

4 Remove from oven and serve immediately or refrigerate for up to 5 days.

Protein Snack Box

Be prepared with a nutritious and well-balanced snack box for when the afternoon munchies hit. Assemble a few of these at the beginning of the week to keep your snack habits on point. It's a great way to ensure that you're meeting your protein goals for the day.

3 ounces sliced deli turkey breast

½ large green bell pepper, seeded and sliced

½ cup cherry tomatoes

1 ounce cubed or sliced Cheddar cheese

1 large hard-cooked egg

SERVES 1	
Per Serving:	
Calories	289
Fat	15g
Sodium	650mg
Carbohydrates	9g
Fiber	2g
Sugar	7g
Protein	30g

1 Pile turkey slices in a stack and roll up to form a cylinder. Cut the cylinder crosswise into four pieces. Place turkey rolls in a glass storage container.

2 Arrange bell pepper slices, cherry tomatoes, cheese, and egg in the container. Cover and refrigerate for up to 3 days.

Lemon Coconut Protein Balls

These chewy bites make a great protein-packed sweet treat. Keep a batch in the refrigerator for a nutritious dessert or snack.

½ cup vanilla or coconut protein powder

½ cup melted coconut oil

¾ cup unsweetened shredded coconut

2 tablespoons honey

2 tablespoons lemon juice

½ teaspoon grated lemon zest

2 tablespoons coconut flour

MAKES 12 BALLS	
Per Serving (1 ball):	
Calories	185
Fat	15g
Sodium	14mg
Carbohydrates	7g
Fiber	2g
Sugar	3g
Protein	5g

1 Line a large baking sheet with parchment paper.

2 Combine all ingredients in a large bowl. If the mixture is too crumbly, add water, 1 teaspoon at a time, until it holds together when squeezed.

3 Form the batter into 1" balls and place on the prepared baking sheet. Refrigerate for at least 1 hour. Serve immediately or refrigerate for up to 1 week in a sealed container.

Broccoli and Cheese Balls

MAKES 24 BALLS

Per Serving (2 balls):

Calories	62
Fat	4g
Sodium	312mg
Carbohydrates	2g
Fiber	2g
Sugar	0g
Protein	4g

PACK READY-TO-GO SNACKS

There are no excuses for veering off your plan when you can grab a healthy snack that's been made ahead of time and already packed. In addition to Broccoli and Cheese Balls, try the Protein Snack Box, Peanut Butter Protein Balls, and Not-a-Million-Calories Maple Granola (see recipes in this chapter). Having one or two of these packed in single serving amounts will help you keep on track.

Make a batch of these vegetable balls on your food prep day and store them in an airtight container in the refrigerator for a quick nutrient-dense snack or addition to a meal.

4 cups frozen broccoli florets, defrosted and excess water removed

½ cup almond flour

¾ cup grated Parmesan cheese

¼ cup shredded sharp Cheddar cheese

2 teaspoons minced garlic

1 teaspoon salt

½ teaspoon ground black pepper

½ teaspoon dried parsley

1 large egg

1 Preheat oven to 350°F. Line a large baking sheet with parchment paper.

2 In a large bowl, mash broccoli using a potato masher. Add almond flour, Parmesan, Cheddar, garlic, salt, pepper, parsley, and egg to the bowl. Stir to combine well.

3 Form mixture into twenty-four balls and arrange them on the prepared baking sheet.

4 Bake for 20–25 minutes until balls turn a golden brown. Remove from oven and allow to cool for 5 minutes before serving.

Sunbutter Falafel Balls

Indulge in a craving for falafel with these not-fried snacks. Try using peanut butter or another favorite nut butter instead of sunbutter.

½ cup rolled oats

1 teaspoon baking powder

1 (14-ounce) can chickpeas, drained and rinsed

½ cup canned pumpkin purée

⅓ cup sunbutter

2 tablespoons lemon juice

2 teaspoons ground cumin

2 teaspoons onion powder

½ teaspoon ground cinnamon

½ teaspoon salt

1 Preheat oven to 350°F. Line a baking sheet with parchment paper.

2 Place oats and baking powder in a food processor. Pulse until oats form a coarse flour.

3 Add chickpeas, pumpkin, sunbutter, lemon juice, cumin, onion powder, cinnamon, and salt. Process to combine, scraping down the sides with a spatula. If the mixture is too crumbly, add water, 1 teaspoon at a time, until it holds together when squeezed.

4 Form the batter into 1½" balls and place on the prepared baking sheet. The batter should make eighteen balls.

5 Bake for 20–25 minutes until lightly browned.

6 Remove from oven and cool on a wire rack before serving, or refrigerate for up to 5 days.

MAKES 18 BALLS

Per Serving (1 ball):

Calories	56
Fat	3g
Sodium	133mg
Carbohydrates	6g
Fiber	2g
Sugar	1g
Protein	1g

SUNFLOWER BUTTER VERSUS PEANUT BUTTER

Sunflower butter is made from nutrient-dense sunflower seeds, which are a great source of protein, healthy fats, vitamin E, and magnesium. Sunflower butter actually contains one-third less saturated fat and twice as much fiber compared to most peanut butter.

Peanut Butter Protein Balls

MAKES 12 BALLS

Per Serving (1 ball):

Calories	107
Fat	5g
Sodium	55mg
Carbohydrates	8g
Fiber	1g
Sugar	4g
Protein	7g

Protein snack balls are so easy to make, and it doesn't take more than 10 minutes to whip up a big batch of them. Make a batch on Sunday and then snack on them all week long. They're a great before- and after-workout snack as well as a sweet treat after dinner.

½ cup smooth peanut butter

½ cup rolled oats

½ cup vanilla protein powder

2 tablespoons honey

1 Line a large baking sheet with parchment paper.

2 Combine all ingredients in a large bowl. If the mixture is too crumbly, add water, 1 teaspoon at a time, until it holds together when squeezed.

3 Form the batter into 1" balls and place on the prepared baking sheet. Place baking sheet in the refrigerator and chill for at least 1 hour. Remove from the refrigerator and serve immediately or refrigerate for up to 1 week in a sealed container.

Chocolate Chip Protein Balls

These no-bake protein balls taste just like little bites of chocolate chip cookie dough, but they're portion-controlled and macro-friendly. They're also customizable—make them with dark or milk chocolate, butterscotch or peanut butter chips, or dried cranberries or cherries. You can also use any flavor protein powder you like.

½ cup almond flour

¾ cup rolled oats

½ cup vanilla protein powder

¼ cup melted coconut oil

¼ cup maple syrup

¼ cup mini chocolate chips

1 teaspoon vanilla extract

½ teaspoon salt

1 Line a large baking sheet with parchment paper.

2 Combine all ingredients in a large bowl. If the mixture is too crumbly, add water, 1 teaspoon at a time, until it holds together when squeezed.

3 Form the batter into twelve balls and place them on the prepared baking sheet. Place baking sheet in the refrigerator and chill for at least 1 hour. Remove from the refrigerator and serve immediately or refrigerate for up to 1 week in a sealed container.

MAKES 12 BALLS

Per Serving (1 ball):

Calories	135
Fat	7g
Sodium	99mg
Carbohydrates	14g
Fiber	1g
Sugar	7g
Protein	4g

REASONS TO EAT OATS

Oats are high in the soluble fiber beta-glucan, which helps reduce cholesterol and blood sugar levels, promotes healthy gut bacteria, and increases feelings of fullness.

Chocolate Peanut Butter Crunch Balls

MAKES 4 BALLS

Per Serving (1 ball):

Calories	75
Fat	4g
Sodium	88mg
Carbohydrates	9g
Fiber	0g
Sugar	5g
Protein	1g

These bite-sized treats taste almost exactly like chocolate sugar wafer cookies. But, thankfully, the recipe makes only four balls, so if you just happen to eat the entire batch, you won't wreck your plan for the day.

1 plain rice cake

1 tablespoon peanut butter

1 tablespoon chocolate hazelnut spread

1 tablespoon honey

1 tablespoon chocolate protein powder

⅛ teaspoon salt

1 Crush rice cake into crumbs and place the crumbs in a medium bowl. Add peanut butter, hazelnut spread, honey, protein powder, and salt. Mix well.

2 Divide batter into four portions and roll each portion into a ball.

3 Serve immediately or refrigerate for up to 1 week.

Three-Minute Peanut Butter Cookie

SERVES 1

Per Serving:

Calories	253
Fat	16g
Sodium	130mg
Carbohydrates	18g
Fiber	2g
Sugar	13g
Protein	10g

When you want a sweet and satisfying treat quickly, how about a single-serving cookie that can be made in just 3 minutes? This peanut butter cookie is delicious and macro-friendly with a well-balanced mix of protein, carbohydrates, and fat.

2 tablespoons creamy peanut butter

1 tablespoon light brown sugar

1 tablespoon liquid egg whites

¼ teaspoon baking powder

1 Coat a microwave-safe bowl with nonstick cooking spray.

2 Combine all ingredients in the prepared bowl and mix well. Scrape the batter down from the sides of the bowl and flatten the dough into a round cookie shape at the bottom of the bowl.

3 Microwave on high for 1 minute.

4 Remove from microwave and cool 5 minutes. Remove cookie from the bowl and serve.

The Best Peanut Butter and Banana Smoothie

Just about everyone has a favorite peanut butter and banana smoothie, but this one is the best for after a workout. It's loaded with peanut butter to help you recover and keep you satisfied. Replace the vanilla almond milk with chocolate almond milk for a delicious peanut butter and chocolate version.

1 medium banana, peeled and frozen

2 tablespoons smooth peanut butter

1¼ cups vanilla almond milk

¼ cup vanilla protein powder

½ teaspoon vanilla extract

¼ teaspoon ground cinnamon

Combine all ingredients in a blender and process until smooth. Pour into a tall glass and serve immediately.

SERVES 1	
Per Serving:	
Calories	451
Fat	19g
Sodium	389mg
Carbohydrates	38g
Fiber	6g
Sugar	20g
Protein	34g

Green Collagen Smoothie

Don't let the name of this smoothie scare you off. It provides healthy fats, vitamin-rich greens, and just the right amount of sweetness from the banana. You can replace the collagen powder with protein powder instead.

2 cups baby spinach

½ medium avocado, peeled and pitted

½ medium banana, peeled and frozen

¼ cup collagen powder

1 cup unsweetened almond milk

Combine all ingredients in a blender and process until smooth. Pour into a tall glass and serve immediately.

SERVES 1	
Per Serving:	
Calories	356
Fat	13g
Sodium	611mg
Carbohydrates	25g
Fiber	9g
Sugar	10g
Protein	37g

Creamsicle Smoothie

SERVES 1	
Per Serving:	
Calories	98
Fat	2g
Sodium	180mg
Carbohydrates	18g
Fiber	2g
Sugar	18g
Protein	2g

JUST ADD VEGETABLES

Smoothies and soups are awesome ways to incorporate vegetables into your diet, especially if you're not the biggest fan of all things green. Add frozen chopped spinach into a smoothie and non-starchy vegetables to a soup for an easy, tasty way to get an extra hit of nutrition while filling up.

This smoothie tastes just like the childhood ice cream treat without all of the sugar and with a heck of a lot more good-for-you nutrients!

1 cup diced frozen peaches
½ cup orange juice
¾ cup vanilla almond milk

Combine all ingredients in a blender and process until smooth. Pour into a tall glass and serve immediately.

Pick-Me-Up Smoothie

SERVES 1

Per Serving:

Calories	294
Fat	13g
Sodium	471mg
Carbohydrates	38g
Fiber	7g
Sugar	21g
Protein	7g

This smoothie has a wonderful, slightly sweet almond and coffee flavor. It almost tastes like dessert, but you can enjoy it guilt-free whenever you need a natural boost of energy.

1 medium banana, peeled and frozen

1 tablespoon creamy almond butter

1 cup unsweetened almond milk

1 ounce espresso or strong coffee

1 teaspoon honey

½ teaspoon vanilla extract

½ teaspoon ground cinnamon

3 ice cubes

Combine all ingredients in a blender and process until smooth. Pour into a tall glass and serve immediately.

Gingerbread Smoothie

SERVES 1

Per Serving:

Calories	195
Fat	4g
Sodium	214mg
Carbohydrates	21g
Fiber	6g
Sugar	13g
Protein	19g

This smoothie tastes just like gingerbread, but much more refreshing.

1 cup unsweetened vanilla almond milk

1 medium pear, peeled, cored, and diced

¼ cup vanilla protein powder

¼ teaspoon ground cinnamon

¼ teaspoon ground ginger

Combine all ingredients in a blender and process until smooth. Pour into a tall glass and serve immediately.

CHAPTER 12

Desserts

Chocolate-Covered Banana Bites with Sprinkles

SERVES 4	
Per Serving:	
Calories	329
Fat	17g
Sodium	2mg
Carbohydrates	43g
Fiber	4g
Sugar	32g
Protein	2g

Here's the perfect summer treat that's quick to prepare, and easy to grab and enjoy. They might just be better than ice cream! You can skip the sprinkles and dip the bites in finely chopped nuts or shredded coconut.

2 medium bananas, peeled and cut into ½" slices
4 ounces dark chocolate
½ cup rainbow sprinkles

1 Line a baking sheet with parchment paper.
2 Place bananas on the prepared baking sheet. Freeze at least 2 hours until firm.
3 Place chocolate in a microwave-safe bowl and microwave 2 minutes or until almost completely melted. Stir until smooth.
4 Place sprinkles on a small saucer or plate.
5 Remove banana slices from freezer. Dip them in melted chocolate to cover, then press them into the sprinkles. Return slices to the baking sheet. Freeze at least 15 minutes before serving.

No-Bake Cookie Bites

With just a handful of basic ingredients, you can whip up a quick and healthy alternative to chocolate chip cookies without turning on your oven. These No-Bake Cookie Bites come together effortlessly and are sure to please!

1 cup rolled oats

1 cup raw almonds

10 Medjool dates, pitted

½ cup water

¼ cup semisweet chocolate chips

1 Line a baking sheet with parchment paper.
2 Blend oats and almonds in a food processor until finely ground. Add dates and continue to process until mixed well.
3 With the processor running, slowly add water until the mixture forms a thick dough. Transfer mixture to a medium bowl and stir in chocolate chips.
4 Roll the dough into eight balls, place on the prepared baking sheet, and refrigerate at least 1 hour before serving.

MAKES 8 COOKIES	
Per Serving (1 cookie):	
Calories	241
Fat	9g
Sodium	0mg
Carbohydrates	36g
Fiber	6g
Sugar	25g
Protein	4g

Cranberry Protein Cookies

Cookies don't have to be a guilty treat. These hearty cookies are made from wholesome ingredients with a punch of protein. Banana and dried cranberries add just the right amount of natural sugar without being overly sweet.

1 medium banana, peeled and mashed

¼ cup vanilla protein powder

1 cup rolled oats

1 cup almond butter

¼ cup unsweetened dried cranberries

½ teaspoon ground cinnamon

1 Preheat oven to 350°F and line a baking sheet with parchment paper.

2 In a medium bowl, mix banana and protein powder. Stir in oats, almond butter, dried cranberries, and cinnamon.

3 Roll batter into eight balls and place them on the prepared baking sheet. Flatten balls slightly.

4 Bake for 20 minutes or until lightly browned.

5 Remove from oven, allow to cool slightly, and serve.

MAKES 8 COOKIES

Per Serving (1 cookie):

Calories	301
Fat	17g
Sodium	22mg
Carbohydrates	22g
Fiber	5g
Sugar	4g
Protein	15g

THE OFTEN-OVERLOOKED BERRY

Did you know cranberries are actually higher in antioxidants than most other fruits and berries? They're lower in sugar than many other fruits, with only 4 grams of natural sugar per cup. Cranberries are also loaded with a variety of health benefits from improving digestion and boosting your immune system to preventing gum disease and urinary tract infections.

Cinnamon Pecan Bites

These sweet addictive bites provide a great source of healthy fats and fiber for sustained satisfaction and energy without wrecking your macro goals for the day.

10 large pitted dates, soaked in water for 15 minutes and drained

2 cups raw pecans

2 teaspoons ground cinnamon

1 Preheat oven to 350°F. Line a baking sheet with parchment paper.
2 Combine all ingredients in a food processor and pulse until smooth.
3 Shape dough into small balls and place 1" apart on the prepared baking sheet.
4 Bake 10–12 minutes. Transfer to a wire rack and allow to cool before serving.

Maple Peanut Butter Protein Cookies

The protein and fat in this recipe will keep you full without adding a ton of carbohydrates or sugar. It's perfect for your sweet tooth on low-carb days.

1 cup natural peanut butter

2 large egg whites

¼ cup vanilla protein powder

¼ cup light brown sugar

1 teaspoon maple extract

1 teaspoon ground cinnamon

1 Preheat oven to 350°F. Spray a baking sheet with nonstick cooking spray.
2 Place all ingredients in a medium bowl and stir to combine.
3 Scoop dough into ten cookies and spread out on the prepared baking sheet, leaving 1" between cookies.
4 Bake for 10 minutes. Transfer cookies to a wire rack to cool completely.

Secret Ingredient Double Chocolate Fudge Cookies

Loaded with extra nutrients and fiber, these cookies are chocolatey, rich, not overly sweet, and very moist, just like a fudgy brownie. They're gluten- and egg-free, so just about anyone with food sensitivities can enjoy them too. Kids and adults alike will love these cookies—just don't tell them about the secret ingredient inside!

1 (15-ounce) can kidney beans, drained and rinsed

½ cup creamy peanut butter

½ cup honey

2 tablespoons unsweetened cocoa powder

1 teaspoon vanilla extract

1 teaspoon baking powder

¼ teaspoon salt

⅔ cup dark chocolate chips

1 Preheat oven to 375°F. Line a baking sheet with parchment paper or a silicone mat.

2 Place beans, peanut butter, honey, cocoa powder, vanilla extract, baking powder, and salt in a food processor and process until smooth. Scrape down the sides with a spatula and process again until a smooth dough-like consistency forms.

3 Transfer mixture to a large bowl and stir in chocolate chips.

4 Scoop batter into 1½" disks on the prepared baking sheet.

5 Bake for 10–12 minutes until almost set. Cool cookies 1 minute on the baking sheet, then transfer to a wire rack to cool completely.

MAKES 18 COOKIES

Per Serving (1 cookie):

Calories	161
Fat	7g
Sodium	127mg
Carbohydrates	21g
Fiber	3g
Sugar	17g
Protein	4g

HOW TO TRACK MACROS ON A BUSY DAY

If you're finding it hard to find time to track everything you eat, track only the macro that you have the toughest time hitting. For many people, it's protein, so pay attention to only that one and do your best to make healthy decisions when it comes to carbs and fat. In the end, you just want your overall grams and calories to be within range of your goals for the day.

Almond Butter Collagen Cookies

MAKES 9 COOKIES

Per Serving (1 cookie):

Calories	133
Fat	7g
Sodium	53mg
Carbohydrates	10g
Fiber	2g
Sugar	1g
Protein	8g

BENEFITS OF COLLAGEN

Collagen powder has many health benefits, from relieving joint pain and preventing bone loss to improving skin health and boosting muscle mass. It contains 12 grams of protein per serving, so it's an easy way to hit your protein goals for the day. It's nearly flavorless and mixes right into hot and cold liquids, as well as foods, so you can add it to just about anything. It's a great alternative to protein powder if you're sensitive to whey or other allergens, like eggs or soy.

The combination of creamy almond butter (protein and fat), collagen (protein), flaxseed (protein, fat, and carbs) and brown sugar (carbs) makes a delicious, macro-balanced treat. If you don't have collagen powder, you can use any flavor protein powder instead.

1 tablespoon ground flaxseed

3 tablespoons water

½ cup creamy almond butter

¼ cup collagen powder

¼ cup light brown sugar

1 Preheat oven to 350°F. Line a baking sheet with parchment paper or a silicone mat.
2 Stir flaxseed and water together in a small bowl. Set aside for 5 minutes.
3 In a separate bowl, combine almond butter, collagen powder, and brown sugar. Stir in flaxseed mixture until fully combined.
4 Scoop batter into nine disks on the prepared baking sheet.
5 Bake for 14 minutes. Transfer cookies to a wire rack to cool completely before serving.

Tahini Chocolate Chip Cookies

Tahini is loaded with healthy fats. In fact, about 50 percent of the fat in tahini comes from monounsaturated fatty acids—the good kind—which means you can eat these cookies in confidence knowing they're checking off the right nutritional boxes.

½ cup tahini

2 tablespoons maple syrup

1 cup almond flour

2 tablespoons mini chocolate chips

½ teaspoon salt, divided

1 Preheat oven to 350°F. Line a baking sheet with parchment paper.

2 Combine tahini, maple syrup, almond flour, chocolate chips, and ¼ teaspoon salt in a medium mixing bowl. Stir until well combined.

3 Scoop out a heaping tablespoon of dough and roll it into a ball. Place it on the baking sheet and flatten with hand. Repeat with the remaining dough. Sprinkle cookies with the remaining ¼ teaspoon salt.

4 Bake for 10–12 minutes. Cool cookies on the baking sheet for 1 minute, then transfer to a wire rack to cool completely.

MAKES 8 COOKIES	
Per Serving (1 cookie):	
Calories	310
Fat	25g
Sodium	143mg
Carbohydrates	11g
Fiber	3g
Sugar	5g
Protein	10g

Edible Cookie Dough

SERVES 2	
Per Serving:	
Calories	262
Fat	18g
Sodium	195mg
Carbohydrates	18g
Fiber	3g
Sugar	13g
Protein	7g

This chocolate cookie dough is eggless and made for eating instead of baking. The taste and texture are almost like the real deal, but it's made from wholesome ingredients that can fit your macros.

2 tablespoons creamy almond butter

¼ cup almond flour

2 tablespoons semisweet chocolate chips

1 teaspoon vanilla extract

1 teaspoon honey

⅛ teaspoon salt

Combine all ingredients in a small bowl. Refrigerate for at least 30 minutes before serving.

Crispy Rice Protein Treats

SERVES 12	
Per Serving:	
Calories	100
Fat	3g
Sodium	75mg
Carbohydrates	15g
Fiber	0g
Sugar	8g
Protein	3g

These treats, made with muscle-building protein powder, marshmallows, and crispy rice cereal, are great for dessert or a post-workout snack.

3 tablespoons salted butter

16 regular-sized marshmallows

⅓ cup vanilla protein powder

2 cups crisped rice cereal

1 Line a small baking sheet or dinner plate with parchment paper.
2 In a large saucepan over medium-low heat, melt butter and marshmallows together. Using a wooden spoon, continuously stir to combine until melted and smooth, about 8–10 minutes.
3 Remove from heat and stir in protein powder. Slowly add cereal and stir until fully combined.
4 Pour batter onto the parchment paper and form into a 6" square.
5 Refrigerate for 30 minutes. Cut into twelve squares and serve.

Healthy Peanut Butter Protein Brownies

Stir up a bowl of brownie batter the next time you have a brownie craving. In seconds, you can be enjoying a warm, gooey, and downright delicious brownie.

½ cup chocolate protein powder

½ cup powdered peanut butter

¼ cup canned pumpkin purée

¼ cup liquid egg whites

2 tablespoons honey

2 tablespoons cocoa powder

1 tablespoon mini chocolate chips

4 teaspoons creamy peanut butter

SERVES 4	
Per Serving:	
Calories	382
Fat	15g
Sodium	449mg
Carbohydrates	29g
Fiber	9g
Sugar	13g
Protein	35g

1 Combine protein powder, powdered peanut butter, pumpkin, egg whites, honey, and cocoa powder in a medium bowl and stir to mix. Divide batter into four microwave-safe ramekins.

2 Sprinkle each with ¼ tablespoon chocolate chips and top with 1 teaspoon creamy peanut butter.

3 Microwave each ramekin separately for 35 seconds (longer or shorter depending on how gooey you like your brownies). Serve warm.

Low-Fat, High-Fiber Brownies

SERVES 20	
Per Serving:	
Calories	121
Fat	2g
Sodium	147mg
Carbohydrates	24g
Fiber	2g
Sugar	16g
Protein	2g

By replacing oil, whole eggs, and butter with a can of black beans, this recipe provides a high-fiber, low-fat treat. It's not exactly low on calories, but it's perfect for high-carb days when fat needs to stay low.

1 (15-ounce) can black beans, drained and rinsed

1 (18.3-ounce) package fudge brownie mix

1 Preheat oven to 350°F. Spray a 9" × 13" baking pan with nonstick cooking spray.

2 Blend beans in a food processor until smooth. Transfer to a large bowl.

3 Add brownie mix and stir until just combined.

4 Bake 22–25 minutes until a toothpick inserted in the center comes out clean. Cool brownies in the pan before cutting and serving.

No-Bake Pumpkin Protein Bars

These bars have a nice pumpkin pie flavor, a hint of sweetness, and a good protein-to-carb ratio, making them perfect for snacking or enjoying at the end of a busy day.

½ cup coconut flour

¼ cup vanilla protein powder

¾ teaspoon pumpkin pie spice

½ cup smooth almond butter

⅓ cup maple syrup

1 teaspoon vanilla extract

½ cup canned pumpkin purée

1 tablespoon unsweetened almond milk

½ cup semisweet chocolate chips

SERVES 8	
Per Serving:	
Calories	246
Fat	12g
Sodium	74mg
Carbohydrates	28g
Fiber	6g
Sugar	18g
Protein	7g

1 Line an 8" × 8" baking pan with parchment paper.

2 In a large bowl, combine coconut flour, protein powder, and pumpkin pie spice.

3 Place almond butter, maple syrup, and vanilla in a small saucepan. Heat over low heat, stirring constantly, until melted and combined, about 3 minutes.

4 Add almond butter mixture to the flour mixture and stir to combine. Add pumpkin and milk and stir until combined. Fold in chocolate chips. (The dough will be very thick.)

5 Transfer the dough to the prepared pan and press firmly with a spatula to pack the dough evenly across the pan. Refrigerate for at least 30 minutes.

6 Slice into eight bars and serve.

Chocolate-Covered Peanut Butter Protein Truffles

MAKES 6 TRUFFLES

Per Serving (1 truffle):

Calories	191
Fat	14g
Sodium	8mg
Carbohydrates	11g
Fiber	1g
Sugar	8g
Protein	6g

MIX UP YOUR NUT SOURCES

Nuts are one of the best natural sources of fat available, and they even contain a little protein. If you get tired of regular peanut butter, try switching up your nut butters. Almond butter, cashew butter, walnut butter, and even sunflower seed butter are all delicious and healthy options you can use for variety.

You'll want to make these truffles again and again. Customize them by switching the peanut butter with another favorite nut butter, trying a different flavor of protein powder and extract, varying the type of chocolate, or by coating them with sprinkles, cocoa powder, or chopped nuts.

3½ teaspoons coconut oil, divided
¼ cup vanilla protein powder
¼ cup smooth peanut butter
2 tablespoons light brown sugar
¼ teaspoon vanilla extract
¼ cup dark chocolate chips

1 Place 2 teaspoons coconut oil in a small microwave-safe bowl. Microwave on high for 30 seconds until melted. Stir in protein powder, peanut butter, brown sugar, and vanilla. Divide batter into six portions and roll each into a ball. Place balls on a plate and refrigerate for 2 hours until firm.

2 In a separate microwave-safe bowl, place chocolate chips and the remaining 1½ teaspoons coconut oil. Microwave on high in 30-second intervals until chocolate is almost completely melted. Stir until smooth.

3 Cover a plate or small tray with waxed paper.

4 Dip balls in melted chocolate and place them on the prepared plate. Refrigerate balls at least 1 hour before serving.

Almond Joy Protein Balls

This high-protein dessert tastes similar to the popular chocolate bar, but without all the sugar and artificial ingredients. This recipe works with a variety of protein powder flavors—chocolate, vanilla, or coconut—and turns out well every time.

4 large Medjool dates

¼ cup vanilla, chocolate, or coconut protein powder

2 tablespoons creamy almond butter

2 tablespoons shredded coconut

2 tablespoons semisweet chocolate chips

1 tablespoon coconut oil, melted

1 Line a baking sheet with parchment paper.

2 Combine all ingredients in a food processor and pulse until smooth.

3 Roll batter into eight balls and place on the prepared baking sheet. Refrigerate for at least 1 hour. Serve immediately or store balls in a covered container in the refrigerator.

MAKES 8 BALLS	
Per Serving (1 ball):	
Calories	116
Fat	5g
Sodium	20mg
Carbohydrates	14g
Fiber	2g
Sugar	11g
Protein	4g

Salted Dark Chocolate Dates

SERVES 12	
Per Serving:	
Calories	83
Fat	4g
Sodium	112mg
Carbohydrates	10g
Fiber	1g
Sugar	7g
Protein	2g

The combination of flavors, textures, and macros are perfect for when you crave a sweet bite. This recipe works with all kinds of nut and seed butters, so feel free to try it with your favorites.

12 large dates, pitted

¼ cup creamy almond butter

2½ ounces bittersweet chocolate, melted

½ teaspoon salt

1 Line a baking sheet with parchment paper.
2 Stuff each date with 2 teaspoons almond butter.
3 Dip a date halfway into melted chocolate and place on the prepared baking sheet. Sprinkle with salt. Repeat with remaining dates.
4 Refrigerate for 1–1½ hours or until chocolate is set.
5 Serve immediately or store in the refrigerator for up to 3 days.

Apple Cinnamon Dips

SERVES 2	
Per Serving:	
Calories	147
Fat	6g
Sodium	28mg
Carbohydrates	17g
Fiber	4g
Sugar	12g
Protein	6g

Apple and cinnamon are a flavor match made in heaven. These apple dips are perfect for a quick and clean dessert or an afternoon snack. Made with no added sugar, this treat will satisfy a sweet tooth.

½ cup low-fat plain Greek yogurt

2 tablespoons unsweetened shredded coconut

1 medium apple, cored and sliced

¼ teaspoon ground cinnamon

1 Line a baking sheet with parchment paper. Place yogurt and coconut into two small separate bowls.
2 Dip each apple slice in the yogurt and then coat with coconut. Place slices on the prepared baking sheet and sprinkle them with cinnamon.
3 Freeze for 10 minutes or until yogurt has hardened. Serve immediately.

Apple Crisp Bowl

Homemade apple crisp sure is delicious, but it's usually high in carbs and sugar. This healthier alternative provides a delicious, lower-calorie option for when you're craving a delicious apple treat.

¾ cup nonfat plain Greek yogurt

2 tablespoons unsweetened applesauce

1 medium apple, cored and diced

¼ teaspoon stevia

¼ teaspoon ground cinnamon

¼ teaspoon ground nutmeg

Mix all ingredients together in a small bowl and serve.

SERVES 1	
Per Serving:	
Calories	198
Fat	0g
Sodium	68mg
Carbohydrates	33g
Fiber	5g
Sugar	26g
Protein	17g

Warm Banana Pudding

If you want a tasty, creamy dessert you can enjoy guilt-free, make this in bulk and keep on hand for when that sweet tooth strikes.

1 medium banana, peeled and sliced

¼ cup vanilla protein powder

⅛ teaspoon ground cinnamon

1 Place banana in a microwave-safe bowl. Microwave on high for 45 seconds.

2 Remove from microwave and stir in protein powder and cinnamon. Mix until well combined. Serve immediately.

SERVES 1	
Per Serving:	
Calories	235
Fat	2g
Sodium	51mg
Carbohydrates	31g
Fiber	4g
Sugar	15g
Protein	24g

Almond and Coconut Chia Pudding

SERVES 1	
Per Serving:	
Calories	408
Fat	26g
Sodium	224mg
Carbohydrates	31g
Fiber	16g
Sugar	12g
Protein	13g

Chia seeds are packed with omega-3 fatty acids, fiber, and protein. Here, they're mixed with chocolate, coconut, and almonds to make a cool, creamy, and satisfying dessert.

2 tablespoons chia seeds

¾ cup almond milk

1 tablespoon creamy almond butter

1 tablespoon shredded coconut

1 tablespoon sliced almonds

½ tablespoon mini chocolate chips

1 teaspoon maple syrup

¼ teaspoon coconut extract

1 In a small bowl or container with a lid, mix together all ingredients until smooth.

2 Cover and refrigerate for at least 3 hours or up to overnight.

3 Serve cold.

Warm Chocolate Chip Cookie Bowl

You can have a warm, gooey chocolate chip cookie in minutes, guaranteed to satisfy the strongest of cravings.

½ medium banana, peeled and mashed

¼ cup almond flour

1 tablespoon creamy almond butter

½ teaspoon vanilla extract

¼ teaspoon salt

1 tablespoon semisweet chocolate chips

1 Combine banana, almond flour, almond butter, vanilla, and salt in a medium microwave-safe bowl. Stir until smooth.

2 Microwave on high for 1 minute. Remove from microwave and stir in chocolate chips. Serve immediately.

SERVES 1	
Per Serving:	
Calories	310
Fat	19g
Sodium	615mg
Carbohydrates	31g
Fiber	6g
Sugar	20g
Protein	7g

Protein Pudding

Creamy, cold, and loaded with protein, Protein Pudding is the ideal macro-friendly dessert treat you can enjoy with zero guilt. Play around with flavors of yogurt and protein powder to customize a decadent treat for yourself.

1 cup low-fat plain Greek yogurt

¼ cup vanilla protein powder

¼ teaspoon stevia

2 tablespoons unsweetened vanilla almond milk

In a medium bowl, mix together all ingredients until combined. Refrigerate for at least 1 hour before serving.

SERVES 2	
Per Serving:	
Calories	150
Fat	3g
Sodium	65mg
Carbohydrates	7g
Fiber	0g
Sugar	3g
Protein	24g

Chocolate Cherry Chia Pudding

SERVES 2	
Per Serving:	
Calories	285
Fat	14g
Sodium	286mg
Carbohydrates	25g
Fiber	14g
Sugar	7g
Protein	14g

CONSISTENCY > PERFECTION

Adjust your expectations for being "perfect" and give yourself some wiggle room with your macro goals. At the end of the day, even if you're 10 grams over or under, you're still doing okay. Just be sure to keep an eye on your overall calories and keep them as consistent as possible to see results.

This superfood treat is great for dessert or even breakfast. It's wonderfully sweet and high in protein.

¼ cup chia seeds

1 cup unsweetened almond milk

¼ cup chocolate protein powder

¾ cup fresh or frozen sweet cherries, pitted

1 tablespoon unsweetened shredded coconut

1 In a large bowl, combine chia seeds, almond milk, and protein powder. Mix well. Cover and refrigerate overnight. If using frozen cherries, place them in a separate covered container in the refrigerator to defrost overnight.

2 Remove from refrigerator and divide between two small bowls. Top with cherries and coconut. Serve cold.

Protein Cheesecake

SERVES 12

Per Serving:

Calories	126
Fat	4g
Sodium	530mg
Carbohydrates	8g
Fiber	8g
Sugar	5g
Protein	14g

Cheesecake is notorious for being a high-fat recipe, but this version is incredibly low in fat with a high protein content and delicious flavor. Top with whipped cream or fresh berries for an extra-special sweet treat.

24 ounces fat-free cream cheese

½ cup vanilla protein powder

¾ cup stevia

1 teaspoon vanilla extract

3 large eggs

1 tablespoon lemon juice

2 tablespoons semisweet chocolate chips

1 Preheat oven to 350°F. Spray a 9" pie pan with nonstick cooking spray.

2 Place cream cheese, protein powder, stevia, vanilla, eggs, and lemon juice in a large bowl and mix with a hand mixer on medium speed.

3 Pour mixture into the prepared pan. Sprinkle with chocolate chips.

4 Bake for 45 minutes. Remove from the oven and cool on a rack for 1 hour. Refrigerate for at least 3 hours before serving.

Blueberry Pie for One

A single-serving fruity treat can be made with just a handful of wholesome ingredients. The small portion also means it won't ruin your macro goals for the day.

1 teaspoon coconut oil

½ teaspoon honey

1½ tablespoons almond flour

½ cup fresh blueberries

1 tablespoon creamy almond butter

1 Melt coconut oil with honey in the microwave in a mug or small ramekin.

2 Stir in almond flour and flatten the mixture with a spoon to make a "crust" in the bottom of the mug.

3 Top with blueberries and almond butter. Microwave on high for 45 seconds.

4 Remove mug from microwave and stir blueberries and almond butter together with a spoon.

5 Allow to cool 1–2 minutes before eating.

SERVES 1	
Per Serving:	
Calories	329
Fat	21g
Sodium	56mg
Carbohydrates	27g
Fiber	6g
Sugar	13g
Protein	9g

BLUEBERRIES FOR BALANCED BLOOD SUGAR

Blueberries won't raise your blood sugar levels as much as other fruits do. These berries are high in fiber and have high concentrations of certain digestive enzymes that slow down digestion. Preventing blood sugar spikes helps to keep hunger levels more stable, so you're better able to stick to your macro goals.

Whipped Berry Bowl

If you're short on hitting your protein goal, here's a dessert that can be assembled in under 2 minutes. It's cool, creamy, and loaded with protein. Top with your choice of fresh berries for some added nutrients and gut-friendly fiber.

½ cup nonfat plain Greek yogurt
¼ cup vanilla protein powder
¼ cup water
1 cup blueberries or sliced strawberries
½ cup fat-free whipped topping

1 Combine yogurt, protein powder, and water in a small bowl, whisking until blended.
2 Place bowl in the freezer for 5 minutes.
3 Remove from freezer, top with berries and whipped topping, and serve.

Lemon Yogurt Mousse

Dessert doesn't need to weigh you down. This lemon mousse is a great way to satisfy a sweet tooth without wrecking your macros.

2 large egg whites
¼ cup sugar
⅛ teaspoon salt

1½ cups low-fat plain Greek yogurt
1 tablespoon lemon juice
1 teaspoon grated lemon zest

1 In a heatproof bowl over a saucepan of simmering water, stir egg whites, sugar, and salt until the sugar fully dissolves.
2 Remove the bowl from heat and beat eggs with a hand mixer or whisk until stiff peaks form.
3 In a separate bowl, combine yogurt, lemon juice, and lemon zest. Fold in the egg white mixture. Refrigerate at least 2 hours before serving.

Piña Colada Ice Cream

All of the fun flavors of a piña colada cocktail (without the booze) in a bowl of ice cream? Yes, please! Banana, pineapple, and coconut combine the flavors of the tropics into a refreshing creamy treat.

1 medium banana, peeled, sliced, and frozen

1 cup pineapple chunks, frozen

¼ cup canned coconut milk

1 tablespoon unsweetened shredded coconut

1   Line a baking sheet with waxed paper.

2   Place banana slices and pineapple chunks on the prepared baking sheet and freeze for 2 hours.

3   Transfer banana and pineapple to a food processor or high-speed blender. Add coconut milk and shredded coconut and blend. Occasionally scrape down the sides and continue to blend until smooth.

4   Scoop into bowls and serve immediately or freeze for at least 1 hour for a firmer texture.

SERVES 2	
Per Serving:	
Calories	171
Fat	7g
Sodium	3mg
Carbohydrates	26g
Fiber	4g
Sugar	15g
Protein	1g

APPENDIX A
How to Calculate Your Macros

The first thing you'll need to know before calculating your macros is your current weight and body fat percentage. Body fat percentage can be measured at a gym or doctor's office, or with a digital scale that measures it. Lean body mass is weight minus body fat. Next, you'll determine your maintenance calorie intake, which is roughly how many calories your body uses every day. To lose fat, you'll eat fewer calories than your maintenance levels, and to build muscle, you'll eat above maintenance.

There are many ways to do this, and none will ever be 100 percent accurate. So to figure out your fat loss calories, which you'll need to track and adjust as you go, you'll need a bit of trial and error in the beginning. Keep in mind that so many factors affect your caloric output—activity levels, genetics, body composition, nutrition, and many more. The math you're about to do will be a best guess, so don't expect to get your calories perfect on the first try.

Step One: Figure Out Your Total Calories

There are plenty of complicated, long calculations out there, but you can keep it simple. If you're a man, multiply your body weight by 15. If you're a woman, multiply your body weight by 14. This will give you a rough guess at your total calories needed to maintain your body weight.

Now that you've come up with a number for your calories, the next step is to consume calories according to this number as closely as you can for seven to ten days. Check your body weight on day one and day ten to compare.

If you lose weight, you've found a caloric deficit. If fat loss is your goal, this is perfect. If you lost more than two and a half pounds, however, that's too fast, and you're undereating. You'll want to bump food up a bit.

If you gained weight, you're eating above maintenance. Lower your food intake by a few hundred calories and try again. You want to start with a 10–15 percent decrease in calories, eat that number for a few days, and then check your weight again, repeating until you find your maintenance level.

If your weight stayed the same, you found your maintenance intake. To lose fat, take about 200–500 calories away from your total carbs and fats. If you want to add muscle, add about 300 calories primarily to carbs with some going to protein.

Step Two: Calculate Your Macros

Now that you have your total calories, it's time to split those calories up into their respective macros. Remember, protein and carbohydrates each have four calories per gram, while fat has nine calories per gram. If you want to plan to include alcohol, it has seven calories per gram but zero nutritional value, so you'll have to lower your remaining calories and simply eat less carbs and fat.

- **Protein:** Set your protein at 1 gram per pound of lean body weight. Write that number down.
- **Fat:** Now set your fat anywhere between .25–.5 grams per pound (lower if you prefer higher carbs, and vice versa).
- **Carbs:** Your remaining calories, after protein and fat, will go to carbs. On training days, set your carbs at 1.25–1.5 grams per pound of body weight, depending on how you ended up setting your fat (higher or lower). On rest days, set your carbs at .5 grams per pound and increase fat by .10 grams per pound.

While protein should stay the same, your fat and carbs can fluctuate based on your personal preference. If you enjoy fatty foods, keep your fat at .5 grams per pound or even higher. This will lower your carbohydrate intake but give you room for foods you enjoy. If you love carbs, keep your fat on the lowest end, .25 grams per pound, and you can enjoy pasta to your heart's content.

Macro Calculation Example

Let's take a 200-pound male with a measured 15 percent body fat and calculate his macros using the previous numbers. Reading the process can seem overwhelming, but following an example will show you how simple it really is.

First and foremost, let's calculate lean body mass. This will be used to determine protein intake. The reason you calculate for lean mass rather than total body weight is to feed your body based on its needs. Since body fat is not active tissue, it doesn't need any nutrition to sustain itself. The rest of your lean mass, consisting of your muscular system, internal organs, bones, and anything that's not fat, does in fact need proper nutrition to function, so that's what you should be concerned with regarding your protein needs.

Total Calorie Calculations

For total calories, use 14 times total body weight for men, so for the sample calculations, total maintenance calories will be 2,800.

For fat loss, it's best to start with a 500-calorie per day deficit. Therefore, our fictional man's total calorie intake goals will be 2,300 calories per day.

For the rest of the calculations, use the following conversion chart.

Macro to Calorie Conversions
- 1 gram protein = 4 calories
- 1 gram carbohydrate = 4 calories
- 1 gram fat = 9 calories

Lean Body Mass Calculation
1. Total body weight × body fat percentage = pounds of fat
2. Total body weight – pounds of fat = lean body mass

Remember, the sample person weighs 200 pounds at 15 percent body fat.

1. 200 × .15 (15 percent) = 30 pounds of fat
2. 200 pounds – 30 pounds = 170 pounds lean body mass

Protein Calculations

Protein should be set at 1 gram per pound of lean body weight. At 170 pounds of lean body mass, this means protein will be set at 170 grams every day.

Protein calories are 170 × 4, or 680.

Fat Calculations

Fat should be set at .25–.45 grams per pound of body weight. Since the man weighs 200 pounds and prefers higher-fat meals, he'll use .45 grams: 200 pounds × .45 grams means fat will be set at 90 grams per day.

Fat calories are 90 × 9, or 810.

Carbohydrate Calculations

To calculate carbohydrates, take your protein and fat calories and subtract them from your total calories for the day. The remaining calories are used for carbohydrates.

Total calories − protein calories − fat calories = carbohydrate calories.

2,300 − 680 − 810 =
810 carbohydrate calories.

Now that you have 810 carbohydrate calories, simply divide this number by 4 to figure out how many grams of carbohydrates are to be consumed each day:

810 ÷ 4 =
203 grams of carbohydrates every day.

Therefore, the final goal numbers for each day are 2,300 calories, coming from 170 grams of protein, 90 grams of fat, and 203 grams of carbohydrates.

Use these calculations to figure out your individual daily needs for total calories and total macros and use those numbers to plan your days and meal plans.

Remember, these numbers are just a best guess and will have to be adjusted as you go. Once you get in the habit of accurately consuming these numbers, which takes practice, it's very easy to adjust your diet when progress stalls. Our fictional man could simply go from eating 203 carbs each day to eating 170 carbs each day, for example. Rather than overhauling your entire diet every few weeks and trying something new, you can simply adjust your ratios whenever progress stops.

Meal Plans

Week 1					
	Breakfast	**Lunch**	**Snack**	**Dinner**	**Macros (approx.)**
Day 1	Tortilla Breakfast Quiche (Chapter 2)	Chicken and Kale Caesar Salad (Chapter 4)	2 Peanut Butter Protein Balls (Chapter 11), 1 medium apple	Pizza Cottage Pie (Chapter 6), 2 cups steamed broccoli with 2 teaspoons butter	Protein: 35% Carbs: 42% Fat: 23%
Day 2	Tortilla Breakfast Quiche (Chapter 2)	Pizza Cottage Pie (Chapter 6)	2 Peanut Butter Protein Balls (Chapter 11), 1 medium apple or pear	Lazy Cook's Cheese-Stuffed Turkey Meatloaf (Chapter 5), Zucchini Fries (Chapter 10)	Protein: 33% Carbs: 44% Fat: 23%
Day 3	Overnight Peanut Butter Protein Oats (Chapter 2)	Lazy Cook's Cheese-Stuffed Turkey Meatloaf (Chapter 5), Zucchini Fries (Chapter 10)	2 Peanut Butter Protein Balls (Chapter 11), 1 medium apple or pear	Mediterranean Chickpea Pita Sandwiches (Chapter 8) with ½ medium avocado, Cauliflower Steaks with Lemon Tahini Drizzle (Chapter 10)	Protein: 27% Carbs: 51% Fat: 22%
Day 4	Overnight Peanut Butter Protein Oats (Chapter 2)	Avocado Egg Salad (Chapter 4), 2 cups mixed salad greens	Green Collagen Smoothie (Chapter 11)	Parmesan-Crusted Salmon (Chapter 7), Roasted Broccoli with Peanut Sauce (Chapter 10), ¾ cup brown rice with 2 teaspoons butter	Protein: 38% Carbs: 36% Fat: 26%

	Breakfast	Lunch	Snack	Dinner	Macros (approx.)
Week 1					
Day 5	Overnight Peanut Butter Protein Oats (Chapter 2)	Parmesan-Crusted Salmon (Chapter 7), 2 cups baby spinach	Roasted Broccoli with Peanut Sauce (Chapter 10)	Garlic Mustard Drumsticks (Chapter 5), Parsnip Mash (Chapter 10), 1 cup steamed Brussels sprouts with 2 teaspoons butter	Protein: 39% Carbs: 37% Fat: 24%
Day 6	Sautéed Sausage and Plantain (Chapter 2)	Garlic Mustard Drumsticks (Chapter 5), Parsnip Mash (Chapter 10), 1 cup steamed green beans	Ham and Swiss Rice Cakes (Chapter 11), 1 large hard-cooked egg	Chicken Taco Skillet (Chapter 5), ¾ cup cauliflower rice	Protein: 33% Carbs: 45% Fat: 23%
Day 7	Sautéed Sausage and Plantain (Chapter 2)	Chicken Taco Skillet (Chapter 5), ¾ cup cauliflower rice	Ham and Swiss Rice Cakes (Chapter 11), 1 large hard-cooked egg	Sheet Pan Kielbasa and Roasted Vegetables (Chapter 6)	Protein: 29% Carbs: 45% Fat: 26%

Week 2

	Breakfast	Lunch	Snack	Dinner	Macros (approx.)
Day 1	Meal Prep Ninja Breakfast Cookies (Chapter 2), 1 cup nonfat plain Greek yogurt	Veggie Burger and Hummus Chopped Salad (Chapter 4)	Protein Snack Box (Chapter 11)	Spaghetti Squash Taco Boats (Chapter 6)	Protein: 35% Carbs: 42% Fat: 23%
Day 2	Meal Prep Ninja Breakfast Cookies (Chapter 2), 1 cup nonfat plain Greek yogurt	Spaghetti Squash Taco Boats (Chapter 6)	Protein Snack Box (Chapter 11)	Thai Veggie Burgers (Chapter 8) with ½ medium avocado, Cabbage Slaw (Chapter 10)	Protein: 32% Carbs: 44% Fat: 25%
Day 3	Egg and Cheese Muffins (Chapter 2), 1 slice whole-grain toast, ½ cup sliced strawberries	Thai Veggie Burgers (Chapter 8) with fried egg, Cabbage Slaw (Chapter 10)	Sweet Potato Wedges (Chapter 10), ¼ cup Cinnamon Tahini Dressing (Chapter 10)	Tuna "Ceviche" (Chapter 7), 2 cups mixed greens	Protein: 31% Carbs: 45% Fat: 25%
Day 4	Meal Prep Ninja Breakfast Cookies (Chapter 2), 1 cup nonfat plain Greek yogurt	Hummus Chicken Salad (Chapter 4), 1 cup baby carrots, 1 cup sliced cucumbers	Sweet Potato Wedges (Chapter 10), ¼ cup Cinnamon Tahini Dressing (Chapter 10)	1½ servings Cheesy Brussels Sprouts with Chicken Sausage (Chapter 5)	Protein: 31% Carbs: 48% Fat: 21%

Week 2

	Breakfast	Lunch	Snack	Dinner	Macros (approx.)
Day 5	Egg and Cheese Muffins (Chapter 2), 1 cup sliced strawberries	Hummus Chicken Salad (Chapter 4), 6" whole-grain tortilla, ¾ cup baby carrots	Protein Snack Box (Chapter 11)	High-Protein Italian Pasta Bake (Chapter 9), 2 cups steamed broccoli florets with 2 teaspoons butter	Protein: 35% Carbs: 43% Fat: 22%
Day 6	Smoked Salmon Avocado Toast (Chapter 2)	High-Protein Italian Pasta Bake (Chapter 9), 2 cups steamed broccoli florets with 2 teaspoons butter	The Best Peanut Butter and Banana Smoothie (Chapter 11)	One Pan BBQ Chicken and Vegetables (Chapter 5), 1 cup cauliflower rice	Protein: 38% Carbs: 38% Fat: 24%
Day 7	Smoked Salmon Avocado Toast (Chapter 2)	One Pan BBQ Chicken and Vegetables (Chapter 5), 1 cup cauliflower rice	French Toast Scramble (Chapter 2)	2 Open-Faced BLATs (Chapter 3), 1 cup steamed sugar snap peas	Protein: 32% Carbs: 44% Fat: 24%

STANDARD US/METRIC MEASUREMENT CONVERSIONS

VOLUME CONVERSIONS

US Volume Measure	Metric Equivalent
⅛ teaspoon	0.5 milliliter
¼ teaspoon	1 milliliter
½ teaspoon	2 milliliters
1 teaspoon	5 milliliters
½ tablespoon	7 milliliters
1 tablespoon (3 teaspoons)	15 milliliters
2 tablespoons (1 fluid ounce)	30 milliliters
¼ cup (4 tablespoons)	60 milliliters
⅓ cup	90 milliliters
½ cup (4 fluid ounces)	125 milliliters
⅔ cup	160 milliliters
¾ cup (6 fluid ounces)	180 milliliters
1 cup (16 tablespoons)	250 milliliters
1 pint (2 cups)	500 milliliters
1 quart (4 cups)	1 liter (about)

WEIGHT CONVERSIONS

US Weight Measure	Metric Equivalent
½ ounce	15 grams
1 ounce	30 grams
2 ounces	60 grams
3 ounces	85 grams
¼ pound (4 ounces)	115 grams
½ pound (8 ounces)	225 grams
¾ pound (12 ounces)	340 grams
1 pound (16 ounces)	454 grams

OVEN TEMPERATURE CONVERSIONS

Degrees Fahrenheit	Degrees Celsius
200 degrees F	95 degrees C
250 degrees F	120 degrees C
275 degrees F	135 degrees C
300 degrees F	150 degrees C
325 degrees F	160 degrees C
350 degrees F	180 degrees C
375 degrees F	190 degrees C
400 degrees F	205 degrees C
425 degrees F	220 degrees C
450 degrees F	230 degrees C

BAKING PAN SIZES

American	Metric
8 × 1½ inch round baking pan	20 × 4 cm cake tin
9 × 1½ inch round baking pan	23 × 3.5 cm cake tin
11 × 7 × 1½ inch baking pan	28 × 18 × 4 cm baking tin
13 × 9 × 2 inch baking pan	30 × 20 × 5 cm baking tin
2 quart rectangular baking dish	30 × 20 × 3 cm baking tin
15 × 10 × 2 inch baking pan	30 × 25 × 2 cm baking tin (Swiss roll tin)
9 inch pie plate	22 × 4 or 23 × 4 cm pie plate
7 or 8 inch springform pan	18 or 20 cm springform or loose bottom cake tin
9 × 5 × 3 inch loaf pan	23 × 13 × 7 cm or 2 lb narrow loaf or pate tin
1½ quart casserole	1.5 liter casserole
2 quart casserole	2 liter casserole

Index

Lose weight and build muscle with the macronutrient diet!

INCLUDES 50+ RECIPES!

MACRONUTRIENT
BASICS

INCLUDES 50+ RECIPES

Your Guide to the Essentials of Macronutrients—and How a Macro Diet Can Work for You!

MACRO GUIDELINES

STARTER RECIPES

LIFESTYLE ADJUSTMENTS

MATT DUSTIN, CSCS

Pick Up or Download Your Copy Today!

adamsmedia
An Imprint of Simon & Schuster
A ViacomCBS COMPANY